THE LONG WAR ON DRUGS

THE LONG WAR ON DRUGS

ANNE L. FOSTER

Duke University Press Durham and London 2023

Printed and bound by CPI Group (UK) Ltd, Croydon, CR0 4YY
Project Editor: Livia Tenzer
Designed by Courtney Leigh Richardson
Typeset in Whitman and Trade Gothic LT Std.
by Westchester Publishing Services

Library of Congress Cataloging-in-Publication Data
Names: Foster, Anne L., [date] author.
Title: The long war on drugs / Anne L. Foster.
Description: Durham : Duke University Press, 2023. | Includes bibliographical references and index.
Identifiers: LCCN 2023009672 (print)
LCCN 2023009673 (ebook)
ISBN 9781478025429 (paperback)
ISBN 9781478020646 (hardcover)
ISBN 9781478027553 (ebook)
Subjects: LCSH: Drug control—United States. | Drug control—United States—History. | Drug abuse—United States. | Drug abuse—United States—History. | Drug abuse—Law and legislation—United States. | Drug abuse—Government policy—United States. | Drug Legalization—United States. | Drug abuse—Social aspects. | Drug Abuse—Prevention. | BISAC: HISTORY / United States / 20th Century | SOCIAL SCIENCE / Criminology
Classification: LCC HV5825 .F678 2023 (print) | LCC HV5825 (ebook) | DDC 362.290973—dc23/eng/20230720
LC record available at https://lccn.loc.gov/2023009672
LC ebook record available at https://lccn.loc.gov/2023009673

COVER ART: Distribution bags. Courtesy Shutterstock/donikz.

For all my History 313 students,
for whom I wrote and who made it better

CONTENTS

ACKNOWLEDGMENTS

I began writing this book to provide a text for students in my course Long War on Drugs. No single, accessible book existed, and I wrote first for them. I asked them for feedback, since I hoped to publish it someday. My first thank you, then, is to all my History 313 students, who provided encouragement, suggestions, and insightful criticism. In particular, I would like to thank Isiah Baxter, Kim Caufield, Sebastian Cummins, Andy Fouts, Jasen Kwok, Brandon Scott, Cassie Souder, Myles Taylor, and Faith Williams.

I have relied on the insights and support of colleagues and friends through the writing of this book. David Aldridge read most of the manuscript, providing invaluable feedback. Fellow drug historians Daniel Weimer and Matthew Pembleton answered questions, suggested readings, and produced their own inspiring work. My colleagues in the Department of History and African and African American Studies at Indiana State University have listened to more about drug history than they ever imagined possible. Thanks especially to Taylor Easum, who heard even more than others. The virtual faculty writing hour during the pandemic kept me on track during those difficult months. Thank you to Lisa Phillips for organizing us, and to Ruth Fairbanks and James Gustafson for reliably showing up. Along with Lisa and Ruth, thanks to Andrea Arrington, Jessica Fields, Colleen Haas, Micki Morahn, Barbara Skinner, and Kim Stanley for some well-timed happy hours, both virtual and in person. Petra Goedde and Naoko Shibusawa have been stalwart supporters and friends, too, offering timely encouragement.

In fall 2019, the Roosevelt Institute for American Studies (RIAS) hosted me for a short-term residential fellowship in Middelburg, the Netherlands. Those weeks of concentrated writing, with few responsibilities and a whole host of accomplished scholars to talk with, helped me through a crucial writing stage. Thanks especially to Giles Scott-Smith for inviting me and for many good conversations. Thanks also to Paul Brennan, Dario Fazzi, Cees Heere, Celia Nijdam, Damian Pargas, Nanka de Vries, and Debbie Esmé de Vugt for making me feel welcome and for our lively conversations over coffee. In a special category at RIAS, thanks to Leontien Joosse for facilitating all our work so effectively, finding me the perfect place to live, and helping me get the most out of my stay.

When I wrote my first book, my children were small and paid attention only to the fact that writing kept me away from them. This time, they were teenagers and now are adults, and whether because the topic is more interesting or they are older, they paid more attention to what I was writing. Naomi had gone away to college before I began writing in earnest, but she listened patiently while I thought out loud about the book during her calls and offered helpful suggestions. Susan didn't complain (too much) when I spent several weeks of her junior year of high school in the Netherlands without her, and she has asked many questions about the history of drugs. Those questions made the class I teach, and this book, better. I couldn't do any of it without support from Jeff. My mom and dad, Bobbie, and Maria all helped in ways they do and don't know.

The pandemic prevented me from taking the research trips I had planned to find images for the book. But as you will see, I was more fortunate than I could have imagined with photographs. Steve Raymer, whose photographs tell stories all on their own, enthusiastically responded to my request for an image or two. He generously supplied many more than that. I am truly grateful.

The continued support and encouragement of Gisela Fosado, my editor at Duke University Press, has been instrumental in prompting me to finish the manuscript. I couldn't ask for a better editor. Thank you to Adriane Lentz-Smith for suggesting I talk with her. The two anonymous reviewers provided helpful feedback beyond what I have ever experienced. The whole Duke UP team, in particular Alejandra Mejía and Livia Tenzer, have been terrific to work with. They have helped me realize my vision for this book. I am sure that a book covering such a large and changing topic contains errors, for which responsibility remains with me.

INTRODUCTION. The Meaning of Drugs

The official death toll from overdose in the United States in 2020–21 totaled more than 100,000 people, more than doubling the overdose death numbers of only five years earlier. Drug overdoses, if counted as a separate category in US Centers for Disease Control and Prevention (CDC) tallies, would have ranked as the sixth leading cause of death.[1] In 2020, approximately 9.5 million Americans reported misusing opioids.[2] The United States, despite having a policy prohibiting nonmedicinal use of narcotics for more than a century, has not solved the drug problem. By some measures, misuse of drugs has gotten worse in recent years. Despite this persistent problem, US policy to prevent drug use and abuse has remained remarkably consistent. The first prohibitionist federal law aimed at restricting recreational consumption of narcotics passed in 1914. Since then, federal drug policy has focused primarily on controlling supply of drugs and punishing users and dealers with prison time. Demand-reduction efforts, such as treatment and prevention, have received inadequate and intermittent funding. Since Barack Obama's presidency, there have been modest steps to provide more federal support for a health care approach to addiction, with the Joseph R. Biden administration even providing some funds for harm-reduction strategies such as needle exchange. These shifts remain modest and controversial. US drug policy remains focused primarily on arrests and seizures. Even though the phrase "War on Drugs" is usually associated with policies originating in Richard M. Nixon's presidency in the early 1970s, I argue that the United States has pursued a War on Drugs approach for more than one hundred years.

Critiques of the War on Drugs approach focus on its ineffectiveness, the militarization of efforts to control the drug supply coming from other countries, the differential policing and prison sentences of racial minorities, and the punishment of people who have had the misfortune to become addicted to drugs. Supporters of the War on Drugs emphasize that these illegal drugs are harmful, and it is the job of government to punish illegal behavior. They hope that this punishment will serve both to repress illegal activity and to serve as a warning to those tempted to get involved with drugs. The problem is a vexing one, and many people are urging that the government rethink the War on Drugs approach. Some of them want to remove all restrictions on this war, devoting more resources to the current efforts and imposing long prison sentences on all involved with the trade. Others find harm reduction, in which users are supported in safer methods of drug consumption to reduce the likelihood of disease and overdose, more humane. Still others urge legalization of some or even all illegal drugs, arguing that humans naturally seek altered states and that many drugs can be used safely, even enjoyably. It is better, in their minds, to tax the sale of these drugs and gain revenue than to spend revenue to control what will not be controlled. This book can help inform these policy discussions by examining how and why earlier policies have been adopted as well as their shortcomings and successes.

The aim of the book is to explore how people have consumed drugs, when legal and illegal, since the early twentieth century, as well as explain why a prohibitionist approach was adopted. It then explores the implications of that prohibitionist approach for medical, social, legal, cultural, and international politics. The book focuses primarily on narcotics, which in the early years was used as an umbrella term to include both opiates and cocaine. It argues that the basic patterns of drug control were set during the years when US actors were most concerned with opiates. The policies adopted to control cocaine, marijuana, and, after World War II, the increased illicit use of pharmaceuticals as well as synthetic drugs such as LSD still relied on the basic methods adopted in the early twentieth century.

Narcotics prohibition developed in a global context, so while the story in many ways centers on the United States, the book draws connections to events around the world in order to better illuminate how policies were made and the consequences of them. US politicians and activists often led the prohibitionist movement, but implementation of drug restrictions required cooperation from actors in other countries. Sometimes these actors shared US goals; other times they had competing needs. US supply-side-control efforts were frequently enforced at the US border or even in a producing country, meaning US policy reverberated, often with devastating effects, around the world. The earliest US attempts to implement restrictions, in the US colony in the Philippines after 1905, were hindered by the differing policies of surrounding countries. Since that date, US policy has depended on enticing or forcing other countries to cooperate.

One goal of this book is for readers to reexamine their own assumptions about not only how and why people take drugs but the kinds of policies that would best control drug use to those that are perhaps beneficial, or at the least less harmful. The problem is a complex one, and the more people who think deeply about it, the better. This book is a work of history, not of policy. It demonstrates that some policies have not worked or have had counterproductive consequences. It draws attention to the choices we have made and the implications of those choices, helpful and harmful. Perhaps most importantly, it encourages readers to think about drugs differently. For as long as there has been recorded history, people have been seeking ways to alter their state of mind. Some drugs and some ways of using them are dangerous; others can be healing or simply enjoyable. This book aims to help readers understand ways they can contribute to reducing dangers to themselves, their family and friends, global politics, and even the broader environment.

The book is organized into thirteen short chapters. The first chapter provides a historical background on the uses of drugs in history. Chapters 2 through 5 comprise part I of the book, loosely covering 1870 to 1940. At the beginning of this period, opium, cocaine, and marijuana were lightly regulated, if at all, and consumed commonly for both medicinal and recreational purposes, especially in Europe, the United States, Central and South America (coca and marijuana), and many parts of Asia (primarily opium but also marijuana in some places). By its end, many countries had instituted some controls over use. These controls varied widely, from requiring prescriptions or registering users to complete prohibition of recreational use. Part II, which covers 1940 to 1980 in chapters 6 through 9, focuses on the implementation of a global prohibition of nonmedicinal drug use. These chapters explore the ways that happened as well as the consequences of that prohibition for both the people who continued to use and the governments attempting to stop that use. Part III, chapters 10 through 13, covers 1980 to the present. This part of the book focuses on continuities in the War on Drugs approach but also some changes, as with marijuana policy in the United States, and new challenges, such as environmental consequences and the increased production of synthetic drugs. A short conclusion returns to the ways the drug issue plays out in the United States and the Philippines, but in recent years rather than more than a century ago, to remind us of continuities in the US approach and the harms stemming from it.

A Note on Sources

I wrote this book to serve as the backbone text for a class I teach with the same title as the book. For that reason, the source base tilts to a reliance on synthesizing the many excellent works by other historians and scholars about drug history. In part I, which is closest to my own research, I draw on both primary and secondary sources equally and often contribute directly to creating new scholarly arguments about this history. In parts II and III, primary sources serve as examples and to extend arguments already made by scholars. In general, parts II and III rely on research done by others. The chapter endnotes cite works I quote directly, of course, and acknowledge specific contributions or pieces of information. Each chapter has a list of suggestions for further reading, found at the end of the book. There, I include the most important works I relied on in writing each chapter as well as articles and books that readers can use to learn more about the topics of each chapter.

1. THE MANY USES OF DRUGS

For as long as there has been recorded history, people have been taking substances to alter their mood, help them relieve pain, and, they long believed, connect to higher or greater powers. In every culture, people sought out those plants that could be eaten or smoked to calm them down, give them visions, or speed up their heart rate and brain function. From the peyote of the Indigenous people of North America to the coca leaves chewed in the mountains of South America to the opium produced from poppies in what we now call the Middle East and Central Asia, mind-altering substances available in local areas have been consumed throughout history.

Before 1500, most of these drugs were consumed only in the areas in which they grew. Peyote, coca, and khat (or qat) are examples of drugs with long histories that until recently were primarily consumed in the regions where they grow. Peyote is the product of a cactus plant, and the Indigenous people of the desert areas of North America sought out peyote for the visions its hallucinogenic qualities provided. The search for peyote and consumption of it were done in highly ritualized ways, meaning that abuse of the drug was rare. It can be dried, however, and shipped, and by the mid-twentieth century was beginning to circulate more widely. Coca originally was consumed in the highland areas of South America in what is now Peru and Bolivia. People chewed, or more properly sucked, on the dried leaves. It provides a mild stimulant in this form, enabling work, staving off hunger, and even helping people physically adjust to life at high altitude. Coca use was integrated into daily life of highland peoples, with consumption something like a modern-day coffee break: enjoyable, often sociable, and reinvigorating. Coca has been consumed for centuries, mostly near where it originally grew. It did not become a global drug until after people learned how to process the leaves to make cocaine, in 1860. Khat, a drug found in the Middle East and Africa, is like coca in that in its unprocessed form, its leaves are chewed for a stimulating effect. Khat is still consumed in this form, and in places like Yemen, where as many as 80 percent of adults use the drug, it is well integrated into social mores. There are people who abuse the drug, but in general, users function well in society while consuming the drug as part of daily life. Khat leaves begin to lose their potency within forty-eight hours of being picked, so while today there is some trafficking of the drug from its place of origin to serve immigrant communities in Europe and North America, there is not a flourishing trade beyond those limited circumstances. These three drugs serve as good examples of the ways that humans have always sought the assistance of substances to alter their mood. Peyote's hallucinogenic visions were perceived as religious and provided a kind of mental health healing from trauma and tragedy. Khat enhanced energy for people working long hours at difficult jobs and promoted social interactions.[1]

Historically, peyote and khat attracted both less scholarship and less concern than many other drugs. Coca has primarily attracted scholarly attention and public concern in its cocaine form. Before 1500, most drugs were like these three. They were consumed where they grew, and people developed cultural traditions for the consumption of the drugs. These traditions meant that there were socially acceptable ways to consume the drugs, and the existence of those traditions limited abuse. If people began to violate the socially acceptable methods of consumption, other people would intervene and help them return to appropriate methods. There were probably some people who engaged in problematic behaviors, but in general drug use was limited by traditions and social pressure as well as availability and cost.

Before 1500, only two substances we identify today as drugs are partial exceptions to the picture painted here. One is alcohol, and the other is opium. Like peyote, coca, and khat, alcohol and opium have been consumed for almost as long as there is recorded history. The first known alcoholic beverages occur as long ago as 7000 BCE in China, and over the next few hundred years, many of the societies with recorded histories also describe alcohol. The first written records of distilled beverages are from approximately 800 CE. Fermented and distilled beverages, unlike substances such as peyote and khat, developed independently nearly everywhere, which is an important difference. Alcoholic beverages were a trade good in the ancient and early modern worlds, but in general, use of alcohol did not spread through trade. People already accustomed to consuming alcohol sometimes traded to get different or better types of alcohol. Both fermented and distilled beverages generated local social customs about proper use, and while there are reports of the abuse of alcohol throughout its history, this abuse often was limited to particular groups (young men, soldiers especially) and particular times (certain festivals, for instance). Alcohol was, in most societies, a significant source of calories and a safer beverage to consume than water or milk or juice, all of which were more likely to be contaminated than was alcohol. Alcoholic beverages stored more easily in the days before refrigeration, and alcohol was an important part of daily life in many parts of the world.[2]

Archaeological evidence shows human use of poppies as early as approximately 5000 BCE, in areas today called Western and Southern Europe, but probably more for food (seeds and oil) than as a drug. The first recorded uses of opium appear between 3000 and 2000 BCE, in the area around the Mediterranean.[3] As with other mind-altering substances, it is likely that poppies were used earlier than they appear in the historical record. Opium use, from the beginning, was a more complex matter than the other drugs discussed in this chapter. People quickly realized that opium not only altered their mood, providing a sense of euphoria or peacefulness for many, vivid dreams for others, and restfulness or calm for still others, but it also had physical effects that were highly beneficial. Opium, of course, relieved pain, and pain was a constant of life in the past in a way difficult to imagine today. Filling of cavities and other tooth care, as well as bone-setting techniques, were primitive and did not necessarily end the pain of toothache or broken bone. Without the ability to vaccinate against illness or take antibiotics after infection or illness, people were often sick and experienced a lot of pain. Drinking alcohol or chewing on willow bark (which has the same ingredient found today in aspirin) might alleviate pain somewhat, but opium actually relieved it. That was invaluable. Opium also relieved symptoms of common illnesses such as malaria and dysentery. One of the side effects that is a great problem of opioids today—the fact that it is constipating—was actually a huge benefit in the past. When food was less hygienic, and when clean water was a rarity, people were much more likely to have various stomach ailments that could be at least partially relieved by a constipating medicine. The incentives to use opium were stronger than for any other drug besides alcohol. Perhaps not surprisingly, then, opium use spread from its places of origin, both throughout the areas in which the poppy plant was cultivated and through trade in prepared opium.

Opium use is recorded before 1500 CE throughout much of Europe and Asia, so it had traveled far from its points of origin. The societies to which opium spread, especially those only purchasing it and not growing it, did not develop as robust a set of social traditions surrounding its consumption as they did for alcohol, peyote, and khat. It's not completely clear why that did not happen. Probably a combination of factors was important, including the fact that the drug was not indigenous to the area, the relatively high expense of it, and the variety of uses it had. Still, because of the expense, it was also rare for people in most areas to become seriously addicted to opium, as far as we can tell from existing records, before 1500. There simply were too many disruptions in supply for people to develop the kind of dependency associated with full-fledged addiction.

Historians generally consider the years since 1500 to constitute modern history. After 1500, the world began to be more closely linked by trade, by the experience of developing nation-states and modern empires, and by innovations and inventions arising from the Scientific Revolution. These changes all influenced the ways that people around the world consumed drugs and the ways that governments promoted and controlled those drugs.

At the beginning of this modern era, three drugs were significantly important to world historical developments: tobacco, alcohol (sugar), and again, opium. This book focuses on the history of opium and then other drugs we call "hard" drugs, but it is useful to remember that the modern era is an era of licit and illicit drug consumption.

Tobacco was one of those drugs, like peyote and khat, that was originally consumed only in its area of origin, and then primarily in religious ceremonies or in highly prescribed social settings. Tobacco grew in many parts of the Americas, and although there was some regional trade in the product, in general its use was confined to that region until the Europeans arrived in the Americas around 1500.[4] Unlike peyote or khat, however, tobacco is a product that is easy to trade. It is not consumed in its fresh form, as khat usually is, but after being dried. So it is easily preserved and a lightweight good, simple to transport. And unlike peyote, it is an annual plant, with a new crop available each year. Once Europeans smoked tobacco with the Indigenous people they met in the Americas, they began to ship it back to Europe and, after settling in the Americas themselves, to grow it for their own consumption as well as for export. Tobacco use and production spread quickly. Crops and domestic trade were well established in China before 1600, for instance.

As anyone who has smoked knows, tobacco is not an immediately appealing drug to take. In fact, most people have a negative response to most drugs when they first take them. For whatever reason, however, many people will persist through that initial bad experience to continue consuming intoxicating drugs. Tobacco is no exception. The nicotine in tobacco is a mild stimulant, helping keep people awake and reducing hunger. Coffee and tea were just becoming available in Europe in very small quantities after 1600, so tobacco was the most readily available mild stimulant for Europeans. Tobacco use followed early modern trade patterns, with sailors and merchants separately spreading the practice to various groups in the places they traveled and lived, often moving from the lower to the upper social classes. Nearly everywhere tobacco spread, men rather than women first adopted tobacco use. European political and religious leaders denounced tobacco for its association with the supposed barbarism of Indigenous Americans, while in the Middle East, leaders feared tobacco was a European plot to undermine them. Even in China, where these particular fears held little sway, societal leaders had some concerns about potential negative health or social effects. New commodities often face this kind of contradictory reception.

Tobacco use had a sociability from its beginning in the societies it spread to throughout Europe, the Middle East, and Asia. Sailors and traders brought it to a new place, instructing merchants and friends alike in how to consume this new product. Once people had smoked a few times, they enjoyed the effects of the nicotine along with the practice of preparing their pipe, lighting and smoking it, and the relaxing moments they took for this task. Rituals grew up around smoking, and the equipment available for smoking became more elaborate. Of course most people used simple pipes they could carve themselves, but wealthy people acquired beautiful pipes, works of art in themselves. These rituals suggest that tobacco smoking was folded into societal traditions and might lead us to believe that the kinds of restrictions that prevented abuse of tobacco by Indigenous people in North America would develop in Europe and by Europeans consuming it in the Americas too. In some ways, that was the case, but the social restrictions on use proved looser. Governments throughout Europe attempted to prohibit tobacco smoking, unsuccessfully. As soon as tobacco was being produced inexpensively and consistently enough, men began to consume it frequently, and the addictive qualities of nicotine overtook any social restrictions. The most important social taboo that persisted was against women smoking. Some women did, more privately than publicly, but until the twentieth century, men smoked more often, with less criticism, than women.

Tobacco was a significant trade good, then, enabling the European settlements in the southern parts of the United States to be profitable. Cotton did not become the dominant export crop from the US South until the early nineteenth century. Before that, tobacco was one of the major products fueling the development of the economy in the southern American colonies, and like cotton, tobacco relied on indentured labor and slavery. Tobacco also was an important consumer product in Europe, addictive and inexpensive enough that ordinary people could afford it. Part of its appeal was that before its arrival, Europeans had little access to drugs that were stimulants. Soon after tobacco came to Europe, Europeans also got access to coffee and tea, and with these stimulants (along with sugar), they consumed products giving them energy to engage in the sustained hard work required for the Industrial Revolution.

Alcohol, unlike tobacco, was widespread well before the modern era. Alcohol as a fermented beverage, either beer or wine, as well as in spirits (distilled) developed independently in many parts of the world. But the availability of inexpensive sugar in the aftermath of European colonization of the Caribbean led to distilled liquor becoming more readily available throughout the world, at inexpensive prices.[5] Sugar itself is not a drug, although many might claim it has addictive qualities! But it is easily converted into alcohol, especially rum, and Europeans used rum as an important trade good in the years after 1500.

People have always sought to add sweetness to their food, but for centuries nearly everyone had access only to the sweetness offered by fruits and honey. Not until after the year 1000 CE was something like modern sugar available, and even then it was so rare and expensive that only the wealthiest people could consume it as a food. Sugar cane grows only in a narrow temperature range, needing a consistently warm climate, and grows best in places where a constant breeze can move among the stalks. Small islands in warm places make the best sugar cane regions, and once Europeans colonized the Caribbean after 1500, they moved quickly to start growing sugar there and in coastal South America.

Producing sugar from sugar cane is difficult and dangerous, however. Europeans initially attempted to coerce the Indigenous people of the Caribbean and South America into working in the fields and processing the cane, but most of them died after initial contact with Europeans from diseases they had no immunity to, or they ran away after learning about how likely they were to be injured or killed producing sugar. Sugar cane itself is sharp, and the machetes necessary to harvest it are naturally as well. Many people were cut, often severely, and even minor injuries were susceptible to infection in the tropical climate. With no antibiotics, these infections often proved deadly. The European solution to this perceived problem was importing slaves from Africa. Africans were more likely to have immunity to the same diseases as Europeans and were less likely to run away since they did not know the area, but they still died at an appalling rate from injury and the effects of malnutrition and climate. Europeans, however, just brought in more slaves.

It was a deadly cycle that we now call the triangle trade. In reality, the trade had four sides, with Europe sending cloth and guns and some rum to Africa in exchange for captured or purchased slaves, who were sent to the Caribbean. The sugar produced in the Caribbean was sent to North America and Europe as sugar and molasses. North America processed the sugar and molasses into rum, consuming a lot of it there but also sending some to Europe and Africa, along with tobacco and furs. It was the beginning of a global system of exchange leading to our modern world economy. It was fueled by global demand for sugar and alcohol. Slave labor was integral to its functioning; Europeans were deeply involved in trading and owning slaves in their effort to continue the global trade in sugar and alcohol, among other products. And it promoted the introduction of alcohol into two parts of the world where it had not otherwise been prevalent: North America and many parts of Africa. The Indigenous people in each of these regions had modest or no experience with alcohol, and the introduction of this new intoxicating substance caused some harm to their societies. They had few or no social traditions to govern appropriate use. The burgeoning global economy raised standards of living for Europeans and Europeans in the Americas during the eighteenth century but actively harmed the Indigenous peoples of the Americas and Africa.

Like alcohol, opium was already spreading through trade and expanding areas of production, even before 1500. After 1500, however, the way the global economy developed accelerated the pace and extent of that expansion. In some ways, this spread was a natural result of the increasing interconnection of the globe. Europeans were exploring and colonizing in the Americas and Asia and engaging in proto-colonization and trade with Africa. As part of all these activities, they brought opium for their own medicinal and recreational needs and in the process traded with the peoples around the world. The medical usefulness of opium meant that it was welcomed everywhere, as medicine.[6] Two factors combined by the beginning of the eighteenth century, however, to accelerate the production and consumption of opiates, first in Europe and then in other parts of the world over the next two hundred years.

Capitalism and the Industrial Revolution joined imperialism as the main drivers of global activity after 1700. Both required that ordinary people around the globe begin to produce and consume at levels not previously seen. These developments prompted massive changes in almost all aspects of daily life. In Europe, people began to move into cities in unprecedented numbers, starting the trend toward urbanization that continues today. People began to produce for a market, often a global market, and had to produce a surplus to sell rather than attempt to supply all of one's family needs by the produce of one's own farm or small business. People in Europe began to work in factories, on larger farms, or in mines for a wage, leading to the monetization of an economy. Europeans colonized much of the rest of the world, transforming work there too. They often sold Africans into slavery, taking all the profit of their labor. In the colonies in the Americas, Asia, and increasingly Africa after 1800, conditions of work were reordered to force the production of a surplus for the benefit of imperialists and capitalists. None of these things were new in 1700; all had long existed. But after 1700, they increasingly began to be the only choice most people had for how to engage with the economy.

In the midst of these transitions, opium production and consumption dramatically increased. European countries were leaders in industrialization in part because they could acquire raw materials in their empire at a low cost. They sourced cotton from the Americas and India. They sourced sugar from the Caribbean. They sourced minerals from South America, Africa, and Southeast Asia. They sourced timber from Asia and North America. Europeans then transformed these raw materials into manufactured goods such as textiles and guns and furniture, selling it not merely to other Europeans but also to people in their colonies. But it was a real question: how to get people in these colonies and in places like China to want to buy the European goods? There are many different answers, but one is that Europeans promoted the sale of opium in these places too.

Opium had all the medicinal benefits noted previously and was a welcome medicine. But for people who were poor, working long hours in difficult and dangerous jobs or far from home trying to earn enough to support a family, opium provided a welcome relief from physical and psychic pain. The British organized the trade most effectively. They forced peasants in their colony in India to switch from producing food crops such as rice to producing opium. This opium was then processed in India and sold in China (not a colony) and in the other Asian colonies of England, such as Singapore and Malaya. People consumed the opium for pleasure as well as medicinally, and many became addicted. Their addiction meant they continued working to buy opium, and the main beneficiary was the British government. It worked well from the perspective of the British.

But opium became very popular and commonly consumed in Europe, especially England, as well. In Asia, opium was mostly consumed by smoking (China and Southeast Asia) or eating (India), but in England, the United States, and most of Europe, people consumed opium most frequently by taking laudanum. This is a preparation of opium in alcohol, and it looks like medicine. It would be much like taking cough syrup today, and indeed it was like an over-the-counter medicine. People took it for headache, toothache, nerves, stomach upset, and to help them sleep. People gave it to

Fig. 1.1. Man slicing opium bud in a garden. From Georg Wolffgang Wedel, *Opiologia ad mentem Academiae Naturae Curiosorum* (Bonn, Germany: Jenae, Sumptibus Johannis Fritschii, 1674), United States National Library of Medicine, Bethesda, MD.

their fussy babies, whether suffering from colic or teething. Many people took it essentially every day. In part, they were suffering the aches and pains that were unavoidable before modern medicine, but also they seem to have been using opium to escape the dreariness of life in industrializing Europe and America.

As long as there has been a recorded history of opium, some writers have been concerned about its effects, even while its medicinal usefulness and pleasurable sensations were also lauded. By the middle of the nineteenth century, though, some groups began to be concerned about the levels of opium consumption in Europe and the United States. They worried about the effects on society, the family, and individuals who were addicted. And they began to agitate against such free use of opium. Many of them worried about other addictive substances, especially alcohol. A prohibitionist approach rose during these years, sometimes led by people concerned primarily with alcohol, sometimes primarily with narcotics, and occasionally concerned with both. This book focuses on the movement against drugs, initially opiates and later others. After some decades, this movement succeeded across the world. It also continues to shape drug policy to the present in most parts of the world.

PART I.
THE BATTLE FOR PROHIBITION, 1870–1940

By the late nineteenth century, a variety of groups began to critique the way narcotics were consumed in Europe, Asia, and the Americas. At that time, narcotics, including opiates, cocaine, and marijuana, were widely available and subject to few restrictions. These groups were not all motivated by the same concerns, but during the last decades of the nineteenth century, they began to argue for restrictions on narcotics; they then organized and advocated for restrictions and even prohibition. By the outbreak of World War II, some parts of the world had adopted prohibition of narcotics, and most of the rest had greatly restricted access to them. In some ways, then, these groups succeeded.

Religiously motivated temperance advocates initiated an anti-opium movement, just as they initiated the anti-alcohol movement. In the United

States and Europe, anti-alcohol groups had a large presence in the nineteenth century, much larger than the movement against opium. People who were engaged in activism to prohibit or restrict alcohol often evoked the danger to or from certain ethnic or racial groups from alcohol consumption, an approach that anti-opium groups adopted. Many anti-alcohol groups also took an anti-opium stance, as with the Women's Christian Temperance Union in the United States or the International Order of the Good Templars, which by the 1890s had chapters on every continent of the world. The religiously motivated anti-opium campaigns often adopted tactics and goals from anti-alcohol efforts. A broader concern about conditions for poor people, especially children, sometimes motivated anti-opium activists. This set of activists usually advocated a number of different reforms, for instance in labor conditions and housing. This kind of advocacy led, in Britain, to laws passed in the late nineteenth century that required that opium be purchased from a chemist (pharmacist) rather than in regular shops. Part of the impetus for that law stemmed from sensational stories of children purchasing opium, even though supposedly these children were merely running errands for their parents. Other times, Christian groups formed around opposition to opium use, and many of these were linked to missionary organizations. Anti-opium activism rather than anti-alcohol concerns or broader reforms motivated these groups. In Britain, for example, the Society for the Suppression of the Opium Trade published *Friend of China* to expose the horrors they believed the British trade in opium caused throughout Asia, and especially in China. US missionaries in China also participated in agitating against opium. Members of these groups deplored narcotics use and urged governments to restrict access to opium unless under a doctor's supervision.

Both China and India had their own anti-opium movements. In China, as British policies of promoting opium consumption succeeded, Chinese people resisted. There was an opium smoking tradition in China, but previously opium had been expensive, viewed as a luxury good or medicine. As more people smoked, more often, many Chinese began to protest against the harmful effects. Similarly, in India, peasants were forced to grow opium instead of their traditional crops by British colonial officials. This change in the economy benefited opium-trading firms and the British government, not Indian peasants. Less food availability was one problem; increased opium consumption was another.

In a few countries, former and serving government officials began to organize to oppose policies allowing easy access to opium. In Japan, for instance, where there was no tradition of recreational opium consumption, the government decided to prohibit recreational use. What officials saw in countries with such use, especially neighboring countries such as China, worried them. In the Netherlands Indies, a Dutch colony, former Dutch colonial officials formed the Anti-Opium Bond. Their experience serving in a government that facilitated the sale of opium had convinced them it was bad for the Indonesian people. As with the missionary and religious groups, these anti-opium activists were often motivated by a paternalistic desire to care for people they believed to be incapable of making good decisions.

Government officials, whether they did or did not support opium consumption, began to study the problem during the late nineteenth century. In Britain, Parliament held a year-long inquiry into the opium trade between British-held India and China, which expanded to include an examination of opium consumption throughout the British empire. This study concluded that in places where opium consumption was traditional and customary, it was not harmful, and it recommended no change in opium policy. Other studies, such as one in the Netherlands Indies, found some problems with the way opium was sold and consumed, and began to recommend government regulation. No study yet recommended prohibition, although the criticisms of opium consumption were increasing.

A few countries had traditionally prohibited opium, and the Chinese government tried, mostly futilely, to outlaw it throughout the nineteenth and early twentieth centuries, but the first country to attempt to prohibit opium in a place where it had previously been legal was the United States in its new colony in the Philippines. Since opium was at that time legal in the United States, prohibition in the Philippines was surprising to some, and a challenge to the existing situation in the region. All other countries in Southeast Asia allowed recreational opium use. US officials quickly realized that it would be difficult to have effective prohibition in a country surrounded by countries where consumption was legal. President Theodore Roosevelt invited other regional powers to attend a conference in Shanghai, which took place in 1909, to talk about the possibility of regional prohibition. This conference was the first of many where the United States promoted its solution to the opium problem: prohibition. The idea was slow to catch on.

The US initiative was only a little ahead of its time, however. Opium had traditionally been useful as a medicine against a variety of ailments.

Like today, it was an important pain reliever. Indeed, in these days before the commercial availability of aspirin or the invention of ibuprofen, opiates provided the only truly effective pain relief. In addition, opium treated symptoms of diseases such as malaria, dysentery, and other stomach conditions. In most of the world, few people had ready access to a doctor. Opium was a standard tool in people's medicine chests at this time. By the early twentieth century, however, the prevalence of some of these diseases was decreasing due to improved public health measures. Modern medicine increasingly had treatments for the diseases, too, so mere relief of symptoms was less necessary. Opium's medicinal role was diminishing, and consumption was becoming more associated with pleasure than with medical treatment.

The next four chapters explore these years of transition for opium. Chapter 2 explores how different groups began to become more concerned about opium use in the late nineteenth century and examines their first attempts to figure out solutions to the problems they identified. Chapter 3 discusses how nonmedicinal prohibition gained traction as a solution, even though many people involved in the opium question did not want it. Chapter 4 follows the course of international opium restriction through the international conferences of the early twentieth century. Chapter 5 shows how changing medical practices and knowledge made it easier for anti-opium activists to promote prohibition.

In 1880, opium was legal, commonly consumed for recreational and medicinal purposes, and integral to many people's lives around the world. It was also a source of important revenue for many governments. By 1940, as World War II raged, some countries prohibited opium and most others restricted it. It remained critical for pain relief, but its other medical uses were greatly diminished in countries having effective public health systems and modern medicine. This transition was a contested one, but by 1940, few people defended easy access to opium. It was the eve of global prohibition.

2. IDENTIFYING THE PROBLEM

Britain went to war with China in the middle of the nineteenth century to force the Chinese government to permit opium sales, even though the Chinese government wanted to ban opium. At the time, some British citizens were disturbed both by the trade and by the need to use military force to enforce the trade. Anti-opium sentiment in England flared. Given the critical role of opium in society in both Europe and Asia, however, powerful groups in society rarely shared this sentiment. This kernel of an anti-opium movement slowly grew, and by the late nineteenth century, some people in China and India, as well as missionaries and reformers in Europe and the United States, had begun to advocate more effectively against opium.

Not surprisingly, even though Britain defeated China in the Opium Wars and gained the ability to sell opium to China, the anti-opium sentiment that had prompted the war persisted in China. A dramatic expression of this persistence came in 1869. Yixin, known in English as Prince Gong, who was the previous regent to his half nephew, the reigning emperor, complained to the departing British minister Rutherford Alcock about the British opium policy. It was a bold move, given China's defeat and perceived weakness and the importance of the opium trade to Britain's finances and imperial status. But Alcock listened carefully and was persuaded. Powerful voices like his had influence back in England. Anti-opium sentiment from China and India continued to grow, become more organized, and express itself to sympathetic ears in England, Europe, and the United States.[1]

Britain had one of the first prominent and long-lasting anti-opium groups: the British Society for the Suppression of the Opium Trade (SSOT), founded in 1874. Most members were religiously motivated, largely due to their involvement with missionary activities in Asia, especially China. They published *Friend of China*, a monthly magazine designed to publicize the horrors of the British opium trade in China. Sometimes articles in the magazine also featured British colonies such as India or Burma, and occasionally they explored the problems with opium in other parts of Asia.[2] The very first issue, published in 1875, featured letters and speeches from British merchants, reformers, and missionaries decrying opium's effects on China. The issue included a speech given at an SSOT meeting by Chan Laisun, guest of Thomas Hanbury, a British merchant. Laisun's rhetoric was typical of the journal: "In order to gratify his passion for the opium which is destroying him, [the opium smoker] will pawn his house and all it contains, he will sell his children and pawn his very wife. . . . No language can describe all the horrors which result from the use of opium in China; it involves a state of existence which the Chinese describe as 'living in a second hell.'"[3] The society's focus on Asia is revealing. Opium was consumed widely in England too, and indeed throughout Europe and the United States. Anti-opium movements targeting opium use in Britain focused primarily on eradicating opium dens and smoking, associated with Chinese immigrants, and limiting unfettered access by children. The more lurid campaigns against use in China touted only the harms of opium consumption.

British reformers wanted to stop the British trade in opium to China, but British imperialism in Asia depended on the production, sale, and consumption of opium. The opium sold by British traders in China largely came from India. In 1870, India produced approximately 5,700 metric tons of opium, the vast majority of it destined for China. Indians themselves consumed little of what remained; most was exported to Southeast Asia and to some extent to the Middle East, Europe, and North America. These large numbers suggest that a lot of money was made in opium, and it was. The government revenue stemming from the opium trade was immense, amounting to 16 percent of the budget of India, and at 40 percent or more, even more important for the budget of the Straits Settlements (Singapore).[4]

Opium-trading firms flourished as well. They purchased opium from the British government or sometimes directly from peasant growers and sold it to governments, private firms, and individuals throughout the world. The demand for opium continued to grow, making it a profitable business venture. British firms were not the only ones involved in the trade. Merchants from France, the Netherlands, and the United States, among others, included opium among the goods they bought and sold. The peasants who grew opium, in India as well as China, Persia, and the Ottoman Empire, did not receive the financial benefit that the traders or governments did and in some cases were impoverished by being forced to grow opium. In most of India, for instance, the British government purchased their produce, meaning the price was set so as to advantage the government. Similar policies were in place in most opium-growing regions. Imperial powers, particularly Britain, required their subjects to grow opium for the benefit of European companies and countries, and they promoted consumption of opium to encourage a more robust market. These policies undoubtedly increased addiction in consumers and poverty in growers.

China is the country most often associated with opium consumption in the nineteenth century, and the use of opium there certainly was growing quickly. During the early decades of the 1800s, after the British had been importing opium into China vigorously for about 50 years, opium exports from India amounted to approximately 4,000 chests per year, while by the end of the century, total opium exports were approximately 70,000 chests per year. A chest was a standard measure of 133 pounds, meaning that exports had reached more than 9 million pounds by 1900. This opium went to China, Southeast Asia, Europe, and the United States, although most of it went to China. In addition, local Chinese production of opium also had increased dramatically, from almost nothing at the start of the century to, by the end of the century, enough to supply about half of China's growing consumption. It's difficult to know how many people actually consumed opium and even harder to assess how many of them were addicted, but clearly the amounts of opium in China helped fuel a massive increase in opium use.

China was far from the only place where opium use increased in the nineteenth century, though. Imperial governments in Southeast Asia, which found that opium was as profitable there as in China, set up systems for them to control and profit from the import and distribution of opium. In part the habit spread there as laborers from China arrived to work in the docks and plantations and mines, but the local population also began to consume. Most commonly, both Chinese migrants to Southeast Asia as well as people already in the region consumed opium by smoking. In Europe and the United States, however, people rarely smoked opium. Chinese immigrants of course did, and sometimes artists such as writers smoked too, but most Europeans and Americans took opium in laudanum or other tinctures. With few exceptions, such as Japan or most of Africa, the number of people taking opium grew dramatically in the nineteenth century for medicinal or recreational purposes, or for some combination of the two.

The growing use is part of what prompted the anti-opium activism of the late nineteenth century. Given the profitable and growing nature of the business, neither traders nor the involved governments welcomed the anti-opium activism of SSOT and similar groups founded in China, India, France, the Netherlands, and, to a lesser extent, the United States during the 1870s. But another group began to raise concerns, and it was harder to ignore: government officials involved in the opium trade, especially in the colonies. With missionaries and local people advocating against opium from a moral and religious perspective, and government officials raising concerns about corruption and evasion of laws, the anti-opium movement gained some ground.

Charles TeMechelen, a government official in the Netherlands Indies (present-day Indonesia), studied the opium problem from his vantage point as the person in charge of preventing smuggling of opium. Unlike Britain, the Dutch government did not have a colony producing opium. But the Dutch government maintained a monopoly over the importation of opium to its colony in the Netherlands Indies. The government then auctioned off the right to sell opium in particular geographical areas of the colony, usually to an ethnic Chinese person or group of people. This system was called the "opium farm," although it does not refer to growing opium, only to the "farmed-out" right to sell opium. The government collected revenue from the auction and benefited by being the only legal source of opium for each opium farmer. TeMechelen's job was to prevent opium farmers (those with the right to sell opium) and opium users from smuggling opium into the country. Smuggling undercut the government's profits.

TeMechelen's report, begun in 1885 and not completed until 1886, thoroughly explored the opium farm system on Java, the most populated island of the Netherlands Indies. He approached the issue of opium sales in a practical manner, not considering whether it was moral. He thought it would be impossible to eradicate use, so he wanted to make sure the government had as much control over sales as possible. The government would then profit, not smugglers. To that end, he advocated working closely with the opium farmers and dramatically increasing the size and prestige of government anti-opium forces. His own efforts were initially successful, and licit sales of opium shot up, suggesting that illicit sales were squeezed. But over time the opium farmers seem to have taken advantage of their close connections with TeMechelen, and several were accused of smuggling opium right under his nose. Still, his report urged the Dutch government to keep the opium farm system and work more on enforcement.[5]

Although TeMechelen's report prompted no substantive change in Dutch opium policy for its colony, its conclusions pointed to issues that were beginning to bother European colonial officials throughout Asia. The people who were given government monopolies over the retail sale of opium were also illicitly importing and selling opium to local people. These illicit sales undercut colonial government control over its territory. Opium farmers were supposed to be providing policing to prevent smuggling but clearly were actually participating in smuggling. Control over borders was spotty at best. In addition, these illicit opium sales hurt government revenue. At minimum, the opium farmers were buying less government opium than they might otherwise, but it might even have been hurting the price at auction for the opium farm itself. At this point, in the 1880s, European officials had little concern about the effects of opium on Asians. Mostly they worried about control and profits.

During the 1880s, however, these concerns grew. By the 1890s, several colonial powers were investigating the opium issue. In the French colony of Indochina (the present-day countries of Vietnam, Laos, and Cambodia), the French government tried to move from the opium farm system to a government monopoly over both importation and sale of opium. French officials believed this system would better protect revenue but also better control who smoked opium. Dutch officials thought the French idea was intriguing and sent Dutch officials to Indochina to study its implementation. Their report, issued in 1890, ultimately did not recommend a government monopoly but drew on some French innovations to tighten up the Dutch system.[6] And in England, a group of reformers and missionaries prompted a parliamentary inquiry into opium sales between India and China, an inquiry that grew in size and scope to include British opium policy throughout its empire and some attention to how other empires dealt with opium.

Eventually published in 1894–95 under the authorship of the Royal Commission on Opium as a seven-volume compendium of all the interviews, supporting documentation, and recommendations, the British inquiry recommended no change at all in British imperial opium policy. The anti-opium activists had placed great hopes in this inquiry, but the tactic backfired, at least for the time being. The members of the commission were not opposed to opium sales, and while they conducted an exhaustive study, traveling for months throughout India and collecting testimony from China, the other British colonies in Asia, and both Indochina and the Netherlands Indies, they were inclined to listen more to the other pro-opium voices. The report's conclusions bluntly said that Britain could not afford to give up opium sales from India if it was to maintain the empire. But the commission also reported that doctors in India generally did not oppose opium use, saying that it "is harmful, harmless or even beneficial, according to the measure and discretion with which it is used." And the commission sought to undermine the nearly unanimous missionary opposition to opium, noting that most of those active against opium were "total abstainers," meaning also from alcohol. By this, they meant that the anti-opium activists opposed opium for ideological reasons and were unable to assess its benefit and harm fairly.[7] Those in charge of the Royal Commission simply sidestepped the anti-opium activism of Indians like Soonderbai H. Powar, who conducted a powerful anti-opium lobbying campaign in England from 1889.[8] British opium policy did not change. But the scale of the endeavor, and the questions driving the inquiry, demonstrated that agitation against opium was gaining strength.

Colonial government reports reflected official concern and showed that new policies were being considered. But popular culture in Asia was beginning to reflect a growing uneasiness with opium and its role in society too. The Indian poet Rabindranath Tagore wrote an article in 1881, when he was a young man, with the title in English "The Death Traffic in China." He critiqued British opium trade in China and by extension the production in India, all the fault of Britain.[9] The Dutch novel *Baboe Dalima*, set in the Netherlands Indies, was published in 1886 and was sufficiently popular that it was translated into English within two years. M. T. H. Perelaer, the author, had been in the Dutch military in the Indies, and during his years there he had come to believe Dutch rule was a corrupting force rather than a good influence on the people of the islands. *Baboe Dalima* is a melodramatic tale of all the ill effects on the Indies and its people from the Dutch opium policy. It interestingly focuses very little on the effects of taking opium but more on the corruption of people involved in its sale. Opium farmers and their employees are rich and powerful, skirting the law and even thinking they can seize young women (the Dalima of the title) for nefarious purposes. The people who try to stand up to the opium farmers in this novel never win. Poor Dalima and the upright young man in love with her come to an unhappy end. The opium farmers don't get all they want but come out of it better than anyone else. *Baboe Dalima* is not great literature, but it is one of many novels published in Asia during the late nineteenth century about the problems opium caused in society.[10]

As printed material, not only books but also newspapers and magazines, became more available and popular in colonial Asia at this time, editors and authors were seeking interesting, even sensational topics that touched the lives of many people. These stories sold. They sold in the United States and Europe too. Thomas De Quincey's famous *Confessions of an Opium Eater* was first published in 1821, became immediately popular, and is still in print today. Less well-known responses followed and were popular at the time. *Doctor Judas* (1895), by William Rosser Cobbe, is the autobiography of an American opium addict who promised none of the allure that De Quincey did. In the typical flowery language of the time, Cobbe said he was writing the book not for sympathy but out of duty: "Inexorable duty, and that alone, has urged the writer to the painful task of recording the terrible story of nine years' slavery to opium."[11] This kind of literature became prevalent, a support to the anti-opium activism growing in those years, whether in the United States, Europe, or Asia.

By the end of the nineteenth century, European and American imperialists justified their rule with reference to some version of the civilizing mission ideology. The civilizing mission claimed that European and US imperial rule was beneficial to colonized peoples. Imperialists noted that they brought education, Christianity, infrastructure, and economic development to their colonies. Even back in the nineteenth century, however, this claim was susceptible to criticism that benefits were not widespread, and imperialism also brought exploitation and impoverishment. The handsome profits that European governments, and some individual Europeans, made from opium sales also undercut claims for a civilizing mission. In the 1890s, criticism of opium was gaining force, despite the significant role of opium in society for both medicinal and cultural purposes.

In China, too, anti-opium forces were gaining strength in the 1890s. Some Chinese, before then, feared that increasing opium consumption in their country was ruining the people and draining the government's hard currency reserves, while others found opium consumption pleasurable, sociable, and a good medicine. The two groups were about equal in influence until the 1890s, when the anti-opium voices began to increase. Japan's defeat of China in the Sino-Japanese War of 1894–95, the increasingly insistent voices of European and American missionaries against the drug, the year-by-year increase in the amount of opium available in the country, and government concerns about the effects of all these developments prompted the government to encourage local elites to form anti-opium societies. After 1895, in parts of China, these societies used meetings, propaganda posters, and pamphlets to change the image of opium from desirable luxury good to a substance that would lead to destruction and poverty. For a period, they were quite successful, and during 1906–16, opium consumption decreased. During the 1920s and 1930s, though, consumption rebounded. The reasons are complicated, but the ongoing political struggles in China and the weak central government meant it was difficult to suppress production. Additionally, opium again was associated with glamor by many in the big cities.[12]

Concerns about opium use in Asia spilled over into concerns about opium use in Europe and the United States as well. The addictive qualities of opium had been known as long as the drug had been in use. As early as the 1820s, some reformers and medical practitioners cautioned against overuse. In England, opium use was so common and so ingrained in society that critiques of opium use made little headway. With few doctors, and little the doctors could offer as treatment in any case, people purchased opium to relieve the pains of toothache, arthritis, stomach upset, and teething in children. Laudanum, a mix of alcohol and opium, was as common in the medicine chest as cough syrup and ibuprofen today, and it was used for a similar range of ailments. Parents gave their children Mrs. Winslow's Soothing Syrup for Infants to help them sleep, and then perhaps took Godfrey's Cordial themselves. It was as easy to go to the store for a tincture of opium as for a loaf of bread. Reformers drew attention to what appeared to be an increasing number of accidental overdoses in the middle of the nineteenth century, and the broader public also began to be alarmed at the ease with which opium could be adulterated, making it dangerous. As a result, the 1868 Pharmacy Act put a few restrictions on opium in Britain, primarily to try to enforce labeling of patent medicines but also to add some modest restrictions at the point of sale.[13]

The missionaries and reformers in England who were trying to prevent British opium trade in China and restrict opium production in India also found recreational use in England harmful. They distinguished opium smoking from other forms of consumption. Opium smoking was associated with Asians, especially Chinese, who were a tiny minority in England in the late nineteenth century but increasingly visible, especially in cities. Alarmist stories about filthy opium dens and the ways British were lured into them appeared in popular magazines. In these stories, the danger was as much in becoming more Chinese in appearance and habits through association as it was in becoming addicted to opium. Many people believed that opium smoking had the potential to harm the British nation, even while they believed more traditional forms of consumption, such as laudanum and tinctures, were not dangerous. In the nineteenth century, this rhetoric did not, however, lead to many legal changes.

In the rest of Europe, opium consumption also seemed to be increasing but appears to have remained below the levels seen in Britain. In France in the early nineteenth century, only pharmacists and doctors with a government license could sell opium, so it appears to have been used less liberally than in England. Still, by the mid-nineteenth century, opium use was on the rise as French citizens began to access doctors more frequently, and doctors prescribed one of the few effective treatments for pain that they had. As in England, the French tended to condemn opium smoking as an alien practice, acquired most often by French soldiers or travelers to the new French colonies of Algeria and Indochina. They also, like the British, had a growing concern about this new form of opium use, combined with their perception that opium use generally was increasing.[14]

Despite not having any Asian colonies until the end of the nineteenth century, the United States had an opium consumption rate nearly equal to that of Britain.[15] Patent medicines, many containing both alcohol and opium, were popular in the United States. Many parts of the United States were sparsely populated, with few or no doctors, and opiates were indispensable. By midcentury, it was increasingly seen as inappropriate for middle-class Protestant women to consume alcohol, and many of them used laudanum as a mood-altering drug instead. After the Civil War, too, many soldiers used various opium preparations as treatment for the lingering wounds of war. The high levels of opium consumption by these two well-respected groups helped make opium a common and accepted drug. Just as many American patent medicines with opium existed as in England. Mrs. Winslow's Soothing Syrup, in versions for children and for women's complaints, originated in the United States, joining Davis's Pain-Killer and Dover's Powder among many other remedies containing opium (and often alcohol).

The growing number of temperance groups in the United States after the middle of the nineteenth century sometimes drew attention to the

Fig. 2.1. A typical patent medicine advertisement from the nineteenth century. Wistar's Balsam of Wild Cherry contained alcohol, cherry extract, and opiates. Image from the History of Medicine, United States National Library of Medicine, Bethesda, MD.

issue of opiates as well. They advocated temperance for all, but much of their message stressed that alcohol-consuming immigrants, such as the Irish, posed a threat to American values, or that alcohol was a particular harm to those they thought in need of special protections, such as Indigenous people. These racialized ways of promoting temperance were echoed in anti-opium campaigns. Ironically, sometimes those who advocated most strongly against alcohol consumption were the very people consuming the patent medicines containing both alcohol and opium. From the 1870s, a small movement developed, advocating against all narcotics and alcohol, typified by the Women's Christian Temperance Movement. As in Europe, opium smoking was universally condemned and associated with Chinese immigrants, against whom there was significant prejudice. In the American press, opium dens were presented as lurid places where Chinese men tried to lure innocent, naive young white women into trying opium so they could ensnare them into a life of addiction and prostitution. The strict immigration laws in the United States, which had the effect of preventing Chinese women from joining the Chinese men who had immigrated to the United States, both stemmed from and heightened this fear among white Americans. In this context, the first laws against opium consumption, most of which banned only opium dens, began to pass in towns and cities in California in the 1870s.[16] Bans against opium smoking followed within a few years in some places.

Unlike in Europe, these local option laws, allowing prohibition in a city or, later, state, allowed the first prohibition movement to take hold in the United States. By the end of the century, a few cities and states, mostly in the US West, had banned opium smoking. Since possession of opium itself was not illegal, only of that prepared for smoking, these laws were even less effective than prohibition laws generally are. But these laws also demonstrated the tactics that would be used to begin to restrict and eventually prohibit opium in the future.

At the end of the nineteenth century, then, opium was commonly consumed in many parts of the world. It was an absolutely indispensable medicine, at that time the only effective pain relief available. Since people around the world generally treated all but the most serious illnesses and injuries without going to the doctor, most people self-dosed with opium. This practice assuredly led to some dependencies, and even addiction, among people suffering chronic low-level pain. But it also meant that many people took opium as needed only, which may have been frequent by today's standards but does not seem to have interfered with their daily life. With the ease of access to opium, many people at the end of the nineteenth century also certainly consumed opium for pleasure. The tradition of opium smoking in Asia, which spread to Europe and the United States to some degree in the nineteenth century, has associations with consumption for pleasure rather than medicine. That connection holds for Europe and the United States, although less so for Asia, and because of the connection in Europe and the United States, this form of opium consumption attracted criticism by the end of the nineteenth century.

In 1899, opium was common if increasingly contested and controversial. Still, probably no observer, whether an opium user or a critic of opium, would have predicted that within two decades, a strong international movement arguing for restrictions on opium, and having the goal of eventual prohibition, would have gained a foothold at the highest international levels. Yet that is exactly what happened.

3. DECIDING ON PROHIBITION

In the late nineteenth century, a wave of reform movements drew attention to the difficult conditions for working people, peasants, women, children, and colonized subjects. Reformers advocated for shorter working hours, safer working conditions, compulsory education, and temperance as well as against child labor, monopolies, and penal labor codes. Because many of these reforms were eventually adopted, first in Europe and the United States, then spreading throughout the world and reaching colonized spaces more slowly, it is sometimes difficult to remember how many people did not see the need for these reforms and worked to stop them. Reformers concerned about opium also faced significant opposition. Some people thought opium remained a useful medicine rather than a dangerous, addictive drug. Others knew that many governments relied on the revenue from opium in order to fund important projects. Many Europeans and Americans also believed opium was only a problem for some types of people. Racism worked in two different ways to influence how they thought. On the one hand, many Europeans and Americans believed some groups, particularly but not only ethnic Chinese, could consume opium without harm to themselves. Since that was the case, they believed, it was fine to sell opium to them. On the other hand, many Europeans and Americans also believed certain groups, including Burmese and Filipinos but also white women, were particularly susceptible to harm from opium. For these groups, a ban was critical.[1] These assessments and categories don't make much sense to modern observers. But in the late nineteenth and early twentieth centuries, these kinds of beliefs shaped the debate about what kind of policies nations, imperial powers, and eventually the international community should adopt regarding opium, and later other drugs. This chapter explores how that debate developed and how prohibition became the answer.

In colonial Southeast Asia before the 1880s, there was not much anti-opium sentiment. Opium was not merely a critically important medicine for its ability to relieve pain, symptoms of malaria, and help with the diarrhea many people experienced for a variety of reasons, but it also provided a significant portion of many colonial budgets, from the modest but significant amount of about 10 percent in Burma and parts of the Netherlands Indies to as high as 50 percent for Singapore. Though opium smoking as a custom had been brought to most parts of Southeast Asia by ethnic Chinese migrants and then reinforced by the actions of colonial governments, by the late nineteenth century many Southeast Asians as well as ethnic Chinese smoked, for pleasure and medicinal purposes. It had become an entrenched, if sometimes contested, practice in many parts of the region. Colonial governments raised their vast sums from opium with low levels of administration before 1890. Each government ran an "opium farm," which was a tax farm, not an agricultural farm. The government imported the opium and then auctioned off the right to sell opium in a particular geographical region to the highest bidder. The successful opium farmer paid the fee to the government but also had to purchase all the opium he sold to customers from the government, at prices it set. The government made a tidy, predictable profit. The opium farmer took on all risk of changes in demand or retail price as well as most policing duties. This approach generated substantial profit for colonial governments but meant they had nearly no idea how much opium was really consumed, who smoked it, when, and where. In addition, it is likely that opium farmers imported some opium illicitly, for a price advantage, and therefore sold more than the government knew about. For some decades, the arrangement suited everyone. By the end of the nineteenth century, though, as concepts like the "civilizing mission" became more important to colonial officials in their justification of imperial rule, it was more difficult to ignore these illicit imports and the higher levels of opium consumption they promoted.[2]

China was also struggling to figure out how to control opium. In the aftermath of the Opium Wars (1839 and 1858), opium imports from India were legalized in some places. The amount of opium in the country increased, as did usage. Previously opium had been too expensive for most ordinary people to consume it, but prices dropped with the increase in amounts, especially after Chinese peasants began to grow opium as well. The Chinese-grown opium was considered of lower quality, but it was affordable. Women even began to smoke, although almost entirely in the privacy of their homes.

The Chinese government had little control over the import or retail sale of opium and mainly worried about the apparent increase in use and the continuing drain of silver from the country to pay for the imports. The government decided to support an even greater increase in opium growing in China as a solution. It would not mean a decrease in consumption in the country, but it would at least reduce the currency drain. By the early twentieth century, domestic opium exceeded imported.[3]

In the early 1890s, Britain, the Netherlands, and France all launched investigations into opium use in their empires. The British investigation, a multiyear, multicountry Parliamentary inquiry discussed in chapter 2, was the most substantial and far-reaching. It had been prompted by missionaries and anti-opium activists, while the Dutch and French ones grew out of concerns held by government officials. The results of the British inquiry were published in a seven-volume report containing all the testimony given to the commission. Much of the testimony was negative, touting the horrors of opium and the dangers inherent in British promotion of the opium trade. But the policy results were negligible. British officials, the vast majority of whom favored continuing the opium trade, focused the inquiry on the Britain–China trade, meaning that even the sections on the role of opium in the empire mostly explored the role of opium in India, where it was both grown for export and consumed. British exports to and promotion of opium consumption in Hong Kong, Malaya, and Burma attracted nearly no attention despite the fact that this trade was large and growing. No changes at all occurred in policy for those colonies. The anti-opium activists had most hoped for action against the trade with China. They were disappointed. The report emphasized that most local observers believed opium consumption was not a serious problem but also argued that if China wanted to forbid opium, China should take the first step. British traders should not be denied the right to trade in a commodity legal in China and even grown there in ever larger amounts. No policy changes occurred, although some people suggested that Britain and China could discuss trade restrictions on a mutual basis.

Dutch and French officials initiated their studies because they were worried about the problems with the opium farms in Indochina and the Netherlands Indies. They thought the opium farmers were importing and selling more opium than they said and that consumption therefore was more substantial than anyone knew. Despite the fact that anti-opium activists were trying to influence these inquiries to promote less opium consumption, the Dutch and French reports mostly recommended changes designed to better control and regulate the sale of opium for the purpose of knowing who was selling and buying rather than for the purpose of restricting use. The Dutch official W. P. Groeneveldt, sent by the Netherlands Indies government to Indochina for an inspection tour, recommended switching from the opium farm system to a government monopoly, but only slowly. He said that if the government was going to change, it needed to be ready to do things properly. First, the government would need to institute a better police force, create an organized packing system for the opium, and hire trained government officials to manage sales.[4] Controlling opium, not necessarily reducing its use, was the goal. Japan had also recently acquired Formosa (Taiwan) as a colony, as a result of the 1894–95 Sino-Japanese War. Japan had previously restricted opium imports into Japan, and recreational use there was modest. But Formosa had substantial numbers of recreational opium smokers, most of them ethnic Chinese. In part to better control opium, as the other colonial powers did, but also to prevent ethnic Chinese from traveling with opium between China, Formosa, and Japan itself, Japan instituted a monopoly over the import and sale of opium for Formosa, with a goal of eventually reducing use.[5]

In the early 1890s, then, colonial governments in Southeast Asia were showing some concerns about the use of opium by their colonial subjects. The concern did not stem from worries about opium use itself as much as from a desire to have efficiently functioning colonial bureaucracies and for those in charge of the colonial governments to have better knowledge of the actions of both government officials and colonial subjects. They were not motivated by a desire to prevent most colonial subjects from buying and using opium. Some colonial policies forbade some groups from using opium. In the Netherlands Indies, for instance, the parts of those islands where opium use had never occurred to that point were considered "forbidden areas." Opium farms could not legally sell in those areas. In other colonies, such as Burma and the Philippines, British and Spanish colonial officials had banned the sale of recreational opium to, respectively, ethnic Burmese and Filipinos. Other ethnic groups in these colonies could legally purchase opium, but colonial officials deemed Burmese and Filipinos to be incapable of using opium without harm to themselves. The reasons for forbidding the drug, however, had more to do with perceptions of the incapacity of Burmese and Filipinos than with dangers inherent in opium. Japan provided a partial exception in its efforts to control and then restrict opium use in Formosa. These were aimed more at controlling the ability of Chinese to travel throughout the Japanese empire with opium than with concerns for the people of Formosa. Even if these initial expressions of concern about opium were limited in various ways, we see in them the beginnings of broader critiques that were extended and used to justify expanded restriction in the twentieth century.

In the United States and Europe, as discussed in chapter 2, agitation against opium smoking was growing during the late nineteenth century. In both places, opium smoking was associated with immigrants, usually Chinese, and considered alien. It was not difficult to get support for actions against opium prepared for smoking and indeed often against the ethnic groups associated with that kind of opium consumption. But opium in medicinal and quasi-medicinal forms (laudanum, patent medicines, and by the end of the century, morphine) was a common drug, part of everyday life. Governments did not control the trade in the way they did in Asia; the economic benefits to the government were less direct, less easy to identify. But in the late nineteenth century, there was not much agitation against even quasi-medicinal use of opiates. Patent medicines were very popular, accounting for as much as 25 percent of all print advertising by 1880 in Britain. Many patent medicines did not contain opiates or cocaine, but a number did. People consumed patent medicines containing opiates without knowing it was an ingredient. In the United States, only after the 1906 Pure Food and Drug Act passed did medicines have to include a list of ingredients. In Britain, the 1868 Poisons Act required any patent medicine containing opium, cocaine, or morphine to be labeled a poison, but this act was rarely enforced. In 1908, the Pharmacy Act stipulated that patent medicines had to contain less than 1 percent cocaine, morphine, or opium.[6] In both countries, though, as in other parts of Europe, doctors could and did prescribe opiates freely to people for a wide variety of ailments. Critics attacked these practices, but both law and custom supported a broad level of opium consumption.

The mention of cocaine in these late nineteenth- and early twentieth-century laws demonstrates that cocaine also had become a prevalent drug, used both medicinally and recreationally. Coca leaf, traditionally grown in what is now Bolivia and Peru, had been consumed for centuries by local people, by chewing and in teas, enjoyed for its mild stimulation and even helpful as a digestive. Coca leaves do not store well, or at least did not under the conditions available before the twentieth century, so coca did not become the global commodity that opium did. Cocaine, first isolated

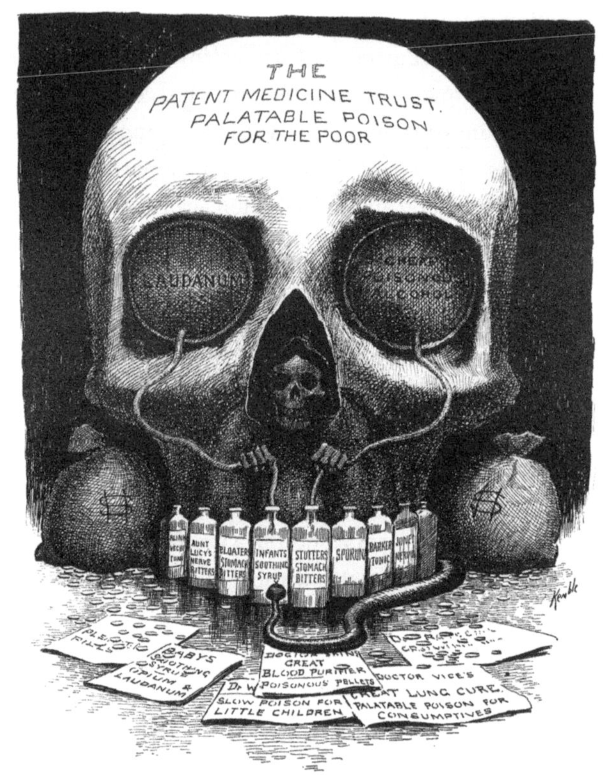

Fig. 3.1. Journalistic investigations of the patent medicine industry in the early twentieth century revealed that these medicines contained significant amounts of alcohol and opiates. From E. W. Kimble, "Death's Laboratory—the Patent Medicine Trust," *Collier's* (1905), Library of Congress, Washington, DC.

from coca in 1860, is a more powerful stimulant and travels well. It quickly became popular in the United States and Europe. Peruvian scientists developed better processing procedures to allow for increased exports. The Dutch government even established a coca leaf plantation in its colony on Java in the 1870s. Nerve tonics included cocaine. Physicians, famously including Sigmund Freud, prescribed it to patients and themselves for depression and other mental health conditions. Until the early twentieth century, cocaine had a mostly positive reputation. Restrictions on it lagged those on opiates, but after World War I they often fell under the same restriction policies and laws.[7]

The forces supporting opium and cocaine consumption in the late nineteenth century looked stronger than the forces opposing it. There was a growing discussion about problems of addiction, but many people at the time believed addiction was a sign of personal weakness rather than a problem with the drug itself. It seemed likely that there might be more regulation of opium sale and use, to protect groups like children, young women, and some ethnic groups. The trade itself seemed too significant to fully eradicate.

When the United States acquired the Philippines in 1898, then, opium policy was a matter of discussion in colonial Southeast Asia, but opium was generally available for most people, and there was no hint of a wholesale change in policy in the near future. Governments were making substantial profit from the sale of opium. Its consumption was common and medically useful, while also sometimes criticized as having negative social or cultural effects. The initial US governmental policy regarding opium differed some from that of other colonial powers, but not substantially. The United States did not end the Spanish opium farm. Instead, the United States imposed a high tariff, meaning an import tax, on opium coming into the Philippines. This policy echoed existing federal law in the United States. It was easy to administer and kept the price of opium reasonably high. US colonial officials had more pressing matters at hand, as the United States fought to conquer the Philippines and then worked to set up a colonial government there. US officials spent no time considering whether the Philippines needed a different opium policy from that in place in the metropole. It is difficult to trace the initial effects of the change in opium policy in the islands from the Spanish to the US era. The ongoing war in the first years of US rule both disrupted usual imports and led to increased demand for opiates as medicine, to treat wounded soldiers for pain and to alleviate the effects of the devastating cholera epidemic sweeping Manila. It is also likely that opium was illicitly imported to evade the import tax and that informal markets in opium sprang up.[8]

One way to interpret the utter lack of concern by US officials about the nature of opium policy for the Philippines is that US officials were not really interested in or prepared to actually rule in the Philippines. However, it is more likely an indication of the lack of concern US officials had about opium consumption. Opium consumption in the United States was common, even if opium smoking was not. But observers perceived the customs as different in Asia. William Howard Taft, the governor general of the Philippines in 1903, wrote to US secretary of war Elihu Root that "in America opium smoking is regarded as very different from liquor habit . . . although a close and impartial observer can see no real or practical distinction." He echoed a commonly held sentiment about ethnic Chinese when writing that "most of them are temperate in smoking it merely as sedative and that effects are probably not worse than those of liquor habit among Americans."[9] Taft was not worried about people drinking alcohol in the United States and likewise not concerned about people smoking opium in the Philippines. As in the British case, though, the first anti-opium activists in the US-ruled Philippines were missionaries. Protestant missionaries, most prominently Methodists but also some Episcopalians, with experience in China launched anti-opium activism shortly after arriving in the Philippines. The leadership of the Methodists proved consequential: they favored abstinence more generally, drew on deep public support for an abstinence agenda by local congregations in the United States, and prepared to mobilize a public campaign. US officials in the Philippines and in Washington initially paid little attention. But when anti-opium activists prompted their followers to send thousands of telegrams in support of anti-opium measures to the White House, President Theodore Roosevelt took notice.

Roosevelt adhered to the tenets of the Progressive movement. Progressives advocated studying a problem before proposing a solution, so US officials set up a commission in 1903 to study opium policy in nearby countries and colonies. The Philippine Opium Commission traveled throughout Asia to interview officials, medical professionals, and leading community members. With the knowledge gained, it returned to recommend a policy. US officials in the colonial government hoped that the time the commission took to investigate would sufficiently delay action until they could regain control over the course of opium policy, but they also wanted to know more about what had and had not worked elsewhere. All the members of the commission began as skeptics of opium regulation. Charles H. Brent, on the commission due to his status as the Episcopal bishop in Manila, believed much as Taft at this point: opium consumption was no worse for Asians than alcohol for whites, and like many Episcopalians, he had no problem with a glass of wine in the evening. The other members of the commission were Jose Albert, a physician in Manila; and the commission's chair, Edward C. Carter, commissioner of public health for the Philippines government and a career military surgeon.

This commission took several months to travel and talk with knowledgeable people throughout Asia. The conclusions reflect that they had good contacts with missionaries, who promoted a prohibitionist approach. The results have done much to shape US thinking about drug policy to the present day in ways that have been problematic. The first conclusion, which appeals instinctively but has created significant tragedy, was the easy assumption that it is easy to establish neat, clear categories of "medicinal opium" and "recreational opium." Once established, if careful rules about proper medicinal use are followed by conscientious medical professionals, opium can be safely used. The commission's report to Congress, published in 1906, consistently distinguished between "legitimate medical practice" and problematic recreational use, or described a restriction or prohibition that should be adopted "except for medical purposes."[10] Medical practitioners, both doctors and pharmacists, were interviewed by the commission. Nearly all of them made a casual distinction between medical use (prescribed by a doctor; obtained from a pharmacist) and recreational use. A few noted that there were dangers of addiction if doctors prescribed opium for chronic pain, but overall, the impression they gave in interviews was that medicinal opium, from a medical professional, should be legal with no government oversight. The doctors did not all agree on the nature and degree of danger from recreational opium but were in accord that opium as medicine rarely posed a danger.

A second conclusion, equally problematic, is that people of different races react to the use of drugs differently. People interviewed and the authors of the report shared a belief that it is more dangerous for some groups to use certain drugs than it is for other groups. They also believed that some groups are themselves more dangerous to society when they use drugs. This assumption was at the heart of the commission's charge, since it was formed in response to a proposed bill to continue the Spanish-era practice of forbidding Filipinos from smoking opium. The commission had been instructed to find methods for "reducing and restraining the use of opium by the Filipinos."[11] Some aspects of the proposal were controversial, but this provision was put forth as an unquestioned benefit. Commissioners, however, asked about the effects of opium on different ethnic groups as they traveled around Asia. The question about protecting Filipinos sounds like a thoughtful one, taking care to protect the new subjects of US rule. But it set up a racial distinction about drug use and abuse that has had a harmful effect in US drug policy to the present day.

Finally, the third conclusion was that the drug problem originated outside the country, meaning outside the Philippines. The solution to the drug problem then was to prohibit the importation of drugs. The report noted that with few exceptions, Filipinos did not have a practice of smoking opium. The habit was prevalent only among the ethnic Chinese. Since US immigration law, including the 1882 law prohibiting Chinese immigration, was extended to the new US colony in the Philippines, that meant "as long as the present Chinese exclusion act continues in force there can be no influx of opium smokers from without."[12] The commissioners believed that since few Filipinos had a tradition of smoking, banning opium would be successful. They also thought that Chinese, whom they believed were very likely to be smokers, would not even want to come to the Philippines if opium was prohibited there. For US officials, this policy was a double benefit, then, getting rid of both Chinese immigrants and opium. In this conclusion, too, racism plays an unfortunate and integral role. After prohibition was adopted in the Philippines, the flaws in each of these guiding principles revealed themselves quite quickly. Opium use in the Philippines was both driven underground and seemed to expand. Rather than examining assumptions, however, US policymakers adopted a similar approach in making changes to federal law governing the United States as a whole. In 1909, Congress passed an act to forbid the importation of opium prepared for smoking. In 1914, Congress adopted the Harrison Narcotics Act, which forbade nonmedicinal opium consumption. The US government also began to promote opium restriction in other parts of Asia, assuming that reduced opium consumption in the region would reduce smuggling into the Philippines.

The 1903 Philippine Commission initially recommended a government monopoly over opium sales, as existed in most of Southeast Asia, for three years, followed by prohibition "except for medicinal purposes." Officials in Washington, DC, were wary about a government monopoly. It would take a lot of money and expertise to set up a government monopoly and then run it for only three years. So they modified the plan. The policy eventually adopted, beginning in 1905, stipulated a high tariff for three years, followed by prohibition except for medical use.[13] As US colonial officials began to think about enforcement, however, they quickly realized that smuggling was likely to be rampant. With licit opium in all neighboring countries, many of which had islands only a short distance from some islands of the Philippines, and with all but the most central ports lightly monitored, if at all, any demand for opium in the Philippines would be met. US officials therefore began thinking almost immediately about establishing an international restriction regime. As early as 1906, US officials were beginning to approach officials in other Asian countries and colonies to ask about a region-wide approach to controlling opium. In calling for the first opium conference, which came to fruition as the 1909 Shanghai Opium Commission, they set in motion the fourth problematic component of US drug policy: a consistent effort to promote an international drug regime designed by US officials, serving stated US interests.

Prohibition in the Philippines did go into effect in 1908 as planned and scheduled. The government tracked the number of people who entered drug treatment programs, the number of people arrested for buying or selling opium illegally, and the amount of opium seized as people attempted to smuggle it into the country. These numbers were all pretty high. At first that did not worry US or Filipino officials very much. They hoped that in these early stages of prohibition, the high numbers of those seeking treatment would mean that later the arrests and seizures would decrease. US officials began planning, however, for a continued effort to prevent opium from entering the Philippines. This emphasis on supply has characterized the US effort to prohibit drugs ever since. The idea has been that eradicating the supply of illegal drugs, often perceived to be entering the country from outside its border, would lead to dramatic decreases in illicit consumption. Reduced supply of course does mean less use, at least temporarily, but without also reducing demand, other suppliers are likely to step in, or at least try to step in, to fill the void.

Still, supply reduction was appealing, and the United States began working to promote international cooperation throughout Asia to decrease supply. The first step in this direction was the 1909 Shanghai Opium Conference, held at the invitation of the United States. That conference begins the story of international efforts at opium regulation, which were contentious but constant after 1909. The beginning of that story is told in chapter 4.

4. INTERNATIONAL CONFERENCES

Before the twentieth century, there were not many international conferences at which a group of nations gathered to address social, economic, or cultural issues. Some existed, such as the Congress of Vienna, for settling diplomatic issues or to negotiate peace after a war. But the kinds of international conferences that became commonplace in the twentieth century, addressing regional or global issues, were rare. A few topics prompted such conferences: postal agreements, so that mail could flow freely around the world, and infectious diseases, so that appropriate quarantines could be established to prevent the spread of devastating diseases such as the plague. Otherwise, nations generally solved problems on their own or in one-on-one negotiations. Problems requiring a broader coalition did not get resolved.

In the second half of the nineteenth century, however, people in a variety of nations across the world began to change their attitude about international gatherings and made an attempt to resolve problems that nations had in common and especially problems that crossed national boundaries. Those interested in health measures pioneered these conferences. The first International Sanitary Conference was held in 1851, with twelve delegations, nearly all from Europe. The conference was prompted largely by the transnational, and growing, threat of cholera. It proved difficult for those attending to find common ground on either the science or the right policy responses. Still, additional Sanitary Conferences occurred over the next four decades because the transnational threat continued. A first success came in 1892 when more than a dozen nations signed the first International Sanitary Convention. Over the next ten years, more nations from all parts of the world joined, and they came to agreements about how to handle a wide range of infectious diseases, such as quarantine measures at ports and transit points, and started to create best practices for clean water and sewage.[1]

A conference about international peace was held at The Hague, in the Netherlands, in 1899, with another in 1907. Concern about what was then called "white slavery," or trafficking in women for the purposes of prostitution, also prompted an international conference, in 1902. These conferences all stemmed from concerns of reformers about the need to improve world conditions. The Sanitary Conferences, like the earlier ones about diplomacy or postal agreements, were attended by government officials who had to make policy for their countries. But the "white slavery" and peace conferences were also attended by private citizens, who would work to lobby their governments.[2]

Shanghai Opium Commission, 1909

In 1906, when US president Theodore Roosevelt was prompted to invite officials from countries in Asia to an international conference about the opium problem, it was not a novel thing but also not a common one.[3] Roosevelt did not think of the idea for the conference himself; it was suggested to him by his friend Charles H. Brent, the Episcopal bishop in the Philippines, a US colony since 1898. Brent had been a relatively unknown Episcopal priest when selected as bishop in the new US colony. His abilities developed there, and he became a leading figure not only in the anti-opium movement over the next few decades but also in promoting better relations among both nations and different denominations. Bishop Brent had participated in an investigation of opium throughout Asia in 1903, and, as a result, he thought the United States should promote opium restriction. Brent wanted US rule in the Philippines to succeed and for the United States to be a moral force in colonial Southeast Asia. US officials thought the conference was a good idea. The United States could show support for the Chinese government, which was trying to suppress use of opium in its country. More importantly from the US perspective, the conference could help gain international support for the US effort to prohibit opium in the Philippines. The invitation from the United States went to all governments in Asia as well as those countries that had an interest in the opium issue in Asia, which meant all colonial governments, like Britain, France, and the Netherlands. Other than China, most of the other governments were not immediately interested in participating. But slowly, US and Chinese officials convinced the other countries to sign on. The Shanghai Opium Commission opened on February 5, 1909.

Attendees had different ideas about what the commission should do and what they wanted to get out of it, as is common. The Chinese wanted to get all the other countries to help them keep opium out of their country and especially to force the British government to put a stop to British opium sales in China. The British already had agreed to stop selling opium in China once the Chinese were able to enforce prohibition inside China, or by 1917 at the latest. Since the time of the Opium Wars in the middle of the nineteenth century, Chinese officials had been trying to get Britain to stop selling opium in China, saying opium was destructive to the Chinese people. British officials and merchants said that a lot of opium was grown in and sold by Chinese, so they thought they should be allowed to continue selling it too. Most other attending nations were not very interested in getting involved in that dispute but eventually agreed to the principle that countries should not allow legal exports of narcotics to nations that had prohibited those drugs. It was difficult to know how to enforce that agreement, but for the time being, the Chinese were satisfied with this assurance.

US officials wanted to get the participating nations to sign on to the prohibitionist approach that they had recently adopted for the Philippines. Only China supported the United States in this endeavor, although Japan, which had adopted a nearly prohibitionist approach for its colony in Taiwan, was sympathetic. None of the European colonial powers were supportive at all. In all the European colonies of Southeast Asia, but especially in the Straits Settlements, Malaya, and the Netherlands Indies, a high percentage of the budget came from the legal sale of opium, as discussed in chapter 3. Singapore, part of the Straits Settlements and a British colony, derived as much as 50 percent of government revenue from the sale of opium. Others were less dependent on this revenue but still got 10–30 percent of government funds from opium sales. The battle for regional prohibition would be a difficult one for the United States, not only because of the revenue but because many people did not think smoking or eating opium was particularly harmful. As discussed in chapter 5, there was a medical debate about that during the early twentieth century.

The US delegation was headed initially by Charles Brent, but he was elected chair of the commission, so Hamilton Wright took over the top spot in the US group. Wright was a dedicated prohibitionist. He also had experience in Southeast Asia. He had served the British Medical Service in Malaya, doing research on the causes of the disease beriberi. While he was in the region, he traveled in the new US colony in the Philippines and published the book *Handbook of the Philippines* in 1907. His combination of interests—in medical research, prohibition, and Southeast Asia—prompted him to spend the rest of his life continuing to work on the international level to restrict opium. His wife, Elizabeth Washburn Wright, took up the cause after he died in 1917 at age forty-nine due to injuries from a car accident. She had accompanied her husband to Southeast Asia, where she admired British activities in the region but thought the United States had opportunities to do better in the Philippines. She remained a prominent anti-opium activist until World War II, continuing to be involved with the issue until her death in 1954.

Even though most delegates who were not from the United States disagreed with Hamilton Wright, the US delegation succeeded in getting the commission to adopt a resolution that all participating nations move toward a policy of "gradual suppression" of opium consumption except for "medical purposes."[4] Everyone thought they had won. Wright and the US delegation were happy that the commission reflected the US principle of prohibition. The other delegates knew they could recommend that their countries take a long time to achieve their common goal, and there was a lot of disagreement about what constituted legitimate medical use. With the benefit of hindsight, one might argue Wright prevailed. Future conferences would all wrestle with how fast to move toward prohibition. And there would have to be a future conference if the agreements at Shanghai were to become binding. As a "commission," the Shanghai meeting could only establish principles. The nations would have to come together at a "conference," to which they would send delegates with official instructions from their governments, in order to negotiate a potential treaty. Only then would these agreements have the status of international law.

Hague Opium Conference, 1911/1912

A few months after the conclusion of the Shanghai Commission, the US government began pushing other nations to agree to participate in a conference at which they would negotiate a treaty. US diplomats stationed in the countries that had participated in the Shanghai Commission approached those governments and asked them when they wanted to convene an official conference. As before, other than China and a few small nations, no nation was very keen to participate in this US-led effort. The Dutch government, for instance, offered to host the conference but then suggested that it should focus on smuggling rather than the restriction of opium. British officials said that opium wasn't the real problem. They suggested the conference also consider morphine, heroin, and cocaine, in addition to opium. These drugs (two of which are processed forms of opium) were becoming significant societal problems, especially in Europe, so adding them made sense. But adding them also meant that there was much less attention to the issue of traditional opium, which is what the United States wanted. Just getting agreement about holding the conference took nearly two years, which is one indication that participating powers were wary about what might happen there.

The conference, which met during December 1911–January 1912, resulted in the first international drug-control treaty. Getting to that was difficult, however, and the results were much less than what the US delegation, again led by Charles Brent (who chaired the conference) and Hamilton Wright, wanted. Both Britain and Germany successfully deflected attention from their main concerns. British officials spent a good deal of energy trying to get the delegates to focus on heroin, morphine, and cocaine and to reduce their attention on opium. Opium sales undergirded the British empire in Asia, and significant restrictions on opium would have weakened British imperialism. Germany had nearly the opposite concern. German pharmaceutical companies produced increasing amounts of morphine, heroin, and cocaine as well as another newly available painkiller, aspirin, in the early twentieth century. As discussed in chapter 5, people had high hopes for the medical value of these drugs. These pharmaceutical companies also contributed significantly to a growing German industrialized economy. German delegates were happy to support proposals limiting illicit production of morphine, heroin, and cocaine, since those would reduce competition for German companies.[5]

Participating nations agreed to adopt laws or pharmacy regulations to restrict access to morphine, heroin, and cocaine and asked producing nations to agree to abide by the import laws of other nations, not sending drugs except as the importing nation permitted. Signing nations promised to prohibit opium (meaning nonmedical opium) "as soon as possible." For morphine, heroin, and cocaine, signatories agreed to the "legitimate medical use" guideline.[6] Some countries began to change their laws immediately after signing the treaty. The United States, even though a leader in the movement to prohibit narcotics, still did not have a national law of prohibition. At Hamilton Wright's urging, Congress adopted the 1914 Harrison

Narcotics Act, which effectively prohibited narcotics in the United States. This law explicitly stated that narcotics, then meaning opium, morphine, heroin, and cocaine, could be sold only by people who possessed a stamp from the government allowing them to do so, and only for the purpose of medical treatment. The strange mechanism of requiring a "stamp" stems from the way the US Constitution was interpreted at the time, in which the federal government did not have the power to prohibit the sale of any good. So in at least one nation, the 1912 Hague Conference quickly led to prohibition. Countries like France, England, and the Netherlands also began passing laws to fulfill their agreements made at The Hague, but not until during and after World War I.

The treaty adopted at the conference did not come into effect until 1922, however. In another effort to dilute its effect, Germany stipulated that the treaty only come into effect when all nations had ratified it. The stated reason, which had validity, was that if Germany was agreeing to restrict the sale of German-produced pharmaceutical drugs only to countries explicitly permitting them, they wanted to make sure all other countries had to abide by the same restriction. Ratifications had been slowly accumulating in 1913 and early 1914 but were disrupted by the outbreak of war in Europe in 1914. Delegates to the Paris Peace Conference at the end of World War I saw an opportunity to gain full acceptance of the agreement. US secretary of state Robert Lansing argued that the treaty provided a "fitting opportunity." Sir Robert Borden, delegate from the British Empire and prime minister of Canada, agreed that the opium agreement should be adopted at the "earliest moment" and supported "any method" leading to that end.[7] With such strong support from Britain and the United States, it was written into the Treaty of Versailles that nations signing and ratifying that treaty were also simultaneously signing and ratifying what came to be called the International Opium Convention.

Geneva Conferences, 1924/1925

One outcome of World War I was the formation of the League of Nations, an organization of nation-states designed to promote peaceful solutions to the world's problems. Most of the time, the League of Nations is remembered for failing to prevent the conflicts leading to World War II, but the league also addressed a large number of social and economic problems, and many times did that reasonably successfully. The International Labor

Office, for instance, investigated oppressive and harmful working conditions around the world and tried to get better working conditions. The Health Section, predecessor to today's World Health Organization, studied global trends in disease and health and promoted vaccines and other healthy measures. Narcotics were also overseen by the league, through the Opium Advisory Committee.

Even though the United States did not formally join the League of Nations, US representatives participated in many aspects, especially the social and economic parts, of the league. The Opium Advisory Committee (OAC) is one place the United States played a significant role. The OAC gathered statistics about the implementation of the International Opium Convention and about the use of opiates and other drugs in countries around the world, and members discussed how best to approach the control of narcotics in the future. By 1924, they were ready to attempt to update the 1912 Convention adopted at The Hague to take account of new realities. As with the previous conference, however, political controversies among all the nations and a variety of goals for narcotics and policy meant it was difficult to get agreement. A first conference met in November 1924, with a goal of controlling opium smoking in Asia. Only governments controlling territory in Asia involved in opium trade participated in this conference, so the United States was not a participant. Disputes among China, Japan, Britain, and its colony India meant that the conference achieved very little. Japan was upset because the British wanted to do extra inspections of Japanese import certificates (essentially a license to trade opium across national borders). Japanese officials believed this was an insult and insisted on equitable treatment of all import and export certificates. British officials said they had reports that Japanese citizens were more heavily involved than other nationalities in smuggling opium. There is no way to confirm British or Japanese claims about who was smuggling. That dispute took so long to resolve that there was little time for attention to key issues. Probably the most important was about opium in China. Delegates from Britain and from the Indian government (who were British, from the British colonial government in India, not Indians) observed that China had been unable to control domestic drug use. The colonial Indian government subsequently asserted it should therefore be able to sell as much opium as it liked. Officials from Britain thought the Indian government's position was a bit extreme and attempted to moderate it, but in the end they supported India.

The 1924 conference resulted in a treaty, but it made only minor changes to what had been agreed in 1912, and only India signed immediately.

The 1924 conference lasted twice as long as scheduled (well into December), and what came to be called the 1925 conference (although it started in late November 1924) had already begun. This conference included all nations having an interest in the narcotics issue, so it had many more attendees. The US delegation, led by congressman Stephen Porter of Pennsylvania, played a prominent role. Congressman Porter was a dedicated anti-opium activist but also, in his role as chair of the House Foreign Relations Committee, a powerful opponent of the League of Nations. He wanted the United States to participate in the 1925 conference only if the United States could get everything that it wanted. Elizabeth Wright, the widow of the Hamilton Wright who had played a prominent role at The Hague in 1912, was also a member of the US delegation, as she had been for several years. Interestingly, she was the first woman ever granted plenipotentiary powers by the US government, meaning she had the power to act on behalf of the US government overseas.[8] Both Porter and Elizabeth Wright adamantly opposed narcotics use, except for strictly medical purposes, and Porter especially attempted to achieve a prohibitionist goal at the 1925 conference. He proposed four things, all designed to promote the US agenda, which most of the other countries either did not like or thought were premature. The first two proposals were expected, and they were adopted in modified form: a permanent control board for monitoring global usage, production, and trade in narcotics. This was created in 1925 as the Permanent Central Opium Board, and in slightly different form it continues to exist today as the International Narcotics Control Board at the United Nations. The other proposal was to more strictly regulate and control import and export statistics. Neither of these proposals was controversial; not everyone thought they would work, but all the main countries were willing to try.

Porter's other two proposals, however, were so controversial that he really only had one staunch supporter among the other nations: China. Porter proposed to enshrine in an international treaty a promise that nations would end opium smoking within ten years and limit production of opium and coca to the medicinal needs of the world. It is worth spending a little time discussing these proposals because they still today form the philosophical underpinning of US drug policy. Nearly all representatives at the conference found the proposal to end opium smoking within ten years to be at best laughable, and more appropriately, worthy of disdain. They just did not think it was a feasible objective. The other proposal, to limit all production to the medicinal needs of the world, sounded appealing but of course was nearly impossible logistically. First, the OAC would have to somehow figure out what the medicinal needs of the world actually were, and then, second, also somehow convince not merely all nations but all opium growers in all nations to agree to quotas of production. Even though most of the people involved in the discussions about how to regulate narcotics thought Congressman Porter's proposals were unworkable, they understood the appeal. If it were possible to control the supply of narcotics so that there was not any left over to use in harmful ways, that would be an easy way to stop addiction. The proposals to end abuse of narcotics by declaring them illegal except with a doctor's prescription and by banning excessive production appealed to people's emotional worry about opium's ill effects. These efforts are part of a supply-restriction approach to ending narcotics abuse, and the United States has pursued this approach consistently in its drug policy. Supply restriction has never fully worked, but it has also never lost its appeal.

Not surprisingly, representatives of other nations, especially of Britain and Germany, objected to Porter's proposals. The debates got quite heated at times, and there was little movement toward an agreement. When it became clear that there would be no movement toward the US demands, Porter walked out of the meeting. The Chinese delegation, still the sole supporter of the US position, soon followed. The remaining nations settled on an agreement that owed a lot to the US proposals, making it all the more puzzling why Porter had not been willing to compromise some. They agreed to end the opium trade among nations within fifteen years and to only allow trade through government monopolies. This agreement represented an acknowledgment that it was pretty difficult to control opium consumption but maybe possible to control opium trade. Also of note, the 1925 Geneva Convention was the first international drug treaty to cover trade in what was called Indian hemp, known today as marijuana.

Geneva and Bangkok, 1931

By the time the Geneva Conference for the Limitation of the Manufacture of Narcotic Drugs met in the spring of 1931, the experiences of running the Permanent Central Opium Board (PCOB) for a few years, plus the growing sense that the recession of 1929–30 was becoming a global and pervasive economic depression, seem to have prompted the delegates to be more in the mood for compromises than they had been in 1924–25. Sir Malcolm Delevingne, head of the British delegation and the nation's foremost expert on opium policy, had high hopes for getting all the producing nations to agree to a quota system. The PCOB had made an effort to collect reliable statistics about the normal amount of narcotics needed for medical purposes. They had good estimates to base an agreement on. Delevingne believed he would get support from the United States and Canada and therefore be able to overcome the objections of nations with expanding production, who would not appreciate getting saddled with a small quota. Delevingne did not prevail, however. Almost no one really wanted a quota system. Producing nations all thought they would get too small of a percentage of the allotted production. Consuming nations were afraid prices would rise in a world of restricted supply.

There could have been a repeat of 1925, with acrimony and nations storming out in a huff. The United States was still pushing for dramatic reductions in available supply, which complicated matters, for instance. But instead, everyone compromised. The 1931 treaty stipulated that countries would determine each year their estimated need of controlled substances (mostly opiates and cocaine products) and only purchase that amount. The PCOB would also determine the amounts needed by any countries not adhering to the treaty, and then manufacturers would agree to produce no more, in whole, than the total estimated needs of the countries as a group. Effectively, it was the supply restriction the United States had wanted. In the event of an emergency (for instance, war or epidemic), nations could exceed their agreed amount. The biggest struggle was over how to define what constituted a "drug." Germany lobbied hard to exempt codeine completely, arguing that it had too small an amount of opiates in it to qualify. In the end, codeine was regulated but less stringently than other drugs, and there was a threshold below which a drug was not a controlled substance. As you might imagine, the production of drugs right at or slightly below the threshold to be considered a "drug" increased dramatically. In the increasingly chaotic world of the 1930s, with economic depression and rising totalitarian states leading by the end of the decade to the start of World War II, the treaty was enforced imperfectly. But it set standards that would inform international drug control for many years.

Later in 1931, many of the same delegates gathered in Bangkok for the Conference on the Suppression of Opium-Smoking. The Geneva Conference had primarily been about the medicinal needs for opium and assumed that if excess production of opiates used as medicine was curtailed, new addicts would not be created. That assumption was overly optimistic since many recreational users existed throughout the world, but the plan would make initial access to opium more difficult. In Asia, though, many people still smoked or ate opium for pleasure, or for both pleasure and medicinal purposes in places where there were few doctors and pharmaceutical medicines were expensive and rare. In many parts of Asia, too, opium for smoking remained legal, if increasingly restricted. The debate at this conference was again between those who advocated an idealistic approach, mandating an early end to legal opium sales, and those who thought it would be difficult, and maybe undesirable, to move quickly to end access to smoking opium. The US delegate, consul John E. Caldwell, attended with the status of observer. He operated under State Department instructions to promote prohibition and cooperation in suppressing smuggling. The group advocating for modest steps mostly prevailed, with this treaty stipulating age limits for access to opium, requiring that it be sold and consumed in government-run shops, and limiting the amount a person could buy. Opium for pleasure remained legal, if restricted, in many parts of Asia. Politics interrupted the ratification of this treaty as well when conflict between Japan and China erupted into war in Manchuria in 1931. That fighting continued off and on, erupting into full-fledged war in 1937 and then lasting until 1945. The Bangkok Treaty was not ratified until after World War II, in 1946.

Illicit Trafficking Convention, 1936

All of these treaties aimed to control how narcotics were grown, produced, traded, and consumed, focusing on what people were allowed to do. In other words, they aimed to regulate the licit market, which increasingly was synonymous with a medical market, where doctors determined access to narcotics and even operated under restrictions established by governments. These efforts to control licit production and consumption of narcotics worked reasonably well. By 1935, PCOB officials estimated that the amount of medicinal narcotics needed approximately matched the amount of pharmaceutical narcotics legally produced. The careful tracking of narcotic consumption and the cooperation of pharmaceutical companies seemed to be paying off. Not surprisingly, though, illicit forms of all the drugs remained easily available and perhaps were even more prevalent.

In 1936, the signatories to the 1931 conventions met to try to address this illegal trafficking.

As with previous conferences, the United States proposed a broader restriction of drugs than other nations were willing to consider. Most of the countries participating wanted to discuss how to prevent illicit trafficking in the drugs controlled by the 1931 Geneva Convention, meaning the versions of narcotics produced for medical use. The US delegates, Harry Anslinger (head of the Federal Bureau of Narcotics) and Stuart Fuller, his deputy, proposed a much broader treaty, covering smoking opium and all raw opium products. These two men played an important role in US anti-narcotics on the world stage. Fuller, assistant chief of the Far Eastern Division in the Department of State, also was in charge of the State Department's anti-narcotics efforts from 1932 until his death in 1941. He excelled in publicly humiliating, in meetings and the press, representatives of nations not living up to their agreements to reduce narcotics trade and consumption. He worked well with the powerful Anslinger, first head of the US Federal Bureau of Narcotics (predecessor to the Drug Enforcement Administration).[9] Anslinger served from 1930 to 1962 and rivaled J. Edgar Hoover of the US Federal Bureau of Investigation in his willingness to use all methods, however controversial, to obtain his personal and professional goals.[10] At the 1936 conference, Anslinger and Fuller had to settle for haranguing; they did not get delegates to accept their more extensive prohibition. Since smoking opium was still legal in some places, the objections could have been predicted. And nearly all delegates argued that controlling these forms of opium would be an impossible task. They wanted to focus on the easier-to-control pharmaceuticals.

In the end, a relatively general treaty was negotiated, calling on countries to severely punish and agree to extradite drug traffickers. The United States called it too weak and refused to sign. Ratification happened slowly, and the treaty barely came into effect before World War II began. During the chaos of the war, enforcement against drug trafficking was nonexistent, and the treaty was not effective. This treaty did, however, represent a turning point in that the nations collectively agreed that international trafficking was a crime that should be punished by jail time in every country. Still, for most nations interested in combatting trafficking, the treaty did not represent a practical, useful approach. Countries concerned about trafficking continued to negotiate bilateral agreements to cooperate closely rather than rely on the 1936 convention.

World War II disrupted the trade in raw materials for drugs, the manufacture of drugs, and the efforts to control them. Legitimate medical use increased dramatically during the war, too, as wounded soldiers needed them. After the war, these conferences of the 1920s and 1930s set the standards for international control through the new United Nations. Chapter 6 picks up the story of the trade in drugs and efforts to control it during and after World War II. Chapter 5 explores changing medical practice in the first half of the twentieth century and the ways opiate use was transformed during those years.

5. CHANGING PRACTICE AND POLICY IN MEDICINE AND PUBLIC HEALTH

Discussions about opium policy during the first half of the twentieth century usually featured one group of people advocating restriction—arguing that opiates should be restricted to medically necessary use, ideally prescribed by a doctor—and another group arguing for looser controls. This second group usually reminded participants that in many parts of the world there were few doctors. In those places, opiates remained a critical part of the ordinary person's medicine chest. Even though full adoption of a medicalized, prescription-only model for opiates did not occur until after 1945, this approach steadily gained ground in the early twentieth century. Anti-opium activists as well as doctors and pharmacists had reasons for promoting stricter controls over opium. Opiates were available in ever-stronger doses, increasing the likelihood of addiction. New ways of addressing disease existed, meaning opiates should be needed less. But this advocacy often ignored that many people could not yet access these new treatments. Equally problematic, some colonial officials advocated for continued easy access to opiates in the colonies but without acknowledging that these more expansive uses were needed in part due to the failure of colonial governments to extend to their colonized subjects the same medical innovations that existed in the metropole.

Understanding how changing medical practice and knowledge influenced the medicinal need for opiates during the early twentieth century helps clarify some of the ways the anti-opium movement succeeded and why it met resistance. This chapter explores some of the diseases and conditions for which opium had traditionally been used. Developments in medicine and public health enabled some people to reduce or stop using opiates. Given the uneven distribution of these developments, though, opiates retained utility in rural and poor areas across the globe.

Today, opioids are prescribed to relieve pain. They have no other medicinal use. The pain-relieving quality of opiates has always been prized, but previously people took opiates to relieve other kinds of symptoms as well. In particular, the constipating effects of opiates, now considered an unwelcome side effect, helped people suffering from gastrointestinal illnesses such as cholera and dysentery as well as the frequent stomach upsets people suffered before the widespread availability of refrigeration and clean water. People also took opiates when they had a number of other diseases, including malaria and smallpox. Opiates did not cure these diseases or directly relieve key symptoms but made patients more comfortable. Even the pain-relieving qualities of opiates had more widespread utility in the past, too, since pain was a more constant feature of life. The success of the anti-opium movement came only as people in the wealthier nations increasingly had access to preventive measures, which meant they did not get as many of the diseases for which opiates provided relief, and they had access to X-rays and surgery to fix some of the problems that had caused pain.

In the 1897 edition of his *Handbook of Materia Medica*, Samuel O. L. Potter advised physicians that "probably no drug in the Materia Medica is so useful as Opium, or has so wide a range of applications." He listed six separate "indications" for prescribing opium: pain relief, to induce sleep particularly when "low fevers" caused insomnia, to reduce physical irritation, "to check excessive secretion" (a wide range, including diarrhea, diabetes, and some kinds of bleeding), to provide "support [of] the system during low fevers," and to induce sweating.[1] Developments in medical knowledge and practice, as well as public health policies, were beginning to reduce the cases that would meet these conditions. Still, the 1917 edition of this book contained the same list of indications, although it did take a slightly more cautionary approach to the potential for addiction.[2] Doctors in the twentieth century began to have other tools, in addition to opiates, for addressing many of these issues.

Vaccines were one of the first medical developments to begin to prevent the illnesses for which opium traditionally had been used. By the early twentieth century, vaccines existed for smallpox, rabies, cholera, plague, and typhoid, although some were relatively ineffective by today's standards. For people with access to vaccines, though, the dreaded threat of many common diseases faded. People with smallpox and cholera often took opium; opium use had been less common with the other diseases for which vaccines existed before 1945.

From its initial availability, vaccination against smallpox appealed to many people, who eagerly lined up for their shot and for shots for their children. Smallpox was the first disease with a true vaccine, in the eighteenth century. People in different parts of the world, including India and China, had observed that the pus from a smallpox lesion could be scratched into another person's skin (a process called variolation). Processing the substance so that people did not have to be near an active case of the disease they wanted to avoid led to vaccines. Most countries, though, did not have the infrastructure for either administering the vaccine or tracking who had had theirs. Many people were skeptical about or even frightened of the vaccine. Vaccinations spread most effectively in places like Prussia (later Germany) and Japan, where the government mandated vaccines. In England, vaccination rates soared during the mid-nineteenth century, when vaccines were compulsory, but dipped in the late nineteenth and early twentieth centuries, when people were allowed to opt out if they had a conscientious objection. In the United States, where people often resisted efforts by the state to control their personal behavior, compulsory vaccination laws at the state and local levels encouraged many to comply but were far from fully effective. Local authorities strove for "voluntary compliance" except in the midst of active epidemics.[3] Even in the parts of the world where most people could access vaccines if they wanted them, compliance was far from complete. But in these areas, sufficient numbers of people got the vaccines to lead to impressive reductions in disease outbreaks.

In the rest of the world, however, vaccines were too expensive, no infrastructure existed to administer them, or people did not have much trust in the groups, whether from their own government or foreign missionary doctors, who advocated vaccination. In China, for instance, vaccination was common in the major cities but in more rural provinces like Yunnan remained below 5 percent of the population until after World War II.[4] Colonial governments often set up public health administrations with mandates to improve all aspects of public health, including promoting vaccines. Their financial resources were not sufficient to meet all the needs, though, and often only workers, especially workers on large plantations or in foreign-owned enterprises, especially those who migrated across a border for work, received the vaccines.[5] With the rates of vaccination low, epidemic outbreaks remained common. And since these early vaccines rarely offered lifelong immunity, some people who previously had been vaccinated still fell ill. All these developments undercut popular belief in vaccines. Where

Fig. 5.1. British officials administering cholera vaccine in India, 1894. From W. M. Haffkine, *Protective Inoculation against Cholera* (Calcutta, 1913), Wellcome Collection, London.

prevalent, and for the diseases they could prevent, vaccines changed the public health landscape. But many people in the world did not experience these benefits until after World War II. The effects on opium use therefore also lagged. Opium was of course not used to prevent or cure the diseases for which vaccines were developed. But it had been used to alleviate symptoms, helping not only with aches and fevers but also with diarrhea.

Diarrhea remains a significant threat to people's lives and health even today, in parts of the world where it affects infants who are not receiving adequate nutrition or where cholera is still prevalent. Public health measures of the late nineteenth and early twentieth centuries began to reduce diseases caused by dirty water and poor sanitation, also leading to a reduced need for the constipating effects of opiates. Observations about the connection between contaminated water sources and diseases such as cholera had been made as early as 1854, when John Snow investigated the water pumps in a part of London experiencing a major cholera outbreak. He found that, of the hundreds of people in that neighborhood who had cholera, almost all lived near, and presumably got their water from, the

Broad Street pump. Only ten did not live near the pump, and almost all of them got some of their water there (such as children in a nearby school). Snow drew a correlation but couldn't prove that something on the pump handle caused the illness. Still, the city council removed the pump and illness decreased. Not until 1885 did Robert Koch isolate the bacterium causing cholera and prove Snow correct.[6]

In the late nineteenth century, scientists had established germ theory, the observation that "germs" (bacteria or viruses) caused disease, and Koch's work with cholera provided yet more proof. Many people found this theory difficult to accept at that time. Fortunately for public health, the other theory people believed for disease causation at the end of the nineteenth century was called the "miasma" theory, which essentially was a belief that bad air or bad odors or decay caused disease. So the proponents of both the miasma theory and the germ theory had reason to promote cleaner water, improved sanitation practices, and more effective sewer systems. Just cleaning up the water and sewer and removing the massive quantity of garbage generated in cities and towns naturally went a long way toward decreasing disease.

People have long understood the importance of clean water and proper disposal of waste in promoting health, but until the late nineteenth century, medical and scientific knowledge about what the specific problems were, and how best to address them, was limited. Before urbanization, though, it might have been acceptable to use the same stream or river as your water source, laundry location, and repository of human and animal waste. The moving water could be counted on to remove the waste products, so long as there were not too many people and animals using the same stream. Cities historically had some mechanisms for bringing in fresh water and removing dirty water, but the massive boom in urbanization that accompanied the Industrial Revolution completely outstripped this modest infrastructure. Even in wealthy urban centers like London and New York, sanitation and clean water were rudimentary as late as the early twentieth century, as the continuing cholera outbreaks demonstrate effectively. Crowded living conditions grew more common throughout the world, too, increasing the prevalence of polluted water.

Imperial powers also devoted resources, sometimes substantial, to building sanitation and clean water infrastructure in their colonies. A massive cholera outbreak in the Philippines that took place during the war the United States waged there in 1898–1901 shaped early US colonial policy.

As happened in many places, the US government instituted plans to completely remake parts of the city to "clean up" areas it thought were too crowded, too susceptible to pest infestation (especially rats), and without effective sewer and water delivery.[7] These infrastructure projects often disrupted the local populations but undoubtedly improved public health for the remaining inhabitants. Such projects did not, however, reach beyond a minority of the population in most of the world.

Cholera and dysentery are two of the diseases most associated with contaminated food and water, so they are most susceptible to reduction by taking public health measures such as improving the water supply and sanitation practices. Refrigeration also helped significantly in improving food safety. Refrigerators began to become important consumer goods in the early twentieth century. In the United States, refrigerators were common in urban homes by the 1920s, and about 80 percent of homes had them by the 1950s. In poorer parts of the world, though, access to refrigerators has lagged. As recently as 2017, only 30 percent of households in India had a refrigerator. Many other countries have similar rates, in part due to the unpredictability of electricity.[8] The rates of cholera and dysentery began to fall in wealthier parts of the world in the twentieth century, meaning fewer people took opium to alleviate the horrible diarrhea that often killed people by dehydrating them. As with vaccines, public health measures could reduce prevalence of diseases whose symptoms prompted opiate use. The more robust the public health infrastructure, the less incidence of diseases for which people might want opiates for relief.

Malaria provides a useful example of the varying effects of modern medicine and public health policy. From about 1500, since mosquitos traveled all around the world along with people, malaria shows up in almost all parts of the world. Only the very cold and the very dry places escape it. By 1900, scientists understood that mosquitos played an important role in spreading malaria, and they also knew that taking quinine could ward off malaria. By removing locations for mosquitos to breed, by using mosquito netting, and by taking quinine, malaria could be prevented. These techniques are similar to the ones in use today, although the range of preventive drugs has expanded. Now, as then, malaria could not be cured but only managed, if you caught it. Through the first decades of the twentieth century, many people managed malaria's chills and fevers with opiates. Although there were some campaigns to drain swamps and use mosquito netting in Asia, Africa, Central America, and the Caribbean in the early twentieth century, both those and quinine were deemed too expensive for widespread distribution in these areas. In the British colony of Burma, for example, British officials in their reports detailed the many measures taken to reduce mosquitos, and therefore malaria, but also noted those efforts were inadequate. As a 1904 report on the efforts to more strictly regulate and restrict opium sales acknowledged, "it is impolitic to refuse to recognise that the habitual use of the drug as a preventive of fever and dysentery is practically a necessity to the dwellers on the sea-coast and in or near the hills and to fisherman in the delta."[9] But in the continental United States and Europe, antimalarial efforts became common, and many fewer people suffered from the illness. Europeans and Americans also were much more likely to take quinine if they traveled to malarial areas than were the people who already lived there. This differential public health experience, in which most Europeans and Americans reduced their own likelihood of contracting malaria without lowering the exposure of most of the rest of the world, led to different types of medical needs for opium in different parts of the world.

As now, in the past the most common, compelling medical reason for using opiates was to relieve pain. Walter Bastedo, a professor of pharmacology at Columbia University College of Physicians and Surgeons, wrote in 1913 that "morphine stands by itself in its power to allay pain . . . and to change discomfort into comfort."[10] Morphine and other opiates continue to this day to provide relief against both chronic and acute pain. Medical developments of the late nineteenth through early twentieth centuries helped eliminate or reduce painful conditions in ways that had not previously been possible. People with access to newly developed forms of anesthesia and the surgeries they enabled, as well as the X-rays allowing for more precision in removing bullets, setting bones, and other kinds of restorative surgery, could be cured of their pain rather than managing it.

Surgery has existed since antiquity as a medical practice, used to remove diseased or damaged tissue, teeth, or bones. Until the invention of modern forms of anesthesia in the nineteenth century, it was impossible to eliminate pain during surgical procedures. In ancient times, people drank various herbal concoctions or alcohol or took opium. For the alcohol or opium to work at all well, the patient had to be very close to unconscious, which had its own negative side effects. Until the invention of modern anesthesia, surgeons, who were feared more than respected, were deemed to be good if they were quick more than if they were accurate or successful. Not surprisingly, people were reluctant to have operations unless absolutely necessary, and this meant that they were often too injured or too far along in an illness for the surgery to make them better. Surgery itself was dangerous, and since many surgeons were not hygienic and antibiotics did not yet exist, many people also died from infection. Still, if the problem of pain during the operation could be solved, then surgeons could be more precise, cut less, operate at an earlier stage in the illness or injury, and perhaps be more successful.

Before 1846, in many parts of the world, alcohol was more likely to be used than opium to attempt to prevent pain during surgery. Sometimes opium was not readily available, but people also worried about the amount of opium they might have to take to be successful as well as the possibility of what we would call an overdose. Alcohol simply does not work well, however, for most surgeries, since it is not very effective at truly blocking pain, wears off reasonably quickly but is not easy to continue ingesting during surgery, and has negative side effects (dehydration, stomach upset, headache), which may prevent good recovery from the surgery. People can often become agitated or belligerent if they have drunk too much alcohol, making it difficult for the surgeon to operate. Everyone was pleased to see alcohol replaced by modern anesthesia as a sedative for surgeries, but it took some time for this to fully happen, even in Europe and the United States. My own great-grandfather, as a young man in the early twentieth century, helped hold down a man in his east Tennessee town who had consumed whiskey in preparation for having his leg amputated. The fact that my great-grandfather remembered that a number of people had to hold the man down suggests the alcohol was only partially effective.

During the nineteenth century, several new techniques developed to reduce or eliminate pain during surgery. Nitrous oxide seemed promising but didn't work reliably. In 1846, a dentist, William T. G. Morton, used information he had acquired while attending a chemistry lecture at Harvard University about ether and its ability to render people unconscious. Morton tried it out on himself and his dog, and before trying it out on a patient, he developed a mask so that whomever was administering the ether could monitor the dosing. It was a great success and immediately began to spread to England and the rest of Europe. Ether, however, posed respiratory and stomach problems and soon was replaced by chloroform. Chloroform was very effective and easily administered, sometimes by just putting a drop on a cloth one held to one's face, but it was powerful and difficult to control.

Sometimes people got too much and never recovered. Overall, however, chloroform made it much easier to do surgery safely.[11] Cocaine provided a good solution to one of the main problems with ether or chloroform as anesthesia: ether and chloroform were so powerful and therefore risky that it seemed dangerous to use them for minor operations. Since cocaine can be used topically (applied on or in a particular part of the body), without affecting the central nervous system, it was much safer for dental, eye, and other kinds of surgeries requiring primarily topical pain relief. This use did not have any feeling of a "high," so it had no possibility of leading to addiction.[12] Novocaine, with the telltale "caine" suffix, is still used today in this way, very effectively (it is trademarked as "Novocain").

The improved access to safe and effective surgery had the potential to significantly reduce the common use of opium. As discussed in chapter 2, Civil War soldiers, like many people, took opium because they had chronic, incurable pain from injury or illness. Surgery could resolve some of these problems. For instance, at this time it was common to leave bullets lodged in one's body in place, unless at risk of killing the person, because the risk of surgery and infection after surgery to remove them was often more dangerous than the presence of the bullets. These bullets often caused permanent pain, traditionally managed by maintenance doses of opium.[13] But improvements in anesthesia meant that these bullets could now potentially be removed, meaning the pain would diminish or disappear. After the discovery of X-rays in 1895, it became even easier to remove bullets because X-rays revealed exactly where they were. Surgery, now under anesthesia, was faster, less invasive, and easier to recover from. X-rays also made it easier to assist full healing from broken bones and fractures and from toothache. All these ailments had been the source of significant chronic pain. The higher rate of healing that these medical innovations brought helped reduce the need for maintenance doses of opiates.

By the early twentieth century, many doctors were advocating surgery for other kinds of pain, and even other ailments, as well. People with chronic headaches, ringing in the ears, neck and back pain, and numbness in extremities were often told that surgery would help them. These surgeries often involved cutting nerves, which of course may have ended the pain but could also result in paralysis or other negative side effects. This "modern" medicine was not necessarily more effective in improving people's quality of life but provided alternate methods for dealing with pain. The fact that these surgeries, which look extreme by today's standards, were embraced so enthusiastically suggests that chronic pain had been a significant problem for a large number of people.[14]

By the early twentieth century, medicine could sometimes offer scientific explanations for disease as well as a host of preventive measures. Doctors increasingly had a rigorous education focused on prevention and cure and expected to be able to help patients get or stay well rather than, as in the past, mostly being able to help them feel better while still sick. Patients began to expect more from their doctors too. Both doctors and patients began to expect that medicine should offer more than just pain relief. Opium should be given temporarily or as a drug of last resort. Many people have the same belief about opioid prescription today. But then, as now, medical science did not always meet expectations. It could prevent many diseases and cure more than in the past, but only for a minority of people. Still, the changes in what was possible prompted changes in how people perceived the usefulness of opium. Increasingly, countries began to regulate opiates.

Many anti-opium advocates focused their efforts on passing laws to restrict the sale of opium and its derivatives, with the goal of not creating new addicts. Sometimes this restriction was instituted abruptly, as in the United States and the Philippines. After the 1908 prohibition in the Philippines and the Harrison Narcotics Act of 1914 in the United States, opiates were highly restricted. Nonmedicinal use was prohibited, and doctors were not legally permitted to prescribe maintenance doses for people already addicted. Many of these doctors continued to supply the maintenance doses, often but not always evading prosecution. In other places, especially throughout the parts of Asia where opium had been commonly and legally consumed, the restriction rolled out more gradually. Existing consumers could register with the government and continue to purchase their customary dose for the rest of their life. Anti-opium advocates thought the drug was harmful, though, and began to promote programs designed to help people stop consuming narcotics safely and effectively. Even in the early twenty-first century, one of the most difficult things a person can do is stop an addictive habit or behavior. In the early twentieth century, the science of addiction was in its infancy. Health care professionals understood that abrupt withdrawal could be dangerous, even deadly. But they did not have much knowledge about how to help people get free of their addiction. Japanese scientists, who were deeply committed to helping addicts in their new colony of Taiwan stop consuming opiates, began some treatment programs. Many times, though, they helped patients through withdrawal by giving them an "opium-based analgesic." As historian Miriam Kingsberg has found, this meant the addicts simply exchanged addiction to opium for addiction to another opiate, often morphine.[15] Other countries, including the United States in its colony of the Philippines, also provided medical support for ending addiction. The programs were not very effective, but doctors and scientists began to study withdrawal and how to end addiction using scientific methods.[16] Scientific approaches developed slowly, even as more and more people found their legal access to drugs they had always consumed was restricted. It was a difficult dilemma for many.

This time period was a confused and contradictory one. For people with access to the best in modern medicine and living in the cleanest of sanitary environments, opiates were less necessary medically, but even they might still have need of them. Disease rates remained high by twenty-first-century standards, and cures were rare. But most people in the world also did not have access to modern medicine, clean water, and excellent sanitation. For them, opiates remained as critical a drug as ever. Yet, as seen in chapter 4, access increasingly was restricted. Not until after World War II, with the availability of antibiotics and major efforts to improve infrastructure around the world, would opiates finally become a medicine used exclusively for pain control. Those years would see renewed efforts to regulate narcotics on the global stage.

PART II.
TO A DECLARATION OF A WAR ON DRUGS, 1940–1980

As the global war we now call World War II approached, opiates had a contradictory status. In most parts of the world, governments increasingly regulated and even restricted access to opiates except through a doctor's prescription. In other parts of the world, not coincidentally those with a small number of doctors per capita, people consumed opium in ways that may have looked recreational but also served medical needs. If you lived in Europe or North America, you probably had access to clean water, vaccination, and reasonably safe surgery, and your medical need for narcotics was modest. If you lived in other parts of the world, your access to these public health and modern medicine innovations was less certain, and it is likely that opiates still helped people suffering from ordinary disease as well as acute and chronic pain.

As discussed in chapter 6, during World War II itself, as with all wars, the demand for opiates increased due to the massive numbers of injuries as well as the exposure to disease for combatants and civilians alike. During this war, supply lines were dramatically disrupted as fighting took place in many opium-producing countries, and other countries were cut off from their usual supply routes. Growers in Central and South America stepped up production, but it was not sufficient to meet the increased demand. Innovations in medicine again helped address medicinal needs for opiates, from better methods of administration on the battlefield to the first fully synthetic opioids. Recreational users in Europe and the Americas found it nearly impossible to acquire the opiates they were accustomed to and often turned to other drugs. The war also saw the rise of the use of other purely manufactured drugs, especially amphetamines.

After World War II, there was a brief moment, lasting about two years, when recreational drug use was relatively rare, having been disrupted by the war, and supply chains were not yet reestablished. Drug producers seized that opportunity more than did those who wished to restrict drugs, and by the end of the 1940s, Europe and the United States were again swamped with heroin. Heroin use soared in the cities. Additionally, as a new issue, prescription use of barbiturates, amphetamine, and tranquilizers rose throughout the United States. The consumer culture of the 1950s in a fully recovered United States and a recovering Europe demanded drugs as much as cars and washing machines. Doctors readily prescribed the new mood-altering drugs, and alcohol consumption also increased. The illegal drugs—heroin, marijuana, and cocaine—were associated with jazz musicians, urban "hipsters," and ethnic minorities. Their use also increased. Drug use became relatively common in the United States, but there was an enormous divide among the types of drugs and types of users, especially by race and class, as further explored in chapter 8. This divide echoed that which had begun to develop after World War I and made it easier for the United States to pass increasingly harsh laws penalizing illicit drug use, even as prescriptions for mood-altering drugs were common and the three-martini lunch was even more so.

The newly created United Nations took over the work of the anti-narcotics groups in the League of Nations wholesale, only changing the names of the organizations handling the issue to the Commission on Narcotic Drugs and Division on Narcotic Drugs, handling political and statistical issues, respectively. Chapter 7 explores how through the United

Nations, most countries in the world signed on to important measures to control narcotics and other drugs, with significant ones in 1948, 1953, 1961, 1971, and 1972. These international conventions have helped regulate and control production, distribution, trade, and use of a variety of drugs. They have also stipulated the ways that countries would collaborate with each other to help enforce both national laws and international agreements regarding the control of illicit drugs. Nearly all of the world's countries adhere to these conventions, although sometimes governments are unable to fully comply due to issues in their own countries. The United States has sometimes been at odds with other major powers about the best ways to regulate drugs, which has caused some difficulties with international control.

In the United States, the focus on a supply-reduction rather than a harm-prevention or demand-reduction approach to drug control has remained the focus after World War II. This approach has meant the United States has emphasized seizing drugs imported into the United States as well as attempting to eradicate supply in the country through aerial spraying, arresting traffickers, and attempting to destroy illicit production. Domestic laws have generally emphasized harsh prison terms, especially for traffickers and dealers and sometimes also for users who are repeat offenders. Racial and class politics have structured the US response to the drug issue, and the ineffectiveness of US drug policy, along with its uneven effects on people of color and those living in poverty, has made the policy controversial.

After the tumultuous decade of the 1960s, when drug use seemed to gain acceptance with young people but frightened older people with its apparent ubiquity, the administration of President Richard Nixon famously declared the "War on Drugs" and gave a name to the policy the United States had already been following for decades. Chapter 9 explores this history. Nixon emphasized harsh prison sentences for dealers and for users of the types of drugs believed to be particularly dangerous. He also reduced sentences for some kinds of drug use and wanted to spend money on treatment and prevention. This policy was applauded by many, but the resources devoted to the treatment and prevention side were always minimal compared to those devoted to law enforcement and supply interdiction. The drug problem did not seem to improve during his time in office, however. The Nixon War on Drugs approach nevertheless continued to shape policy for many years.

6. OPPORTUNITIES OF WORLD WAR II AND ITS AFTERMATH

As war broke out between Japan and China in 1937 and in Europe in 1939, the global struggle to control narcotics, already embattled, faced additional challenges. The first significant challenge was to the system of control that the League of Nations had been attempting to institute. The United States had long pressed for a supply-side approach to reducing narcotics production. After 1925, the League of Nations had implemented this approach by attempting, each year, to determine the global level of need for narcotics. It then published target global production goals for the upcoming year, designed to meet the previous year's stated needs. As the war expanded to include more countries, more soldiers, and more territory, the need for narcotics expanded as well, much faster than production quotas anticipated. The careful system set up by the League of Nations had been designed for relatively steady consumption of narcotics. It could not keep up with this rapidly expanding, legitimate medical need.

The most significant need, of course, was to treat soldiers injured in battle. Pharmaceutical companies enthusiastically stepped in to fill this need, out of a desire to support the soldiers but also sensing that they could make a lot of money. Innovations in synthetic versions of opiates and in methods of administration promised to bring new profits to the drug manufacturers while also serving medical needs. One significant improvement, for instance, was the syrette, developed by the pharmaceutical company Squibb, now part of Bristol-Myers Squibb. The syrette was a single dose of morphine, packaged in a single-use syringe, able to be kept sterile until needed, and then able to be administered quickly and safely in a manner that would swiftly relieve a soldier's pain on the battlefield. The syrettes also helped combat shock, whose treatment increased a soldier's ability to survive until he could be transported to a field hospital for more extensive care.[1] One Army combat medic later recalled that medics attached the empty syrette to "the patient's clothing to insure that the patient did not receive a second dose" since they rarely had time to fill out the transfer form stating what they had done to each injured man.[2]

Injured soldiers were rarely close to high-quality medical care and sometimes could not reach even a makeshift hospital. For example, British troops in Burma sometimes had no choice but to leave wounded soldiers behind with Burmese villagers if the wounded could not walk. When they did so, they also left morphine, food, water, and bandages, along with letters of instruction for care in several of the local languages.[3] Even with the improved medical care available in World War II, the extended supply lines and massive scale of the war meant that cleaning the wound and offering pain relief were sometimes all medics could offer. In these cases, readily available, easy-to-administer opiates played a critical role in providing appropriate care to soldiers.

The push to develop another innovation, synthetic opiates, initially was strongest in Germany. The country was largely cut off from access to its traditional sources of the raw materials for its opiates in Asia and parts of the Middle East. Scientists sought ways to create opiates from chemicals rather than natural products, and those at I. G. Farbenindustrie developed methadone in 1937. Today, methadone is most commonly used as an alternative maintenance drug for people addicted to heroin because its effects last longer and allow people to live a fuller, more normal life. During World War II, methadone worked well to address the pain experienced by German soldiers injured in battle. It also appears, however, that many high-level German officials, including Adolf Hitler, used synthetic opiates and amphetamines to manage their sleep and alertness. Hitler had a number of ailments, and during the war he also experienced injuries. His personal doctor recorded regularly giving him both opiates and amphetamines, sometimes in high doses.

Amphetamines were not a new invention for World War II but had been synthesized in 1887, forgotten, and then produced again in 1927. They became widely available only in the mid-1930s. Their quality as a "pep pill" was well known. Doctors quickly realized amphetamines were useful in treating narcolepsy and depression, and there even were some early experiments treating what we now know as attention-deficit/hyperactivity disorder (ADHD). All these uses remain. But amphetamines were much more widely used, often without prescription, in the 1930s and 1940s. German soldiers received amphetamines, which helps explain their grueling march, averaging twenty-two miles a day, after the 1939 attack on Poland and in preparation for the attack on France. Allied soldiers used amphetamines as well. Both British and US soldiers took Benzedrine (an amphetamine) during the North Africa campaign. General Dwight D. Eisenhower ordered half a million tablets, a sure sign of its perceived effectiveness. In 1943, the US Army included Benzedrine in its regular first aid kit, with instructions to take only under conditions of "extreme fatigue." Soldiers could interpret that as they liked.[4] Amphetamines, indeed, were used liberally by soldiers, especially pilots. It seems likely, although it is difficult to research, that many civilians also used amphetamines during the war. It was not difficult to obtain them, with or without a prescription, and many people were working significantly longer hours than usual in support of the war effort.

As the example of amphetamines suggests, civilian use of narcotics and other drugs also increased if they could access them. Civilians in war zones were also likely to be injured. If they could reach a functioning and well-supplied hospital, which was far from guaranteed, they also would need the pain-relieving effects of morphine or other forms of opiates. In addition, in war zones the diseases that public health measures had begun to vanquish—such as dysentery, cholera, typhoid, and malaria—reemerged. These diseases often struck thousands of people, as sewers and sanitation failed, as water supplies were disrupted, and as people fled their homes to live in temporary and crowded conditions. People could rarely access opium, but they used it for symptom relief when they could. Even in places less directly affected by the fighting, people were often overworked, living with a lot of stress, and prone to injury and illness in addition to mental health problems. The drugs they may have liked to have taken were often not available, but the demand for these drugs, for legitimate health reasons, was high. Illicit drug use was down, but when people could access drugs, whether from their doctor or in some other way, to deal with their many physical and mental health problems, they did.

The United States had attempted to prepare for this increased demand by stockpiling narcotics, mostly opiates. The head of the Federal Bureau of Narcotics, Harry Anslinger, had been stockpiling opiates since at least 1935. Soon after war broke out in Europe, Anslinger reported having enough stockpiled to supply US needs and even to "take care of the whole Western Hemisphere."[5] One strategy he had was to keep all drugs seized in raids of illicit trafficking. He used these drugs to build the stockpile.

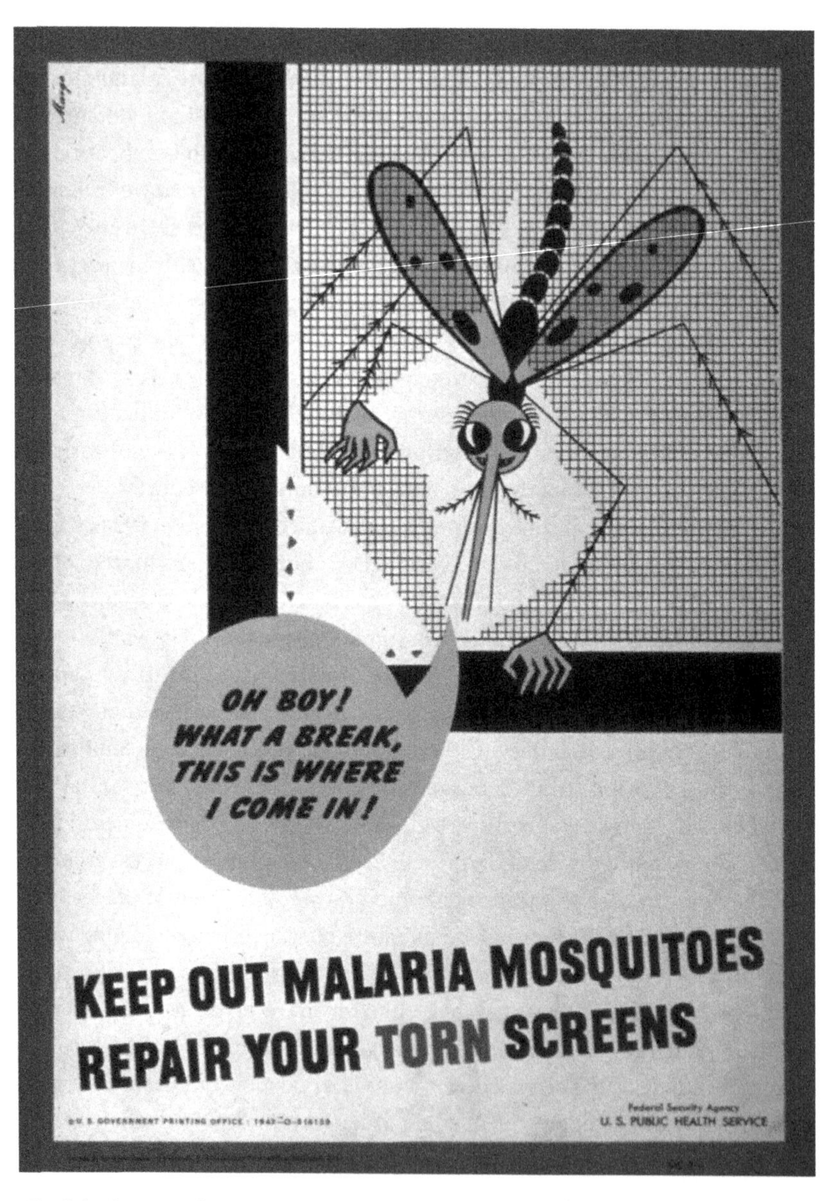

Fig. 6.1. The US military promoted public health measures during World War II to try to keep troops healthy. From World War II Posters, RG 44, Records of the Office of Government Reports, 1932–1947, United States National Archives, Washington, DC.

A number of US agencies were stockpiling key strategic materials, such as rubber and tin, so Anslinger's plan fit with what other officials were doing. His efforts meant that the US government held a substantial amount of narcotics when the war began.[6] Some medical professionals were concerned, however, that these narcotics were not in a form that would be useful to them in their medical practice. Opium prepared for smoking or heroin prepared for illicit injections were difficult to dose, administer, and provide consistently.

As the war got closer, and especially after 1939, Anslinger made purchases above and beyond the US statement of need as prepared for and provided to the League of Nations. Since the United States had promoted the supply-restriction policy, strongly backed by Anslinger, he was reluctant to do this. But even he recognized that legitimate need was growing fast. His long-standing concern that increased purchases stimulated increased production as people sought to profit was overcome by his recognition of the wartime need for more opiates.

There were other, more political, reasons that the United States purchased additional opium. Sometimes, purchasing opium from a country might help make or keep it friendly to the Allied side in the war. In 1941–42, for instance, Iran was authorized to sell opium to the United States despite the fact that Iran had not complied with international opium regulations. Usually the United States would not purchase opium from countries that were out of compliance. The State Department memo explaining this unusual circumstance provided no reason for the unusual approval. Perhaps the fact that Germany was also interested in purchasing this opium helps explain why the United States made this exception. Turkey was an even more important case. Turkey was neutral in World War II until severing diplomatic relations with Germany in late 1944 and formally joining the Allies in early 1945. But Germany was trying hard to entice Turkey to join the Axis. From the earliest days of the war, Britain had purchased significant products from Turkey: not only opium but also copper and antimony. In addition, Britain supplied Turkey with important foodstuffs and war matériel in return. By 1942, Britain was unable to continue this trade, and Germany had promised to step in to both purchase from and supply to Turkey. Germany, however, was slow to fulfill its contracts. The United States took advantage of German delays and seized the opportunity to purchase Turkish products, including opium, and supply Turkish needs, thus cutting out Germany. Officials in the State Department hoped that US opium purchases from Turkey would help sway it to be a neutral country leaning toward the Allies.[7] Whether this purchase was influential or not, Turkey maintained a careful neutrality until near the end of the war.

Germany's quick expansion to seize most of the territory in Western and parts of Eastern Europe increased the magnitude of the problem Allied countries had accessing sufficient drugs for their medical needs. Germany had been a major pharmaceutical supplier. These pharmaceutical companies no longer sold their product to countries Germany was at war with. But German pharmaceutical companies also had difficulty accessing raw materials and could not supply even the needs in countries under German control. There were pharmaceutical companies in France and the Netherlands, but they were also under German occupation. Even the companies in Switzerland, neutral in the war, had difficulty getting their products out to willing buyers, given that the country is landlocked and was essentially surrounded by Axis countries. In Europe, the only Allied nation that could still manufacture narcotics was Britain, and it could in no way keep up with demand. Anslinger's decision to stockpile looked wise, and he enjoyed being able to control the amounts of both raw material and manufactured drugs released to Allied and neutral countries. He saw it as a way of enhancing US power, both politically and economically. It also enabled him to promote the US approach to solving the drug problem.

Anslinger was not shy about using US power. Upon the outbreak of war in Europe, the drug-control agencies of the League of Nations carried on as usual, to the extent possible. Their base in Switzerland was neutral, and the statistics they gathered were invaluable to belligerent nations. Renamed the Drug Control Service, and with a bit more independence from the League of Nations than before, the opium services continued. Within a few months, however, rumors of a possible German invasion of Switzerland as well as conflict within the League of Nations itself about how to operate in wartime meant that most of the technical (not political) agencies moved to the United States. The Drug Control Service moved a bit later than the others, in the late fall of 1940. By that time, Switzerland was almost completely surrounded by Axis allies or countries occupied by the Axis. As the personnel attempted to leave, they had to cross France into Spain as the only way to reach the Atlantic Ocean. But there were some problems with transit visas across Spain. Spain's status at this point was "nonbelligerent," reflecting that political views in the country were divided about who to support. Spain also simply wanted to stay out of the war. In this context, Spanish officials did not want to upset the powerful Germans by granting visas if the Germans disapproved. They were particularly afraid of German anger because some of the officials of the drug-control agencies were Jewish. Anslinger let the Spanish government know that if it did not move positively to allow these people to cross its territory to leave for the United States, Spanish requests for narcotics supplies would be ignored. The Spanish government quickly complied.[8]

In that case, Anslinger used the significant power of the United States to achieve a narrow goal of helping people escape the possibility of Nazi German harassment or oppression. But other times, he used US power for more expansive purposes, usually the US goal of promoting a particular approach to the drug problem. Mexico, for instance, wanted to experiment in 1940 with a maintenance harm-reduction program. This program would have allowed registered addicts to receive a supply of morphine as part of their treatment program. When they announced this plan, Anslinger banned narcotics exports to that country until it promised to stop the experiment. His heavy-handed tactics plus the huge demand for narcotics during the war combined to prompt Mexico to increase domestic production of opiates, which it had not much produced before.[9] Later, the increased production in Mexico meant that a large supply of opiates was available just across the border from the United States, which contributed to illicit supply. Anslinger's power was as great inside the United States too. Pharmaceutical firms in the United States had to apply to the federal government both to get an allocation of raw opium to manufacture their products and to get a license to sell their products to pharmacies and consumers after manufacture. Anslinger obtained presidential authority granting his agency sole authority over allocations and licenses. Despite the increased demand for medical narcotics, Anslinger refused to expand the number of licenses. As a result, small pharmaceutical companies had no chance to benefit from the new opportunities during the war. Larger pharmaceutical companies profited immensely and then could be depended on to support his goals.

Even with drugs already primarily grown in the Americas, where the supply was not disrupted by war, Anslinger used wartime to reorganize the market to fit his perception of US needs. Historian Suzanna Reiss has explained how Anslinger used the disruption to Peru's trade in coca and cocaine with Europe, along with the fact that the only other significant supplier of coca leaves (the Netherlands Indies) was cut off, to solidify US control over manufacture. Anslinger steadfastly refused to budge on the US policy of importing only raw materials. Peru could export only coca leaves and lost the financial benefit of doing some manufacturing in Peru. Its pharmaceutical industry was starved for customers for the duration of the war, harming that business.[10] Anslinger had significant power to shape US domestic and international drug policy during World War II.

Anslinger thought ahead, too, to the postwar situation. He worked to outmaneuver all international efforts to maintain a variety of options for drug policy after the war. He wanted to continue to push the US effort to prohibit nonmedicinal use of narcotics and to use the supply-restriction approach to achieve his goal. His most significant, and risky, move came in early 1943. He wanted to get international agreement on a policy of narcotics prohibition in Asia after the war ended, achieving a longtime goal of ending nonmedical opium use there. He pursued a classic strategy. First, he implied he had official backing of the US government when he approached the British and Dutch governments about his goals. He intimated that it was official US policy that the United States would participate in joint occupations of areas in Asia (after Japanese defeat) only if the government for the area agreed to ban narcotics. Anslinger had not consulted the US Department of State about this policy, nor had he consulted US president Franklin D. Roosevelt. He was acting on his own authority. He had substantial authority, but it did not extend to making policy about the conditions under which US military personnel would participate in occupying a defeated territory. Before Anslinger approached British and Dutch officials, he made his position look stronger by getting China and some Allied personnel from countries having no Asian colonies to sign on.

With the initiative already underway, the US State Department played catch-up. Not everyone agreed that Anslinger's approach was ideal. Most US officials supported the overall goal, however, of extending the US approach, prohibition of nonmedical narcotics, to the areas the US military would occupy after the war. Rather than challenge the powerful and controlling Anslinger, State Department officials belatedly initiated the usual policy formulation process to implement what Anslinger had started on his own. They consulted with the Army, Navy, and Treasury departments during the summer of 1943. By then, British and Dutch officials were already considering the proposal that Anslinger had offered. Fortunately, the US departments all agreed with what Anslinger had already done. The State Department drafted a memo for an official communication with the

Netherlands and Britain that was sent on September 21, 1943. The replies were swift. The Dutch reply came on September 29, 1943, reporting that the Dutch government had decided "several months ago to prohibit completely the use of prepared opium in the Netherlands Indies after the liberation."[11] The British response was slower, but the answer was the same. Officials wrote that even before receiving the US communication, they "had been considering this question, and had reached the same conclusion as the United States, namely that opium smoking should be prohibited . . . in British territories to be freed from Japanese occupation."[12] Neither the Dutch nor the British wanted to follow this policy, but given the overwhelming strength of the US military and the depleted nature of the British and Dutch militaries, they thought they had no choice. They believed they would be relying on US personnel for the postwar occupation, so they had to compromise in order to plan to retake their colonies. By the time it became clear that Anslinger had been ahead of his government, Allies had already acquiesced. Perhaps ironically, although the United States provided substantial funding for the reoccupation by Britain, France, and the Netherlands of their former colonies in Southeast Asia, US troops did not participate in the occupation.

Anslinger effectively used the various advantages of the United States during the war years, including control of a substantial percentage of the raw materials for and manufactured quantities of narcotics medically necessary, to promote the US policy agenda of narcotics prohibition. Another activity he engaged in during the war, that of developing intelligence and spy networks, seems to have undermined US prohibition efforts, especially over the long term. Anslinger believed that to effectively control the flow of drugs around the world during the war, he had to know as precisely as possible the amounts of raw materials being grown as well as the amounts being produced and made into consumable products in countries all around the world. He asked governments to supply this information, and they usually stated they would comply, but he naturally (and rightly) did not trust them to provide fully accurate information. Sometimes they may not have known themselves. Other times they may not have wanted to share complete information with a US official. Anslinger cultivated another information source: spies, especially spies who would know about illicit drug production.[13] During the war, these spies also proved helpful in collecting other kinds of information, especially about troop movements, the economies of enemy countries, and the like. Anslinger worked with the Office of Strategic Services (OSS), the US government's overarching intelligence agency during the war, to recruit and deploy spies. One group he relied on was Italian Americans who were members of organized crime groups. They had the knowledge he, and the OSS, sought. Unfortunately, they also had a different set of motivations and purposes for participating in spying than did the government agencies hiring them. Both US intelligence agencies and some US antidrug efforts in the years after 1945 would be infiltrated by those engaged in drug trafficking, both on their own and serving secret (and not lawful) US governmental goals.[14]

During 1944 and 1945, as it became increasingly clear that the Allies would be victorious, drug-control advocates stepped up their efforts to be in a position to realize their goals at the end of the war. They saw that the League of Nations would end, to be replaced with the United Nations. They navigated carefully in these international organizations to ensure that the supply-control approach to drug control would prevail. They were largely successful due to the power of the United States, which advocated that approach, and the bureaucratic maneuvers of former League of Nations officials in favor of it. Everyone celebrated the end of World War II, but prohibition advocates had multiple reasons. It appeared they finally, after decades of struggle, would have widespread agreement on prohibition and supply control, the moral authority of the United Nations to support them, and the power of an active United States to back them.

During World War II, purely recreational use of narcotics dwindled even as the demand for medically appropriate narcotics soared. The supply of narcotics couldn't keep up even with medicinal demand, but governments also gained much greater ability to regulate and control production and distribution, largely because transportation methods were also in short supply and therefore carefully monitored. People, especially in countries like the United States that did not see fighting in the country, sometimes substituted alcohol, marijuana, and, when available, amphetamines, but even these had been relatively limited in supply. The end of the war seemed to offer those who wanted to strictly regulate and limit access to drugs an important opportunity to achieve their goals. Many officials around the world had come to accept them, and the relative dip in recreational use meant it might be able to get people to stay off drugs. Despite great success in getting agreement about these goals, achieving them remained elusive. Even before the end of the war in Asia, for instance, it was clear that agreement did not necessarily mean compliance. In mid-1944, following a

Congressional resolution after lobbying from Elizabeth Wright, the State Department contacted a number of countries, including Iran, Afghanistan, and Britain, to ask about whether they were intending to limit opium production in areas under their control. There had been complaints that US servicemen fighting in and then occupying some areas were being exposed to narcotics. US officials also wanted to get a start on the postwar opium policy. Responses were slow to come in. For war-torn countries, any lucrative crop was appealing, legitimate medical demand remained high, and government officials had more pressing concerns.[15] Although most governments told the United States they would move to comply with supply restrictions, many times the situation on the ground was already shifting to encourage supply. A new phase in the struggle to control drugs was just beginning.

7. US LAWS AND INTERNATIONAL CONVENTIONS

The end of World War II brought monumental changes throughout the world. Millions of refugees and displaced persons attempted to return home or find new places of safety. Previously colonized peoples declared their independence. Former allies became adversaries while former enemies forged alliances as a Cold War developed. Within individual countries, too, the change seemed overwhelming. War-torn countries struggled to feed, house, and clothe their citizens. All countries wrenched economies from defense production to rebuild civilian infrastructure and industry. Previously marginalized and oppressed groups deployed the idealistic language used to motivate the Allies in World War II to claim fulfillment of those ideals, revitalizing rights movements. The work of recovering from a world war often seemed overwhelming, if also full of promise.

Many people thought the moment offered unparalleled opportunity. Those involved with drug-control efforts before and during World War II agreed. They maneuvered carefully in the planning and early stages for the United Nations to get an international control regime that corrected the problems from the old League of Nations system. In the United States, many of those involved with these international efforts also had significant influence over domestic legal and policy developments. Harry Anslinger continued to dominate this group, participating in international efforts from his position as director of the US Federal Bureau of Narcotics (FBN). In 1946, he also became the US representative to a new United Nations body, the Commission on Narcotic Drugs (CND). He was joined by his longtime ally, the Canadian representative Colonel C. H. L. Sharman, head of the CND, and by American Herbert May, head of the Drug Supervisory Body (DSB), an agency continuing from the League of Nations to the United Nations. Helen Moorhead and Elizabeth Wright, two American women long involved in narcotics control, continued to work effectively in unofficial capacities.[1]

This group believed they had a chance to effectively implement a far-reaching supply-control regime. As discussed in chapter 6, during World War II, traditional recreational use of narcotics had decreased. Supply had been disrupted and legitimate medicinal use absorbed nearly all drugs that were available. If the United Nations as well as individual countries could act quickly to implement stringent controls over growing, producing, and distributing, maybe they could prevent a resurgence in illicit and recreational narcotics use. More pessimistic observers might have noticed that new countries had taken up growing and producing drugs during the war, in particular Mexico. They might also have predicted that countries devastated by war, such as China, might find it enticing to encourage narcotics growth and production again, as perhaps the fastest, simplest way to generate revenue. Anslinger, May, and Sharman were optimistic, if realistic, and thought they had a window in which to achieve their goals.

Despite all the changes following World War II, the US approach to the narcotics problem was largely unchanged. The country embraced a supply-side-control effort even more forcefully. The model was even extended to other commodities, in particular nuclear materials. An editorial in the *New York Herald Tribune* said that the "opium poppy," both "potentially beneficent" and "detrimental in the extreme," was like the atom. The editorial ended with this call: "The need for international controls to preserve only the good, eliminate the bad, applies to the one as to the other."[2] US support for supply control extended to celebration when other countries used military methods to eliminate poppies. In 1948, both China and Mexico used their military and, in Mexico, helicopters to uproot opium poppies. The story in the *New York Herald Tribune* lauded the way the effort "aids the international campaign" and "averts ruin" in the lives of potential drug users far from Mexico or China. The reporter acknowledged that those whose crops were destroyed might "first deem themselves its victims" but claimed that this practice over time would give even them a "better life."[3] These core elements of the War on Drugs approach—using any means necessary, including military means, to eliminate supply—were part of the post–World War II effort against illicit drugs.

At the United Nations, the new CND, along with the continuing agencies of PCOB and DSB, moved quickly to reestablish narcotics-control regimes in countries where they had disintegrated due to war. In this effort, they were reasonably successful. They reestablished monitoring, reporting, and enforcement throughout Europe, in Japan, and to some extent in China. The changed political situation began to hinder them from achieving their goals, however. The Soviet Union before the war had usually declined to cooperate with League of Nations efforts against narcotics. After the war, Soviet officials stated they would cooperate, but it quickly became apparent that they did so only on their own terms. Many areas of Central Asia, where Soviet influence was strong, had the potential to emerge or reemerge as significant producers of opiates if the Soviet Union decided the international control regime was not serving its interests. Any successful control efforts had to at least satisfy the Soviet Union.

Decolonization also meant that international control efforts required new approaches. Many areas of Asia and the Middle East gained independence right after World War II, with some countries in Africa joining them a few years later. Before the war, European colonial powers had been indifferent or hostile to opium prohibition, as discussed in chapter 4. For opium-control advocates, the only benefit to the prewar situation was that there were only a handful of imperial powers, so fewer people were around the negotiating table. After 1945, UN officials had to convince a much larger number of officials, many of whom had reason to continue growing or selling narcotics. For instance, the leaders of the independence struggle in what is now Indonesia were fully in agreement with narcotics prohibition but sold stocks the Dutch colonial government had accumulated in order to fund their independence fight. Other leaders did not have a strong commitment to the issue either way or were actively involved in selling narcotics, such as the Nationalist government in China. And in some places, such as the French colony of Vietnam, the former colonial power was selling opium to gain revenue to support its efforts to reassert imperial control. In general, the newly independent countries backed restrictions on narcotics, not least because of their bad experiences with colonial opium regimes. But not surprisingly, they had diverse views about how to achieve that goal, making negotiations complicated.

The Cold War also began to hinder US efforts to fully support its own policy of supply control. The "War on Drugs" conception of the drug problem that has shaped US policy since the first decades of the twentieth century has always been open to the criticism that any real solution requires focusing on both the demand and supply sides of the issue. Official policy and most of the time also the private US citizens working for drug control have emphasized supply solutions. They focused on the dangers of a substance coming into the country from somewhere else rather than trying to help reduce the demand from Americans for narcotics. Before World War II, though, the US activists were at least consistent in advocating for supply control throughout the world, without exceptions. As discussed in chapter 6, though, during World War II, Anslinger began to recruit spies from among organized crime groups, whose commitment to drug reduction was not complete. During the Cold War, US willingness to compromise on the principle of supply restriction as needed to fulfill other political interests only grew.

In the early 1950s, Burma, which before World War II had produced a negligible amount of opium for global markets, suddenly became a major exporter. Burmese were growing and exporting some opium, trying to find a product to help them rebuild their war-ravaged economy. But by far the more important reason for this sudden surge in opium production was that Guomindang (Nationalist Chinese) military and government officials fleeing after their loss to the Chinese Communist Party came to Burma to hide out and regroup for a potential reinvasion of China. To fund these efforts, they became major drug growers and exporters or encouraged local people in Burma to grow the drugs for them to export. Since the United States supported the Guomindang, US Central Intelligence Agency (CIA) officials at least ignored and in some cases facilitated this narcotics production. This production entered the illicit market, meaning US policy both encouraged and condemned the post-1945 surge in opiate production. A similar resurgence in opium production in Iran, estimated at four million pounds in 1947–48 (more than four times the estimated annual legitimate medical need for the entire world), prompted criticism from the CND. Iran was a longtime supplier of opium to pharmaceutical companies. Anslinger was so angry about this overproduction that he prohibited US companies from importing opium from Iran. But Iran was a site of competition between the United States and the Soviet Union, so the United States needed a friendly Iran. The United States also needed to rebuild its opiates stockpile after it was depleted in World War II. Anslinger had to backtrack. He needed to buy Iranian opium, especially after a poor harvest in Turkey and the complete suppression of opium production in newly Communist China after 1949. He negotiated through US pharmaceutical companies to purchase Iranian opium, with the effect of continuing to stimulate production there. These were some of the first times, but they would not be the last, that US officials actively supported a narcotics operation in service of US Cold War policies. The War on Drugs approach was often counterproductive, but these actions demonstrated that US implementation was also hypocritical.

Officially, though, Americans took the lead internationally to try to create a new, robust narcotics restriction regime and passed laws at home that echoed those commitments. During the 1950s, both international and domestic legal efforts to curtail drugs emphasized restrictive laws similar to but more far-reaching than those of the 1920s and 1930s. The international effort proved more complicated and contentious. Bureaucratic politics more than principles and ideals shaped many of the struggles and meant that even though a treaty was produced in 1953, called the Opium Protocol, it did not have full support of the nations negotiating it, and it was not ratified for ten years. The Opium Protocol reflected the priorities of nations, especially the United States, that believed supply control was most important for narcotics restriction. Anslinger proposed, and was able to get agreement on, a statement that the treaty ban "quasi-medical" use. Countries with a tradition of use that bridged the line between recreational and medicinal had long resisted this proposal from the United States. They were unable to prevent the ban from being included, for the first time, in a treaty, setting a precedent for future agreements. The most important parts of the 1953 Opium Protocol, however, set strict production controls, limited to previously reported amounts needed for medicinal need. A well-elaborated bureaucracy for reporting the amounts of needs and production was intended to reduce excess production, since any excess would be likely to enter the illicit market. All manufacturers would have to buy their raw material supplies from nations specified in the Opium Protocol. Initially, only four nations were named: India, Iran, Turkey, and Yugoslavia. After some protest and maneuvering, the Soviet Union, Bulgaria, and Greece were added. There was no mechanism for adding other nations at a later date.

For supply-control advocates, this treaty represented their best hopes for a successful restriction of narcotics. It stipulated that the global medical need for narcotics be established and publicly stated. A small set of nations agreed to produce that specific amount for a reasonable price. Manufacturers agreed to purchase only that amount from only those producers. The anticipated result: only medically necessary opiates would be available. Illicit supplies would be easier to detect and destroy before they entered the market. Given how easy it is to grow and process opium into a consumable form of an opiate, the enforcement challenges seem insurmountable even to a casual observer. But the 1953 Opium Protocol faced a different hurdle first: it proved impossible to ratify. Neither Mexico nor Peru, for example, signed it. Mexico's opium and Peru's cocaine production had increased in previous decades, especially during World War II. Any comprehensive treaty limiting narcotics would have to do more to take their interests into account than the 1953 Opium Protocol had. It languished for ten years, until Anslinger pushed it through. It was a hollow victory. The Opium Protocol was in effect only a few months before the Single Convention was ratified and superseded it.

In 1948, the UN had called for those involved in the oversight of narcotics control to update and simplify the treaty system governing international narcotics. More than ten treaties had been negotiated since 1912, with various levels of adherence. Many newly decolonized countries, for instance, adhered to few or none. Sometimes they simply had not made the effort to ratify; other times the treaties contained components they objected to. Even the 1953 Opium Protocol was intended just to supplement, not replace, existing treaties. Negotiations to create what became known as the Single Convention took thirteen years, but finally in 1961, a new treaty, eliminating all but one of the previous treaties, was agreed on. Within three years it had obtained sufficient support to be ratified. The Single Convention, as with most compromises, did not fully satisfy any group, but each different group got something important to it. Anslinger was the most disappointed with the outcome. His opposition meant the United States was slow to ratify.

The Single Convention retained the supply-control emphasis of the past. The very first person to speak at the UN conference called to discuss and approve the Single Convention, T. C. Green of Britain, noted that a key purpose was "limitation of production to legitimate purposes." Perhaps Anslinger should not have been as upset as he was. Producing countries, meaning countries growing the raw materials used in making drugs, would be required to report their production of raw materials as well as create a governmental body to oversee purchases and distribution. The Single Convention allowed more countries to grow opium than had the 1953 Opium Protocol, but in most other ways, producer restrictions increased. Coca and marijuana production were brought into the supply-control regime. Licit production was only for legitimate medical use. Countries such as India and Iran, which previously had permitted quasi-medical or even recreational consumption of opiates, instituted restrictions. Countries such as Mexico, which did not have a history of producing significant amounts for the licit market but where production was increasing, tread carefully. The

Mexican delegate, J. Barona Lobato, noted that Mexico already had strict laws against illicit growth and trafficking, and it welcomed the "world wide" scope of this treaty. He emphasized that an effective campaign would allow each country to "be responsible for control within its borders" and include "no violation or infringement of the sovereignty of States." These words seemed aimed at the United States, which as chapter 6 discussed was already trying to control Mexican drug policies to support its own supply-control approach. Producing countries embraced the Single Convention to avoid the even harsher restrictions of the 1953 Opium Protocol but also to gain some control over the production of fully synthetic drugs. As the representative from India, B. N. Banerji, noted at the beginnings of the proceedings to adopt the Single Convention, people commonly claimed "the control over national drugs at source was greater than that of control of the more refined products," but Banerji had "doubts on that point."[4] Synthetic drugs posed a threat to the economic advantages held by licit producers of agriculturally produced drugs. As Banerji seemed to be suggesting, both would prove difficult to control.

Manufacturing nations, meaning countries where pharmaceutical companies turned raw materials into drugs and/or created synthetic drugs from chemicals, embraced the Single Convention for several reasons. Most importantly, they wanted a larger number of producers than the 1953 Opium Protocol permitted. But they also wanted a simplified oversight system and predictability. Even if some parts of the Single Convention were stricter than they would have preferred, they accepted the regulation in order to get stability. Like producers, they also had to keep records demonstrating that all their purchases of raw material were converted into legitimate medical products. Synthetic narcotics came under UN regulation for the first time, so they had to include those in their production figures. Participants in the conference to adopt the Single Convention narrowly rejected extending treaty oversight to synthetic nonnarcotic drugs such as amphetamines, barbiturates, and tranquilizers as well as the first synthetic hallucinogens. They split over the issue of whether such drugs were addictive, but all agreed that consumption of these drugs was increasing.

The 1961 Single Convention codified a more elaborate version of the Schedules for drugs first introduced in the 1931 treaty. These Schedules list specific drugs on one of four Schedules according to their medical usefulness and potential for harm if used inappropriately. This system is still used both by UN oversight agencies and by the US government to stipulate the

Fig. 7.1. Indian laborers stirring thirty-five-kilogram trays of opium paste at the Government Opium and Alkaloid Works at Ghazipur in the state of Uttar Pradesh, 1985. The factory began life as the Benares Opium Agency, an entity of the East India Company, in 1820. India retained the right to produce opiates for medical purposes after World War II. Photograph © Steve Raymer.

level of regulation required for a particular drug. In theory, this approach is responsive. Drugs can be classified according to their dangerousness. Oversight and law enforcement resources can be distributed effectively. In practice, the Schedules have not been free of politics, as is discussed further in chapter 9. In addition, since drugs are listed by their chemical makeup, illicit producers can make synthetic drugs, and by changing one molecule, they can create a harmful drug that is not listed on the Schedule and therefore not subject to oversight. The United States initially opposed the 1961 Single Convention, but most other nations quickly ratified it. It went into effect in 1964.

Even though participants in the 1961 conference voted not to include amphetamines, barbiturates, tranquilizers, and hallucinogens (collectively called psychotropics) in the Single Convention, use of these drugs worldwide seemed to be ballooning in the 1960s. Given what was also happening with marijuana and to a lesser extent heroin consumption in the United States and some other parts of the world in the 1960s, people believed illicit drug use overall was widespread, at levels not seen since the 1920s. Chapter 8 explores further who was using drugs illicitly and why during this time period. United Nations members negotiated and signed a treaty regulating psychotropics in 1971. During negotiations, nations like the United States and Germany, usually at the forefront of demands for strict control over narcotics at the producer level, now took the opposite stance and argued for relatively light regulation. Most psychotropics were manufactured by pharmaceutical companies in their countries. In his initial statement, the US representative to the UN, J. E. Ingersoll, stated that the United States supported the aim of the conference but also that he "agreed with an earlier speaker that the treaty should not unduly encumber the medical profession or the pharmaceutical industry."[5] The convention mandated that pharmaceutical companies record production and distribution numbers in a way that looked similar to the narcotics-control methods. The 1971 Psychotropic Convention did not regulate either precursors (the chemicals used to manufacture the drugs) or derivatives (altered forms of the main types of drugs), due to pressure from manufacturing countries like the United States. These loopholes meant it was easy to evade the restrictions of the convention for those determined to do so.

Until the 1971 conference on psychotropics, a small set of delegates from the United States, Britain, France, and Canada, and to some extent Japan, the Soviet Union, and Germany, had dominated the negotiations. These countries had their differences, but they were also used to each other's stances and ways of negotiating. Even the personnel of some delegations, such as the US one, stayed consistent through much of the time period. Harry Anslinger continued to play a dominant role in US drug policy, both domestically and internationally, until 1964.[6] His legislative goals shaped the Congressional agenda, and his agency, the FBN, dominated other government entities such as the Departments of State and Treasury, in shaping official US policy.

Anslinger had long advocated for mandatory minimum sentences for drug possession and dealing. For Anslinger, the best way to prevent a drug problem was supply control, or making sure no one had access to drugs except by medical prescription. But if that failed and people accessed drugs illicitly, he believed they should be harshly punished. He called drug dealers "insidious, sordid" but also claimed that mere addicts were likely to commit a range of crimes. He did not say the drug itself caused the crime but that the "destruction of moral sensibilities" and "insatiable burning desire" for the drugs made them "ready and willing to violate the law."[7] Prison was the appropriate response. In the aftermath of World War II, when the United States had been relatively free of narcotics, sympathy for Anslinger's approach grew. Hearings in Congress during 1951, with FBN agents prominent among those testifying that the Mafia was flooding the United States with heroin, helped set up passage of the Boggs Act. It was true that heroin imports were up dramatically in the late 1940s. The nature of Mafia involvement is less easy to establish, but the testimony was dramatic and effective. The Boggs Act set a required minimum sentence of two years in prison and a fine of $2,000 for anyone who "imports or brings . . . receives, conceals, buys, sells, or in any manner facilitates the transportation, concealment, or sale of any narcotic drug." No minimum quantity of drug was mentioned. Indeed, "possession" of the drug was "deemed sufficient evidence to authorize conviction."[8] Harsher penalties, and no ability to offer a suspended sentence or parole, followed for subsequent offenses. Given that the average annual family income in 1951 was $3,700, the fine alone was a significant penalty. This was a federal law, and then as now, most drug crime was prosecuted at the state level. States quickly moved to bring their statutes in line with the federal law. Both federal and state laws, as shown in the case of California, drew on a rhetoric of "dope peddlers." Using at best anecdotal evidence, promoters of these laws claimed urban Black and Latino drug dealers threatened to ensnare "innocent" white youth in the drug scene, and used this rhetoric to justify the harsh mandatory minimums. Real developments did not reflect this rhetoric. At the same time that newspapers in Southern California hyped the dangers of "rat packs" composed of Mexican American youth selling drugs to unsuspecting white suburban teenagers, juvenile crime actually was decreasing and those white teens usually got any drugs they consumed from other white people.[9] In the 1950s, as in every wave of heightened concern about drugs, white Americans portrayed the problem as stemming from racialized minorities.

Drug use appeared to continue to increase, and the Boggs Act was strengthened in 1956 with the Narcotics Control Act. This law focused on increasing the maximum penalties, particularly for those with second and subsequent offenses, while leaving the mandatory minimums in place. A first offense for possession could net two or more years, the same as in the Boggs Act, but maximum penalties increased from five to ten years for a second offense. Subsequent offenses likewise had substantially increased penalties. On a third offense for possession, the sentence was at least ten and up to forty years, with a fine of $20,000. Penalties for selling drugs were at the higher end of these stated sentences. Sale of heroin by an adult to a minor called for a sentence of life in prison, and at the jury's discretion could result in the death penalty. State laws echoed the focus on punishment, and the standards of proof were often minimal, with the mere existence of needle tracks in some places sufficient for conviction.[10] Ironically, the high prices and increasingly bad quality of heroin in the early 1950s had already begun to erode usage even before these laws fully took effect. Commissioner Anslinger took credit for reported decreased usage. It looked like the combination of a strict supply-control policy overseas and harsh punishment regime at home had solved the drug problem, and those who supported this War on Drugs approach touted it as the most effective answer.

As discussed in chapter 8, though, the 1960s challenged the notion that the US approach worked. New types of drugs did not fall neatly under existing control mechanisms. Production overseas skyrocketed. And many young people did not think drugs were all that dangerous. People were questioning the harsh mandatory minimums, which on closer examination did not seem to have any significant effect on the amount of drug use in the country. Even groups like the American Bar Association and the American Medical Association (AMA), not known for taking radical positions, had come to see harsh drug laws as counterproductive in solving problems of addiction and crime. Their joint report, published in 1961, while agreeing that "drug peddling" was a "vicious and predatory crime," also said "a grave question remains whether severe jail and prison sentences are the most rational way of dealing with narcotic addicts." In the main, they recommended more study, but their criticism of the existing policy, which mandated jail time rather than treatment, was clear.[11]

In the early 1960s, it appeared that US government policy might be ahead of the curve on these issues. President John F. Kennedy led a charge to reexamine some of the basic principles of US drug law. He established the Presidential Commission on Narcotic and Drug Abuse, whose report was finished just before Kennedy's assassination. His successor, President Lyndon B. Johnson, had to figure out how to respond to the more than twenty-five recommendations. They were far-reaching, including adding more regulation of prescription drugs with addictive capacity such as barbiturates and amphetamines, trying to balance treatment and punishment for users, organization of antidrug law enforcement within the federal government, and reforms to the Narcotics Farms, which since the mid-1930s supposedly had offered treatment but functioned more like jails. For both philosophical and bureaucratic reasons, some of the proposed changes were highly contentious. Johnson initiated some changes in July 1964, with an executive order tasking any federal agency with responsibility in this area to prioritize ending illegal drug trade, preventing drug abuse, and supporting rehabilitation for users. Perhaps more important than these vague directives, Johnson claimed the federal government's authority in the area of drugs stemmed not from its taxation powers (the legal basis for all actions to that point) but from the interstate commerce clause in the Constitution. The change seems subtle and legalistic but had the effect of expanding the types of activities the federal government could control. And, importantly, it meant that the FBN, which had been placed in the Department of Treasury because of the connection to taxation, was likely to experience substantial change. Many people thought this change was long overdue. Initial steps spread out the responsibilities for oversight and enforcement of drug laws among several different departments. By spring 1968, the FBN was dissolved, with its responsibilities (and those of several other agencies) transferred to the Bureau of Narcotics and Dangerous Drugs (BNDD) in the Department of Justice. After 1973, the BNDD became the Drug Enforcement Administration (DEA), which still exists today.

The Johnson administration faced many additional challenges related to drugs, and efforts to address these were made in Congress. Two pieces of federal legislation attempted to realize the administration goal of prioritizing rehabilitation over punishment for people whose only crime was using drugs. Both the 1965 Drug Abuse Control Amendments and the 1966 Narcotic Addict Rehabilitation Act (NARA) reflected the mixed thinking about drugs and their effects as well as the difficulty of turning away from beliefs that drug use and abuse were synonymous. The administration's proposal in the NARA legislation attempted, for instance, to offer civil commitment for anyone whose crimes could be shown to have stemmed only from their attempts to support their own drug habit, but Congress changed the legislation to make it harder to avoid jail time. Rates of drug use were increasing in the mid-1960s, especially of marijuana and hallucinogens. Many Americans, especially younger ones, believed these drugs were not harmful or addictive. Many took them recreationally, seeing only benefit in their use. They supported efforts to decriminalize and to focus on problematic behavior rather than simple drug use. Many other Americans, however, found the increased drug use in society frightening and dangerous, reflective of a whole host of changes they didn't like in the 1960s, including strides toward racial equality and protests against the government. This latter group was more well represented in Congress, as these questions from Representative Robert Ashmore (D-SC) demonstrate. He asked an administration official: "In many ways it [marijuana] is as bad as heroin, morphine and what have you?" and "It [marijuana] can cause one to commit murder, another sex violence, another something else?"[12] Reefer madness was alive and well in Congress, and it blunted the reform impulses behind these two bills.

The Johnson administration continued to attempt to balance between the competing visions of how to address what appeared to be a growing drug problem in the United States. Sometimes the conflict was referred to as being between "cops and docs." The "cops" wanted to maintain mandatory minimums, viewed users as addicts and criminals, and believed strict laws enforced by well-resourced police reduced drug use. Many of them wanted to maintain the independent status of the Federal Bureau of Narcotics, so as to have only minimal oversight, and to treat marijuana, psychedelics, cocaine, and heroin as equally dangerous drugs. The "docs" accepted the new medical insights finding addiction a disease needing treatment more than a crime needing punishment, wanted medical and scientific knowledge of drugs to structure their regulation, and advocated for a variety of government agencies to be involved in the oversight of drug policy. It was difficult for the Johnson administration, wrestling with an unpopular war in Southeast Asia, dramatic and widespread movements for change in the United States itself, and, along with all that, apparent massive increases in drug use, to resist the calls for a "tough-on-crime" policy that would favor the vision of the "cops" more than the "docs." Johnson administration officials also recognized that many of the policy revisions of the mid-1960s had been incomplete and confusing. The 1960s saw both increased acceptance of drug use in the United States and continued emphasis on the dangers of drugs and the people who used them. In the last year of the Johnson administration, officials were working on legislation to improve treatment options, including methadone; to distinguish between users and dealers; and to continue the age-old focus on source control by using US funds to encourage other countries to destroy opium crops. The legislative efforts were a mixed bag, with some elements looking like a medical and treatment approach to drugs and others like a punitive, War on Drugs approach. In the midst of waning influence and other priorities, this legislation did not get finished before a new president, Richard M. Nixon, took office. Passage of that legislation occurred under Nixon, as a prelude to his declaration of the War on Drugs.

8. WHO IS USING?

Drugs and the period of the 1960s–1970s go together in many people's minds: hippies, college students, and pot; heroin in the inner cities and used by soldiers in Vietnam; and the rise in cocaine by a partying crowd at the disco or at big-money parties in cities, with rolled-up hundred-dollar bills used to snort the cocaine. The image is not necessarily wrong, but it's far from complete. Illicit drug use rose and fell during the entire post–World War II era, in both the United States and the rest of the world. Licit drug use also rose significantly, especially in the United States. This chapter explores who was using which kinds of drugs but also which kinds of drug use by which kinds of people caused alarm. Not surprisingly, drug use, whether licit or illicit, by wealthier and white people often prompted calls for increased spending on prevention and treatment. Drug use by marginalized or minority groups, especially Black Americans, or even the perception that these groups were using drugs, often led to harsh laws, focused on punishment, instead. Sometimes the harsh laws stemmed from carefully orchestrated campaigns to accuse people from marginalized groups of luring young white Americans into drug use. Racialized rhetoric about the dangers of drug abuse in post–World War II America hid the more diverse and widespread patterns of drug use actually occurring, making it impossible to develop effective policies.

One important consequence of World War II was the massively increased use of newly available drugs such as amphetamines and barbiturates.[1] Soldiers and factory workers alike, as discussed in chapter 6, had used amphetamines to stay awake during long work hours in wartime. By the end of the war, it is estimated that 10 percent or more of US soldiers had taken amphetamines. Amphetamines were considered the new miracle drug for treating depression but also for weight loss, with two million or more pills produced each day for these purposes in the United States in 1945. Soldiers and workers often used barbiturates to finally sleep after forcing themselves to stay awake for long periods or to calm their nerves after battle or other stressful situations. They were sold for anxiety and to help with sleep in the more general population too. Both amphetamines and barbiturates were easy to obtain in the United States in the 1940s and into the 1950s, with some kinds even available over the counter, without a doctor's prescription, until 1951. Although some people raised concerns about their addictive nature, and especially about how easy it was to misuse these drugs, their ubiquity in wartime also meant that many people had experience with them and found them useful.

In the 1950s, despite the need for a prescription for both barbiturates and amphetamines, people used them to an extent that would today seem extreme. When people visited their doctor, more than 60 percent of the time they left with a prescription. Doctors prescribed barbiturates and bromides most frequently, intended to calm and aid sleep.[2] Doctors' prescribing patterns were nearly never investigated, but even if they were, these drugs had been marketed as useful for a wide range of common conditions, such as obesity, "pre-obesity," and even common "mental and emotional distress."[3] The Food and Drug Administration (FDA) had less authority in the 1950s to regulate prescription drugs than it does today but put these drugs on its "prescription only" list. Enforcement fell to the FBN, which instructed its agents to focus on illicit drugs and marginalized groups rather than potential misuse of prescription drugs. White women and wealthy people used prescription drugs most heavily. Statistics are difficult to obtain, but a 1967 survey found that in the previous twelve months, 26 percent of white respondents and 13 percent of Black respondents had taken a psychotropic drug. The question about gender revealed 31 percent of women and 15 percent of men had taken one. The disparities by income were discernible but not as stark, with 31 percent of top earners (more than $10,000 annually) having consumed a psychotropic, compared with 22 percent of those earning the least (under $5,000 annually).[4] In the heated postwar economy, working-class men and women took amphetamines while trying to stay awake on long shifts at demanding jobs. White middle-class men took barbiturates along with alcohol for an intensified feeling of drunkenness but then also to fall sleep despite their work and financial worries. White middle-class women used the same drugs to deal with the increased boredom and anxiety of modern domestic life. Black men and women, along with other ethnic minorities, took these drugs much less often despite facing the same societal disruptions.

The common use of these mood-altering prescription medications with alcohol, which was also enormously popular in the 1950s, meant that many people, particularly white people, took combinations of powerful drugs on a regular basis. Many middle-class white Americans in the 1950s embraced the three-martini lunch and cocktails before dinner. By contrast, the working class engaged in heavy consumption of beer, both at home and in bars. Perhaps after years of reduced alcohol consumption in the 1920s, 1930s, and 1940s, people were just having fun. But other developments may also have prompted anxieties that promoted use of alcohol and prescription drugs, often together. The growth of the suburbs meant many people had longer commutes. People believed that they lived in an age of affluence, and so they felt social pressures to consume more and to present an image of perfection to the outside world. In both blue- and white-collar jobs, many workers faced a faster pace in the work world. The 1950s were far from a placid, drug-free prelude to the wilder 1960s. White Americans consumed significant amounts of drugs in both decades, although of different kinds and to some extent by different groups. One pharmaceutical company even developed a combination barbiturate/amphetamine with the trade name Dexamyl. One physician who tested it on his patients was so satisfied that he claimed, "This is a Dexamyl age, an age of unrest; probably no other period in history has been dominated by a mood of uncertainty and disquiet."[5]

The 1950s also had their own counterculture activists, especially people who identified as Beatniks. They often wanted to reject the consumerist, conformist society of the 1950s. To demonstrate that commitment, they purposefully lived in poverty, engaged in artistic endeavors and journeys of self-awareness, and took drugs. They sometimes consumed amphetamines and barbiturates. More often they wanted to consume drugs that would expand their mental horizons, by causing them to experience the world more deeply or by prompting hallucinations and other kinds of mind journeys. They commonly smoked marijuana but also took peyote (a drug used in religious ceremonies by Native Americans), hallucinogenic mushrooms, and LSD. Lysergic acid diethylamide (LSD) is a psychedelic drug that alters one's experience of reality for a period of a few hours. It was invented in Switzer-

land in the late 1930s and began to be used in the Unite
War II to treat various psychiatric conditions. Those in
took it for the "trip," and it was very popular for a period o

Initially neither prohibition laws nor prescribing regu
LSD. During the 1950s, scientists conducted significant re
possibility that LSD could assist people in overcoming alco
They also believed that LSD, and possibly other hallucinogen ... help people with mental illness, and they studied those possibilities as well. These scientists believed the hallucinations people experienced after taking the drugs offered insight into the origins of a variety of mental health conditions, whether chemical or a result of disordered thinking. Many of these experiments showed promise to offer real relief, but others were conducted unethically or without sufficient care. The bad press from failed experiments stressed the frightening nature of some of the powerful hallucinations, and government officials began to warn against these drugs by the early 1960s.

Officials in the CIA, founded in 1947, thought LSD might have useful properties for them. One section of the CIA had been given the task to find out whether certain drugs and techniques, such as sleep deprivation, might facilitate mind control. These efforts were, and in some cases still are, shrouded in secrecy. Chemists and other scientists devised experiments, conducted without consent on unwitting or unwilling people, including soldiers and students, to test drugs, especially LSD. The CIA officers could lead people on their LSD trip and prompt them to reveal secrets. Sometimes subjects did not, later, even recall that they had revealed this information. The experiments did not in the end produce reliable methods of gaining intelligence. Worse yet, some subjects suffered permanent damage or even death. This use of LSD couldn't be more different from the ways it was used recreationally. The CIA experiments lacked all ethical standards and oversight. It is difficult to know, since the program was secret, but given the conditions under which people took this LSD, they probably were more likely to experience harm than a voluntary user might.[6] Although LSD is not addictive, people's experiences with it vary, and taking LSD in circumstances that are already frightening or uncertain enhances the likelihood of a negative outcome, such as paranoia.

Even heroin saw an initial resurgence, but then usage declined during the 1950s. In contrast to the drugs discussed so far in this chapter, heroin use was prohibited. Other opiates could be legally prescribed by a doctor, [illegible] heroin. In the aftermath of World War II, as we saw in chapters 6 and 7, heroin use rebounded after the war had disrupted both production and trade. In the United States, only major cities, primarily those on both the east and the west coasts, saw significant heroin use, although it appeared throughout the country. In contrast to their perceptions of licit drug users, many people viewed heroin users as poor, marginalized, urban, and often from an ethnic or racial minority. To the extent that this perception echoed reality, one explanation may be that these populations may have found it easier to buy heroin than to access the licit prescription drugs. Teenagers, especially in urban areas, also became more likely to use heroin than in the past, although the numbers were still low overall.[7] Heroin use rose and fell swiftly in the 1950s, though, partly in response to the strict prohibition laws passed in 1951 and 1956 but also due to global production and trade conditions.

By the time the supposedly drug-filled 1960s arrived, Americans already consumed a lot of mind-altering substances. Doctors prescribed a large percentage of these drugs. Still, the 1960s represented change. One change began to rein in the massive use of prescription drugs, first with the additional power given to the FDA in 1962. Starting then, pharmaceutical companies had to prove their drugs had the medical effects they claimed, which led to a reduced number of prescriptions. Americans still consumed, and do to this day, significant amounts of prescription mind-altering substances. Prescriptions for amphetamines and barbiturates have never again reached the levels of the 1950s and early 1960s, though. People turned to so-called minor tranquilizers (such as Valium) for a period, and prescriptions for those remained at extremely high levels through the 1970s.[8] The other change was the large increase in the number of Americans, especially young Americans, using illicit drugs, particularly marijuana. More than any change in the amount of drug consumption in society, this shift toward more recreational use by young Americans did most to prompt people to see the 1960s as an age of drugs. These young drug users often claimed, unabashedly, that they used drugs because they liked the effects rather than to cure some illness. They did not hide their drug use, either, at least so long as being open did not lead to legal trouble. Any claims about the rise or fall in absolute amounts of drug use during a particular time have to be treated with skepticism. Statistics on illicit consumption will always be unreliable. But it felt like drug use was increasing because people talked about it and even advocated for it.

Young people led much of the social upheaval and change that characterizes the 1960s in the United States. Students, mostly college but also high school students, played a leading part in the civil rights movement, marching and organizing, and traveling throughout the country or being willing to be arrested in their hometowns. Young people had significant roles in the growing antiwar movement that developed after the mid-1960s, as they protested the US war in Vietnam. Both political movements happened in the midst of a massive cultural and social change, as young people were more likely to go to college, have independence from their parents, listen to music their parents found radical (rock and roll), and reject the consumerism and conformity they believed had made their parents unhappy. Recreational consumption of drugs often accompanied these changes and movements. Although both Black and white members of these political and cultural movements of the 1960s consumed drugs, white young people did so at a higher rate.

For most young people, the drug of choice was marijuana. Before the 1960s, people like jazz musicians or other artists, or people living in areas near Mexico, where most marijuana for the United States was grown, were most likely to consume marijuana. As white, middle-class young people began to use marijuana, mainstream America revived its concerns about reefer madness, the belief that marijuana use was more harmful than even drugs like cocaine or heroin. The reefer madness propaganda of the 1930s had emphasized that marijuana could make a user become out of control and violent. The 1960s version of this propaganda argued that it was a gateway drug, softening up users for trying harder drugs and providing a path to heroin addiction, for instance. An article in the *Saturday Evening Post* claimed that while it was difficult to discern a set pattern, many teens started with over-the-counter cough syrups containing small amounts of narcotics, then "may graduate to marijuana, which is not addictive, and later perhaps to barbiturate pills or heroin, which are extremely so."[9] It's true that marijuana use is associated, statistically, with the use of other drugs. This means that if you are a marijuana user, you are more likely than someone who does not smoke marijuana to also use another drug. But it's not clear if marijuana use is what prompts the other drug use, let alone how or why. In both the 1930s and the 1960s, too, reefer madness propaganda emphasized the sexual dangers to innocent young women, nearly always portrayed as white, if they began to smoke marijuana. Lurid images suggested that marijuana lowered inhibitions, prompting "good girls" to

Fig. 8.1. Two people sharing what appears to be a joint at a concert in San Francisco, 1967. Photograph © Steven Clevenger, Corbis/Getty.

engage in sexual activities they otherwise would not or make them vulnerable to control by drug pushers, who would lure them into prostitution.

Young people in the 1960s mostly said that they used drugs to have a good time, experience reality a bit differently, and "tune out" a society they found judgmental, repressive, or confining. These reasons frightened many of the older members of society, who worried that young people were "dropping out" of society and were not going to be willing or able to take over in a competitive world. There certainly were young people, commonly called hippies, who deplored what the older generation had created, a world of war and oppression and spending all of one's time working hard for someone else's benefit. Young and old alike often used the phrase "generation gap." But most young people were not hippies, and they may have used drugs occasionally, but not often. A 1969 Gallup poll found that only 4 percent of adults had ever tried marijuana. Assuredly most of that 4 percent were young people, but even so, that wasn't a particularly high percentage even of them. And the majority of young people who did smoke marijuana were not dropping out of society or rejecting their responsibilities. They did it to relax, to have fun, or often as a small act of rebellion.

Use of other drugs also increased in the 1960s, and this increase was less well accepted than marijuana use. For example, LSD was a popular drug, not addictive, and it offered the kind of expansive, mind-altering experience many young people sought. Harvard psychologist Timothy Leary experimented with the drug and found it potentially had benefits, under the right circumstances. His advice to young people to "turn on, tune in, and drop out" was reported more widely than some of his cautions about how to use the drug safely, but he was one of many who thought this drug could be helpful. Mainstream society found LSD worrisome, in part because of what its users found beneficial: the hallucinogenic visions. But many people also worried about the side effects and the fact that its long-term use had not been well studied. Increased recreational use in the 1960s led to LSD being completely outlawed in the United States in 1970.

Heroin also saw an upswing in usage during the 1960s and especially into the 1970s. The increase had several causes. In part, urban usage by minority groups, especially men, had grown already in the 1950s, and it began to spread through nearby neighborhoods and to other socioeconomic groups. The availability of the drug meant more people tried it. In addition, some of the young people who were experimenting with other drugs also tried heroin. Often this usage remained experimental or casual, but not always, and addiction rates for heroin among middle-class youth reached higher levels than in many decades. The most visible users of heroin, and the biggest worry for mainstream Americans, were returning soldiers from Vietnam. Soldiers often turn to drug consumption during war, and the availability of very inexpensive heroin in Vietnam meant that a relatively large percentage of US soldiers at least tried the drug while there. Many were regular users, and some became addicted. The high rates of use caused worried social commentary about the harm that would be caused in the United States, as well as to these men, if they returned from serving as addicts and continued to use after arriving home. As historian Jeremy Kuzmarov argues, the actual situation was much more complicated. He found that the vast majority of men who used marijuana or heroin in Vietnam stopped that use when they returned to the United States.[10] Their use was situational, triggered by particular experiences or particular settings. We see, even today, higher rates of addiction among returning soldiers from all wars, the US war in Vietnam included, than in most groups of people who did not go to war. This heightened use, even if much less than the public concern in the 1960s and 1970s, led to an increase in heroin consumption in the United States.

A final reason that drugs became so much more prevalent in the 1960s and 1970s is that, in some countries, US foreign policy encouraged drug production. Sometimes this result was an indirect one, in that the kinds of economic development policies that the United States promoted prompted some farmers and local businessmen to view drug production as a good business opportunity. Sometimes, the result was more direct. In Vietnam, for example, the United States partnered with political allies who made money by growing and selling drugs. US officials did not attempt to get them to stop. Indeed, they often facilitated the drug trade, since it generated significant funds to support US causes and allies. The CIA used these illicit funds to secretly support groups and causes, sometimes in defiance of stated US policy.[11] Even the environmental destruction of the US war in Vietnam made it more likely that farmers would turn to growing opium, which required little infrastructure, tending, or fertilizer. In Bolivia, coca had long been grown and consumed, but the remoteness of the region where it grew meant a commercial enterprise had not developed. Ironically, US development aid from the 1950s facilitated growth of an infrastructure that could support illicit cocaine manufacture and export, much of it destined for the United States.[12] As the world produced more and more heroin, cocaine, and marijuana, the price of each dropped. The low prices and ample supply meant that it became easy for people to try drugs. Most remained recreational users, but with even a small percentage of a large group becoming addicts, Americans began to worry about a serious drug problem during the 1960s and 1970s even while many still thought that some drug use was nothing to worry about.

During the 1960s and 1970s, the US response to the perception that drug use was growing included both more focus on treatment and President Richard Nixon's famous War on Drugs approach. That response is discussed in chapter 9. By the later 1970s, many Americans thought marijuana should be treated more leniently, perhaps even legalized, although they still worried about increased heroin and cocaine use. Also by the later 1970s, many Americans perceived that drug use was still increasing, despite the efforts the Nixon administration had instituted to curb it. As in every decade after World War II, the perception that young people, especially young white people, were using more drugs drove social policy. As the 1970s came to a close, two divergent attitudes about drugs shaped people's perceptions of drug use in the country. A large group thought at least some drug use, especially marijuana, was not harmful and should at least be decriminalized if not legalized. Another large group thought all illicit drug use was harmful, or at least that it was harmful for young people, and that more availability of drugs in general meant more young people would try drugs and experience that harm. The second group had more influence in the 1980s.

If one judges by media coverage and perception, the 1980s was the decade of cocaine, with usage believed to be rising significantly, particularly of a newly popular form of cocaine: crack. During the 1980s, the word *cocaine* appeared in the *New York Times* more than nine thousand times, while the words *marijuana* and *heroin* appeared only approximately three thousand times each. Cocaine use among celebrities, particularly athletes, seemed rampant. The stories touted the dangers of the new "potent" form of cocaine. Crack cocaine is made from dissolving powder cocaine in water with either baking soda or ammonia, and then boiling it until only the hard solid is left, ready to be broken into "rocks" that are usually smoked. The delivery method means the high is more immediate but shorter in duration. Both media and antidrug public relations campaigns claimed that crack was instantly addictive, with one use sufficient to hook someone. This is not true; many people used both cocaine and crack either occasionally or only a few times. For those who did become addicted, though, the powerful urge to maintain that short-lived high drove them to many dangerous behaviors. Cocaine use rose, relative to use of the drug in the past, during the 1980s. And crack was part of that rise, particularly visible because usage was concentrated among the urban poor, whose drug use is always heavily monitored. Panicked media coverage of cocaine use emphasized its addictive nature, the desperate choices of addicts, and dangers to children, especially so-called crack babies. It is not good for babies if their mothers use cocaine during pregnancy, but the effects are less serious and less permanent than on babies whose mothers drink alcohol heavily while pregnant, an activity attracting much less attention. Societal fears about the effects of cocaine drove efforts to renew the punitive side of the War on Drugs approach Nixon had taken, and under both President Ronald Reagan and President George H. W. Bush, new harsh laws passed.

Concern about drug use by teens and even younger people also rose in the 1980s, this time driven more by concern about marijuana use. Already in the late 1970s, groups of white parents, mostly from suburbs, began to organize against what they perceived to be lax laws and policies around drugs. By 1980, more than three hundred of these groups existed in thirty-four states. Many of them banded together into the National Federation of Parents for Drug-Free Youth (NFP) in the spring of 1980. Ronald Reagan's presidential campaign happily seized the issue of opposing drugs generally, in particular drug use by young people, and NFP members actively worked for his election. First Lady Nancy Reagan adopted youth drug use as her cause, funding some antidrug programs in schools and co-opting an existing Just Say No program for her own public relations purposes.

For all the public concern about marijuana and cocaine use in the 1980s, the actual incidence of drug use in that decade was, overall, on par with or slightly less than in the 1960s and 1970s. To be sure, cocaine use was higher than it had been and rose throughout the decade. Marijuana use remained at a relatively high level compared to pre-1970s usage. It is always difficult to know precisely how much drug use is occurring in the country, but starting in 1975, the National Institute of Drug Abuse began surveying high school seniors about their use of drugs. This survey continues to the present, and the ability to compare this data over so many years provides a reasonably good window into trends, although the absolute numbers may not be fully reliable. Those running the survey also return to the same set of people over the years, asking them to provide information about drug use in later years, meaning that by the mid-1980s, the survey was beginning to provide useful information about drug use by adults as well.

The trends for high school senior drug use from the mid-1970s through the end of the 1980s are revealing. The survey asked about a number of different kinds of drugs, with questions about use in the past thirty days, past year, or ever. For marijuana, for all three questions, reported use rose steadily from 1975 to 1979, then tailed off each year to 1989. For instance, in 1975, 47.3 percent of high school seniors said they had used marijuana at least once in their lifetime. In 1979, usage peaked at 60.4 percent, then by 1989 had decreased to only 43.7 percent. After the 1960s upswing in marijuana usage, it has remained a popular drug. By contrast, heroin was not at all popular with teenagers in the 1970s and 1980s. In 1975, only 2.2 percent of high school seniors reported that they had ever used heroin, and that number decreased to an average of 1.2 percent in the 1980s. Cocaine followed a different arc, suggesting its popularity was growing in the 1980s. Reported lifetime usage in 1975 was 9 percent, rising to a high of 17.3 percent in 1985, and then falling back to just over 10 percent in 1989.

For both use in the past year and use in the past thirty days, the percentages for each of these drugs was significantly lower than the percentage who had used at least once, suggesting that a large number of people tried each drug once or a few times and didn't use again or used only rarely. For context, this survey also found that more than 90 percent of high school seniors had tried alcohol, with the percentage bouncing around in the low 90s throughout this time period. Of those, 82.7 to 87.9 percent had used alcohol in the previous year, and 60 to 72.1 percent had used in the previous thirty days. Alcohol was the most commonly consumed drug by high school seniors, far ahead of all the others.[13]

These numbers reveal only whether drugs were readily available and used by high school students. The decrease in initial use of drugs in high school might not mean much if people simply delayed initial drug use until they were adults. Later survey data suggests that at least 76 percent and perhaps as much as 84 percent of Americans who became adults in the 1980s used some kind of illicit drug at least one time. Experimenting with drugs in young adulthood was common. But the questions asking adults about use in the previous year or thirty days also showed the same decline trends seen in high school senior usage. For all drugs except cocaine, use rates peaked in 1979 or 1980, falling through the 1980s. For cocaine use, rates peaked in 1985 or 1986 and then began to decline. Still, about 25 percent of adults aged 19–30 reported use of marijuana in the previous year in 1989, and between 10 and 15 percent reported use of cocaine. Those are relatively high numbers. It's difficult to assess addiction from this report, since it did not ask about daily use except for marijuana. Only about 5 percent of adults 19–30 reported daily use of marijuana over the previous thirty days in 1989, a percentage also in steady decline from a high of approximately 10 percent in 1979. These statistics suggest a few tentative conclusions about drug use in the 1980s. First, young people commonly tried an illicit drug, and some persisted in that use. Cocaine, whether in powder or crack form, was more prevalent than it had been in past decades, with occasional use not uncommon among young people. Marijuana remained persistently appealing even as use declined somewhat. Second, drug use, except for cocaine, seems to have peaked in 1979 or 1980, before Ronald Reagan was elected president, so also before Nancy Reagan's famous Just Say No campaigns, and before the harsh punitive laws passed during Reagan's presidency, as discussed in chapter 9. Third, the panic about increased crack cocaine use in the 1980s, like the similar panic about LSD in the 1960s and heroin in the 1950s, drew on an actual increase in consumption of these drugs but also obscured the larger picture of illicit drug consumption. People who use drugs a few times or rarely outnumber, by a lot, the number of regular or addicted users.

Despite representing a low percentage of all drug users, those who injected illicit drugs received significant negative attention at the end of the 1980s too. The first US cases of HIV/AIDS were identified in 1981, although the disease was not yet understood. By 1983, though, reports noted that people who injected drugs were among the high-risk groups for infection with HIV/AIDS, as were men who had sex with other men, and people with hemophilia. Nancy Reagan's Just Say No approach seemed as applicable to sex as to drugs in this context. US Health and Human Services secretary Otis R. Bowen said, "I can't emphasize too strongly the necessity of changing life-styles."[14] Sex proved even more difficult to restrict than drugs, however. A safe(r)-sex movement grew, especially promoting condoms but also testing, improved partner communication, and alternative sexual activities. Safer-sex strategies can be compared to harm-reduction efforts for drugs. Harm reduction aims to make illicit drug use safer rather than to eliminate it. In the 1980s and early 1990s, the push for harm reduction through programs to assure clean needles came as much from HIV/AIDS activists as from those concerned primarily with drugs.

By the end of the 1980s, many observers thought the harsh tactics of Reagan's approach to the War on Drugs were working. Illicit drug use appeared to have decreased. These assessments proved wrong, as developments from the 1990s to the present demonstrate. These changes in illicit drug use are discussed further in chapters 10 and 13.

9. WAR ON DRUGS DECLARED

President Richard M. Nixon is usually credited, or blamed, for initiating the US War on Drugs. As we have seen, the United States began using War on Drugs tactics by the first decades of the twentieth century. The Nixon-era changes drew on the prohibitionist, supply-control approach accompanying the first legal US restrictions on drugs. His policies, like those since the late nineteenth century, both drew on and reinforced racially biased ideas about drug users and specific drugs. The policy, legal, and political developments during Nixon's years in office represented significant change, though. Starting with Nixon's presidency, the War on Drugs was institutionalized and funded at higher levels than in the past. The contradictions and unintended consequences of the US effort to prohibit drugs since the late nineteenth century intensified after 1971.

President Richard Nixon's Special Message to Congress on June 17, 1971, could be read as the declaration of the War on Drugs. He opened the speech by declaring, "America's public enemy number one is drug abuse. In order to fight and defeat this enemy, it is necessary to wage a new, all-out offensive."[1] His language was combative, referencing fighting and battles and the need for victory. It was also therapeutic and sociable, emphasizing the human cost of illegal drugs, the effects on families, and the tragedy of addiction. He was responding to a perceived crisis. Heroin use and abuse appeared to be at an all-time high and to be making inroads into parts of the American public not touched by opiate abuse since the 1890s. It is notoriously difficult to estimate numbers of users of illicit drugs, but historian David Musto used data such as the rise in rates of narcotic-related hepatitis to estimate that the number of heroin users in the United States totaled approximately fifty thousand in 1960 and rose to nearly five hundred thousand in just a decade.[2] Regardless of any doubts about the accuracy of these numbers, the perception of such a dramatic rise prompted fear. Crime rates had increased; overdoses and deaths from heroin were also up. Nixon had campaigned for president in 1968 with promises to address these problems. His 1971 speech called for the United States to build on actions already taken, such as passage of the 1970 Comprehensive Drug Abuse Prevention and Control Act (hereafter Prevention and Control Act) and the new United Nations treaty regulating psychotropics, signed in early 1971. He called for additional action, particularly spending substantially more on the traditional policy of supply eradication. He balanced that with proposals to also substantially increase spending on prevention and treatment.

The phrase "War on Drugs" did not appear in this speech, but the mix of treatment emphasis, arbitrary tactics, and harsh punishments in the Nixon approach soon made it clear that the effort was as comprehensive as a war. A variety of policies and laws resulted from the effort this speech advocated. The most far-reaching policies were domestic. Sentences for mere possession were reduced but for dealing remained harsh. For some dealers, conviction could even bring life in prison. Methadone received official support, but with it came more oversight and scrutiny, from both the Food and Drug Administration and law enforcement, to ensure there was no illicit diversion of methadone. Police gained increased rights to search properties where suspected drug dealing was occurring. The 1970 Prevention and Control Act initiated the right of police to acquire no-knock warrants if they thought giving suspects notice would lead to destruction of evidence. Bureaucratic changes streamlined and simplified the US effort against illicit drugs by 1973, concentrating them in the new Drug Enforcement Administration (DEA). Other changes shaped US policy at home and abroad. The federal government sponsored research into herbicides for eradication that would be more environmentally friendly, as discussed in chapter 11. These herbicides increased eradication in foreign countries as well as the United States. The DEA facilitated a more intrusive interdiction policy at US borders and inside other countries, taking the US drug war into those spaces. At the United Nations, the United States played a leading role in negotiating the 1971 Psychotropic Treaty, which placed strict controls on hallucinogenic drugs. This treaty also gave pharmaceutical companies relatively free rein to develop other psychotropics for medical use. The United States also actively participated in crafting the 1972 update to the Single Convention, which strengthened the authority of the International Narcotics Control Board (a UN agency) to investigate and regulate and brought synthetic

Fig. 9.1. Richard M. Nixon signing the 1972 Drug Abuse Office and Treatment Act. From White House Photo Office Collection, January 20, 1969, to August 9, 1974, United States National Archives, Washington, DC.

narcotics under greater scrutiny. Although adding some attention to the demand side of the narcotics problem, the United States retained its now decades-long focus on supply eradication and punishment for users and dealers.

Even before Nixon's War on Drugs speech, the 1970 Prevention and Control Act included one of the most important developments in drug control: creation of the drug schedules (see table 9.1).[3] Different drugs were placed on the "schedule" according to their perceived dangerousness and medical utility. The US schedule drew on, but differed slightly from, similar schedules embedded in United Nations treaties. The US schedule put heroin and marijuana in Schedule I, drugs deemed to have a high likelihood of abuse and no medicinal benefit, while putting preparations with low levels of narcotics (for instance, less than 200 milligrams of codeine per 100 milliliters of preparation) in Schedule V, drugs deemed to have medicinal benefit and low likelihood of abuse. Some people advocated for the schedules as providing flexibility. As new medical information or new drugs were developed, drugs could be moved around. Politicians could make laws stipulating controls and punishments based on the schedule rather than a specific drug, reducing the need to update laws as medical knowledge changed.

Table 9.1. Schedules and Sample Drugs from 1970 Controlled Substances Act

Schedule category	Potential for abuse	Medical use	Effects of abuse	Examples
Schedule I	High potential for abuse	No currently accepted medical use	Not safe to use even under medical supervision	Heroin, marijuana, psilocybin, methylenedioxymethamphetamine
Schedule II	High potential for abuse	Has a currently accepted medical use, with severe restrictions	Abuse can lead to severe psychological or physical dependence	Opium, coca and derivatives, fentanyl, methamphetamine when an injectable liquid, methadone
Schedule III	Less potential for abuse than Schedule I or II	Has a currently accepted medical use	Abuse may lead to low/moderate physical or high psychological dependence	Amphetamine, methamphetamine other than injectable liquid, barbiturates, morphine, many codeine preparations
Schedule IV	Low potential for abuse compared to Schedule III	Has a currently accepted medical use	Abuse may lead to limited physical or psychological dependence, relative to Schedule III	Barbital, chloral hydrate, phenobarbital
Schedule V	Low potential for abuse compared to Schedule IV	Has a currently accepted medical use	Abuse may lead to limited physical or psychological dependence, relative to Schedule IV	Preparations with very low levels of opiates (e.g., cough syrups, antidiarrhea medicines)

The schedules also appeared to rationalize policy about drugs, stipulating more control over more dangerous drugs. The schedules have provided predictability and flexibility, but the placement of a particular drug in a particular part of the schedule can be influenced as much by politics as by science. Pharmaceutical companies lobby for their new drugs to receive favorable placement.[4] The fact that marijuana, a drug most people even in 1970 agreed was not addictive, has always been on Schedule I demonstrates the political nature of the schedules. All subsequent legislation and policy in the United States regarding drugs rely on these schedules.

The Nixon war on drugs approach offered more opportunities for treatment and prevention, to balance the harsh prison sentences and supply-control policies discussed here and in chapter 10. The spike in heroin use prompted particular attention to ways to treat heroin addicts. Some small studies of a new treatment, methadone, suggested that it might be beneficial. A treatment facility in the early 1960s was testing different approaches to helping addicts and observed that only one small group, those taking methadone, was able to manage their addiction. Methadone is also an opiate, and it can be highly effective in relieving severe pain. For treating heroin addicts, it works by taking away a person's craving for their opioid fix, since its narcotic effect lasts over a longer period of time. Usually people who use methadone to manage their addiction take it for a long time, sometimes for the rest of their lives. The methadone users in the 1960s study relied on the drug, but when taking it, they were able to function in all aspects of daily life, whether going to school or a job or maintaining family relationships. They were not involved in crime.[5] Methadone looked like a promising treatment for the growing problem of heroin addiction in the 1970s.

One of the new agencies created as a result of Nixon's War on Drugs was the Special Action Office for Drug Abuse Prevention, headed by Dr. Jerome Jaffe, an addictions expert and advocate of methadone use. Under his leadership, the government encouraged the creation of methadone clinics. The number of people using methadone to control their addiction increased from nine thousand in 1971 to seventy-three thousand by the end of 1973. Despite the fact that methadone worked for a large percentage of serious addicts, the treatment method also provoked a lot of controversy and involved a number of unresolved problems. Some people criticized methadone because it provided a maintenance drug to addicts. They were not cured of addiction but given a substitute drug on which they relied to function. This criticism is as much philosophical as scientific. Some people believe it is always problematic if people are dependent on drugs. Others believe that the best possible solution helps addicts function well in society, regardless of whether they are still using.

But methadone as a treatment method also prompted many scientific questions, also difficult to resolve. How addicted did someone need to be before they should be put on methadone? Was it appropriate for all addicts, or would some relapse from methadone use as well? Was this a lifetime maintenance program, or should treatment programs attempt to wean

Fig. 9.2. A former heroin addict receiving methadone, a mild narcotic painkiller used in the treatment of addiction, at a Southern California clinic, 1985. Photograph © Steve Raymer.

users off methadone at some point? And, what about the problems with diversion of methadone into the illicit market? This last issue proved to be vexing, as it was difficult to even understand how much methadone was being diverted and what the effects were. An article in *Smithsonian Magazine* conveyed a typically conflicted message about methadone: "Methadone is not necessarily a *good* treatment, but nevertheless, for the time being, it is the best available."[6] The federal government exerted some legal authority over the issue but left distribution regulations to the states, meaning that treatment programs did and do vary. It has proved difficult to have effective scientific studies of the issue, meaning that addiction treatment programs vary wildly in quality. Even the best programs don't always have good science to rely on in devising an appropriate program for patients. The FDA stipulated how the methadone itself was distributed, but programs took different approaches to auxiliary services such as counseling, job and educational support, and other social programs.

Nixon's attempt at a wholesale attack on the narcotics problem has been roundly criticized, both because it seemed to have failed and because its harshest consequences fell heavily on minorities and people living in poverty. Despite his claim in the 1971 message to Congress that drug addiction was no longer a class problem but a universal problem, one outcome of Nixon's War on Drugs was treatment and lenient sentences for middle-class users, both because of the types of drugs they tended to use and their access to lawyers and sympathetic doctors. By contrast, Black people, Latinos, and those in urban poverty-stricken areas more often faced prison sentences and a dearth of treatment options. The early 1970s saw a dramatic increase in the number of middle-class youths using marijuana and psychedelics; law enforcement showed little interest in policing marijuana, while heroin remained the cheap drug of choice and under intense scrutiny. Chapter 10 explores the differences in legal and economic ramifications of the War on Drugs approach for different communities in the United States.

Harmful as these policies were to ordinary Americans, the War on Drugs failed even more spectacularly to control the supply of drugs, which traditionally had been the US priority and remained important in Nixon's strategy. The supply of heroin remained at historically high levels, despite the temporarily successful suppression of production in Turkey. The Golden Triangle area of Southeast Asia increased production to fill the gap. In 1972, for instance, this area grew 70 percent of the illicit opium supplied to world markets, and the United States received 30 percent of its illicit opium from Southeast Asia. The Nixon administration redoubled interdiction efforts and managed to disrupt the supply of heroin from Southeast Asia during 1972–73. The War on Drugs seemed to be working, as the number of active addicts appeared to be cut in half and the price of heroin rose during 1973 and 1974. Illicit markets respond to supply-and-demand imperatives too, however, and illicit drug producers in Mexico ramped up production of the poppy to take advantage of the high prices and frantic demand of addicts. Mexican-produced heroin accounted for about 90 percent of US heroin supplies by the mid-1970s, and the close proximity of the supply made it all the more difficult to cut it off. Heroin coming in by ship or plane from Turkey (before 1971) or Southeast Asia (in the early 1970s) generally had to come in through a major port. Mexican heroin could be walked or driven across lightly or unguarded borders. In a 1974 interview, DEA administrator John R. Bartels Jr. acknowledged that smuggling had become much easier in some ways: "People rent planes, fly down to Mexico, pick up a couple hundred pounds of marijuana, an ounce or two of cocaine, and bring it back."[7] The shift in heroin production for US consumption to Mexico has made it much more difficult than it was before 1971 to pursue a supply-control method for narcotics restriction.

The United States could claim some victories in the War on Drugs. Turkey stopped licit production of opium, and distribution networks to France were interrupted; interdiction prevented Southeast Asian heroin from reaching the United States. On a global level, however, US efforts against heroin failed. Countries involved in trafficking suffered even more from the effects of the US War on Drugs. From 1945 to 1971, to the extent that US officials were involved in opium or heroin production in the Golden Triangle, it was to condemn it publicly but ignore or even facilitate it secretly. Cold War imperatives meant US State Department and CIA officers needed local contacts and allies, especially in the border areas near the People's Republic of China, precisely the areas where opium was one of few profitable crops. During the US war in Vietnam, US CIA operatives relied on intelligence from people involved in drug trafficking in Thailand, Laos, and Burma. In exchange, CIA operatives provided some logistical assistance to these drug traffickers. Nixon's War on Drugs changed the emphasis. US policy had to be more explicitly antidrug, but as historian Alfred W. McCoy has argued, in Southeast Asia the United States primarily targeted the opium dens that still operated freely in Laos and the trafficking networks to the United States. Closing the opium dens pushed a large percentage of former smokers to switch to using heroin, which was more dangerous. Disrupting trafficking networks from the Golden Triangle to the United States resulted in increased prices and reduced purity for heroin in the United States but also prompted the Southeast Asian traffickers to seek new markets in Europe, Australia, and Japan. Before the mid-1970s, only the United States had a significant number of heroin users. The War on Drugs crackdowns helped motivate dealers to diversify their networks, spreading heroin use more widely throughout the world.[8] This pattern, in which more emphasis on prohibition enforcement in one area leads to increased trafficking in and to another area, has been repeated many times in the War on Drugs.

Tactics later used against opium, marijuana, and coca production in Central and South America initially were tried out on a smaller scale in the Golden Triangle. Much of the opium in Southeast Asia was grown in the hill regions, which were difficult to access. The Thai, Burmese, and Lao governments exercised light or no effective control in these spaces. Opium warlords, leading armies that might serve to protect only the opium field, heroin production sites, and transport to market but which might also be fighting for national liberation or revolutionary purposes, exercised control, fighting each other as often as the government. Khun Sa is probably the most famous of these warlords. Born in the 1930s in the northern Shan States near the Chinese border, he had a Shan mother and Chinese father. He grew up navigating the political and cultural diversity of that region and served briefly in 1950 in the US-sponsored Guomindang army that funded itself with opium, as discussed in chapter 7. Khun Sa and his Shan United Army worked first to control the transport routes by which opium left Burma for Thailand, then to also control the processing plants along the Burmese–Thai–Lao borders, and finally, by the 1980s, to gain control over opium-growing territories too. He was hugely successful, with McCoy reporting that by the end of the 1980s, Khun Sa "controlled over 80 percent of Burma's opium production and half the world's heroin supply."[9] The amounts produced had increased dramatically as well, from just over five hundred tons in the early 1980s to more than twenty-five hundred tons by the end of the 1980s. The Thai government and especially the Burmese government wanted to stop Khun Sa. The United States supplied both with helicopters and training for troops to attack Khun Sa, with a goal of stabilizing the Thai and Burmese government and eradicating the opium crop. Both tasks proved difficult, with successes at best temporary. The United States would continue the strategy of supplying training and war matériel to governments for the purpose of eradicating drugs, knowing those could be used against local rebels as well as government opponents. As drug production grew in Central and South America, the United States supplied training, helicopters, and planes there too.

Marijuana production increased, both in the United States and in Mexico and Central America. A main driver of increased production was the resurgence in popularity during the 1970s. In part, this upswing was due to societal factors as marijuana use became more mainstream, used by a relatively large percentage of young people, as discussed in chapter 8. Even a report on marijuana commissioned by the Nixon administration that became known as the Shafer Commission noted in 1972 that casual marijuana use was not particularly harmful and recommended decriminalization. Nixon was furious; this conclusion did not mesh with his increasingly

Fig. 9.3. A Thai Army Ranger surveying a farmer's illegal opium poppy field in a remote village of ethnic Hmong, 1985. Carrying an M-16 assault rifle, the ranger holds a thick-bladed scraper or sickle favored by Southeast Asian farmers to harvest the opium gum, recently confiscated from the farmer. Photograph © Steve Raymer.

harsh views of people who used marijuana. Marijuana kept its Schedule I status. Marijuana also benefited from the economies of scale for drug production in the Americas more generally. As heroin and cocaine production increased in Central and South America, marijuana producers could use drug-smuggling routes and protection schemes for their product as well. Marijuana is bulkier, and therefore more difficult to smuggle, and yields a lower profit per pound of production. But given the increased ability to smuggle, production made sense, especially with a ready supply of users.

In June 2021, media coverage of the fiftieth anniversary of Nixon's speech emphasized the devastating toll of the War on Drugs on Americans, particularly Black people and other racial minorities, and in recent years spreading throughout rural white America as well. The effects on people outside the United States have been as brutal, arguably even more so, but not as visible to Americans. One typical story reported extensively on the domestic implications, mentioning the effects outside the United States only twice, and briefly. Most telling, it noted that in 2021, the United States spent $37 billion on the War on Drugs, "much of it devoted to interdiction," without explaining what interdiction is or where it occurs.[10] Historically, the United States has pursued a supply-control approach to controlling drugs, as discussed throughout this book. From the inception of the Federal Bureau of Narcotics in 1930 until the early 1960s, the FBN had to struggle with the US Department of State, US Customs agents, and, after World War II, even the CIA to place its agents in foreign countries in efforts to prevent smuggling. President John F. Kennedy announced in 1962 that the FBN had been successful in its efforts to "strike at the foreign sources of illicit narcotics traffic intended for United States consumption" and that he would be expanding the number of FBN agents abroad. He also reported that he and the president of Mexico, Adolfo Lopéz Mateos, had discussed mutual efforts for "the eradication of illegal drug traffic."[11] President Lyndon B. Johnson reorganized the FBN into the Bureau of Narcotics and Dangerous Drugs, in part to further professionalize efforts against illicit drugs both inside and outside the United States, not least because of credible accusations of corruption in the FBN. Until the late 1960s, though, US policy focused on stopping drugs at the US border, preventing smuggling, and getting other countries to agree to control drug production in their own territory.

President Nixon ramped up efforts at border control early in his presidency with Operation Intercept. In September 1969, more than two thousand US agents went to the US-Mexico border with the intent of carefully searching every entering vehicle for drugs. Very few drugs were found, but crossings were delayed by hours. The economic disruption, to border towns as well as Mexican exporters, was massive. Operation Intercept officially lasted twenty days, but searches reduced significantly after ten days due to complaints from Mexican president Gustavo Díaz Ordaz as well as US businesses and travelers. To get the United States to stop the action, President Díaz promised to intensify antidrug efforts in Mexico; the Nixon administration promised to provide technical support. Mexican officials were wary of accepting some kinds of aid and even more wary of allowing US agents to operate inside Mexico.

Cocaine, not a major drug of choice since it had been prohibited in 1914, grew in popularity in the 1970s. The stimulant cocaine became popular among a new type of drug user: the high-powered, high-achieving middle-class or wealthy person. It was associated with nightclubs and partying, enabling people to stay up all night dancing and still go to work the next day. In many ways, it was a status drug. A different form of cocaine, crack cocaine (discussed in chapter 8), became common in the 1980s. Crack was consumed largely by people who were poor, in an effort to provide energy and a sense of well-being to get through the difficult circumstances of their lives. As Nixon's War on Drugs became Reagan's War on Drugs, the efforts against cocaine ensnared Americans through starkly differentiated sentencing guidelines for powder and crack cocaine, as discussed in chapter 10, and in the ways that US supply-control efforts facilitated the growth of increasingly powerful criminal gangs in Central and South America who controlled drug production and trafficking.

Agricultural drug production for the US market had largely shifted to the Americas, where the United States exerted a lot of control through its foreign policy. Nations dependent on US military and economic aid or unable to resist the demands of their powerful northern neighbor permitted the US government to exert supply-side-control efforts in their countries. This meant US agents, or people paid directly by the US government, went into countries to destroy crops. US efforts to eradicate crops, particularly in Central America, had serious environmental consequences in those countries from the toxic sprays used to kill the plants. US involvement also had political consequences, as when authoritarian rulers gained access to helicopters and other technology that was used in drug eradication but could also be used to control or intimidate the population. Massive illicit drug production in Central and South America, particularly in Colombia and Mexico, nearly all for the US market, enriched and empowered those who controlled this trade. US drug policy and foreign policy in the 1980s often seemed at odds, though, with financial support going to political allies who had ties to the drug trade.[12]

The Nixon War on Drugs grew out of serious and real concerns about the increase in drug use and abuse in the United States in the 1960s and early 1970s. Some people took heart from the emphasis on treatment and prevention, and some important educational and scientific lessons were learned in these years about how to mitigate the effects of drug use and how to help people not use or more safely use drugs. But these efforts were soon overwhelmed by the policing and supply-side-control approach, which was punitive, interventionist, and resisted by dealers and users alike. Each attempt to squash drug production and use seemed only to encourage agricultural production to move to a new country, smugglers and dealers to adopt new methods, and users to switch to a new drug.

PART III.
BLURRING THE LINES, 1980–PRESENT

President Nixon's declaration of the War on Drugs intensified antidrug policies the United States had pursued for decades. In the years after Nixon left office, that intensification continued. Advocates of punitive rather than treatment approaches to addiction quickly regained prominence in shaping the US governmental response. Supply-control efforts both inside and outside US borders continued unabated but with added complications due to increased concerns about the environmental effects of production and eradication. And marijuana continued to chart a slightly different path than other illicit drugs, attaining popular acceptance early in the twenty-first century to rival its status a hundred years earlier. In the twenty-first century, the War on Drugs approach retains its appeal in the United States, but it faces more and new challenges.

After President Jimmy Carter had softened some aspects of the War on Drugs during his term in office, President Ronald Reagan reversed course, explicitly declaring a War on Drugs in a 1982 speech. He then increased the funds dedicated to fighting drugs, spending almost five times the 1980 amount by 1987. Nearly all this funding was devoted to stopping drugs from entering the country and arresting those who used or dealt drugs. The Reagan administration passed two pieces of legislation establishing mandatory minimum prison sentences for drug offenses. Chapter 10 explores how these approaches developed, why many Americans thought they were the appropriate solution, and the legacies of them for equity, justice, and efforts to reduce illicit drug use. The vast spending on incarceration meant reduced or flat funding for education, prevention, and treatment. First Lady Nancy Reagan made antidrug efforts one of her main priorities, appropriating a Just Say No campaign created in Oakland, California, that tried to reach schoolchildren, to prevent them from using for the first time. These efforts received only modest federal funding but significant public attention. By the end of the 1980s, drug-use rates had not declined significantly if at all, the number of people incarcerated had mushroomed, and drugs were more available than ever. Some people thought these apparent failures only demonstrated that the efforts had not been stringent enough; others began to question the whole War on Drugs approach.

In the 1980s, US efforts to suppress supply in producer countries caused substantial chaos, as explored further in chapter 11. The United States pursued aerial spraying in Central and South America, destroying coca crops but also polluting the water and soil. These spraying campaigns often were carried out using US funds, equipment, and materials that had been given to local governments. The helicopters and planes were then used for control and suppression of groups opposed to those local governments, implicating the United States in local political struggles in ways that sometimes harmed US foreign relations more generally. The aerial-spraying campaigns were used against illicit crops in the United States, too, especially on the massive marijuana production that sprang up when border security made it more difficult for marijuana to get into the United States from Mexico. States such as California and Tennessee, with large acreage in remote areas, increased marijuana production, sometimes growing it in state and national forests, protected from discovery by the dense forest and limited roads. The fact that growers did not use their own land also made it more difficult to catch them. The environmental consequences of illicit drug production and attempts at eradication receive little public attention but are far-reaching.

The modest successes during the 1970s achieved by the movement to decriminalize marijuana seemed to all fade away during the Reagan-era renewed War on Drugs focus. As chapter 12 discusses, however, a temporary setback for this effort occurred in the 1980s. An initial movement for medical marijuana grew slowly in the 1980s, and then more quickly beginning in the 1990s. Continued efforts at decriminalization and then legalization of recreational marijuana also gained ground in the wake of the medical marijuana movement. Although still illegal at the federal level, and still classified as a Schedule I drug, marijuana has gained significant social acceptance.

The drug-production market began to splinter and proliferate in the 1990s in ways that law enforcement had difficulty tracking. Heroin use surged as cheap heroin periodically flooded the market, in part due to political strife in heroin-producing areas. But probably of more significance, illicit use of synthetic drugs, both those produced by pharmaceutical companies and those produced outside legal markets, grew significantly. Chapter 13 explores these new developments in the illicit drug market since the 1990s. In some ways, the circumstances echo ones that we have seen throughout this book. In other ways, however, the vast increase in drug production overall and the variety of production methods available to illicit dealers mean supply-control techniques face even starker challenges than they have in the past.

10. MANDATORY MINIMUMS

Debate around mandatory minimum sentencing for drug possession and sale focuses on its association with differential sentencing, prison overcrowding, and racial disparity. Advocates and detractors both often evoke a starting point in the 1980s, when Ronald Reagan's administration endorsed and passed laws imposing strict sentencing guidelines. Judges had no discretion about the minimum sentence for those convicted of some drug crimes. The laws also stipulated longer sentences for drugs or behaviors identified as more harmful. The idea of a mandatory minimum jail or prison sentence for drug offenses predates the 1980s, though.

Commentators often associate mandatory minimum sentences with drug possession and dealing, but other crimes at the state and federal levels in the United States also have mandatory minimum sentences, including for such crimes as murder and child pornography. One purpose of adopting a mandatory minimum is to deter people from committing the crime by stipulating in advance that they will definitely face a particular, usually harsh, punishment. Another is to keep those convicted of the stipulated crime off the streets for a long period of time, under the assumption that then society will be safer. This chapter explores the history of mandatory minimums for drug offenses in the United States. Mandatory minimum sentences historically have harmed racial minorities more than whites to such an extent that lawyer and activist Michelle Alexander famously argued they constituted a "new Jim Crow." They are often associated with an initial reduction in crime rates, but not always, and not always for a long period of time. Public support for mandatory minimum sentencing is often strong in the United States, partly because people want to do something they think will be effective against an intractable problem. Campaigns to promote these laws also stress the outsider status of those likely to be convicted or how dangerous they are to society. When people are afraid, they often support this apparently effective solution. Both times that mandatory minimums have been adopted for drugs in the United States, in the 1950s and 1980s, though, criticism of their fairness and effectiveness followed.

The passage of the Harrison Narcotics Act in 1914 was the culmination of years of growing concern about the prevalence of narcotics consumption in US society, as discussed in chapter 3. State and local laws, passed starting in the late nineteenth century and up to the time of the passage of the Harrison Act itself, varied tremendously in how they identified the drug problem and how they regulated legal drug sellers such as doctors, pharmacists, and patent medicine companies. Virtually all of them, however, saw the problem as primarily one of unscrupulous drug sellers. Even when users and addicts were painted in an unflattering light, the laws at this time rarely targeted them for jail sentences for their drug use alone. As historian David Musto recorded, in states as diverse as Tennessee and New York, early twentieth-century legislation provided for registration of addicts to allow them to receive free or low-cost maintenance drugs. Those advocating such legislation did not think drugs were harmless. They thought addiction was a medical condition, or sometimes a disease, and rarely the addict's fault. Even people working to regulate and restrict drugs tended to believe it was humane to provide drugs to those already addicted.[1] Before 1914, then, while some states and localities had laws banning the sale or consumption of opiates, the group most often punished for violation of those laws was sellers, not users.

Passage of the Harrison Narcotics Act in 1914 changed the US legal approach from widespread tolerance of narcotics consumption, sometimes with various regulations, to prohibition of nonmedical use of narcotics. This federal law enforced prohibition by restricting the ways that narcotics could be sold. The law makes no direct mention of users. If a person was found to be in violation of the distribution methods stipulated in the law, the law stipulated a maximum punishment rather than a mandatory minimum punishment. The most serious consequence of conviction was a fine of $2,000 or a jail sentence of five years, or both.[2] The next five years saw significant legal challenges to the Harrison Narcotics Act, as the Departments of Justice and Treasury claimed it not only required all narcotics to be distributed by doctor's prescription but also that doctors could not legally write prescriptions for maintenance of addiction. Doctors, joined by pharmacists, protested. Some believed in prescribing maintenance narcotics, as they had done so for years. Of those, some were responsible in helping people with chronic pain live as fully as they could. Others were unscrupulous, selling prescriptions to people who were merely addicted and offering no medical care as usually understood. In 1919, the Supreme Court, by a vote of 5–4 in both cases, settled the disputes with two cases. In the first, *United States v. Doremus*, the Court found the law constitutional. The federal government could use revenue laws to stipulate aspects of the ways a doctor practiced medicine. In the second, *United States v. Webb*, the Court declared bluntly that using a doctor's prescription to provide maintenance of addiction was a "perversion" of the term prescription. They disallowed it.[3]

These legal disputes did not touch on the issues of punishment. The provisions of the Harrison Act still fell most heavily on those who sold drugs in unauthorized ways, whether a street dealer or a doctor prescribing outside government regulations. Addicts increasingly got sent to jail too, though, usually because they had in their possession sufficient narcotics to look like a seller or because they committed other crimes and their addiction was a contributing factor. By the late 1920s, a third of the people in federal prisons were there for drug offenses. Then, as today, people with untreated addictions who were imprisoned continued to seek their drugs, which prison officials found disruptive. In an effort to reduce the number of addicts in federal prisons, Walter Treadway of the US Public Health Service and James V. Bennett of the US Bureau of Prisons worked to get legislation to establish the Narcotics Farms, treatment facilities for people convicted of violating federal narcotics law. The law passed in 1929; the first US Narcotic Farm opened in Lexington, Kentucky, in 1935, and then in 1938, the second one opened in Fort Worth, Texas. Many of the residents had been sent there to serve their sentences. They did not have a choice about whether to go there, and they served out their sentences there, sometimes confined even longer if not deemed cured. Given the dearth of treatment options, though, many other people voluntarily entered in hopes of getting help. The farms represented a recognition that jail was not going to lead addicts to end their addiction. Their success rate was very low, though, and the farms were usually far from family and support groups. The last of these farms closed in 1974.[4] During the period from 1914 to 1950, governments at the federal and state levels passed laws designed to impose increasingly serious maximum sentences for repeat offenders, dealers, and especially anyone who sold to a minor.

In the aftermath of World War II, heroin again flowed into the United States, as discussed in chapter 6, setting off a new wave of concern about addicts and addiction. This time, the idea of mandatory minimum sentences gained popularity. Mandatory minimums were not completely novel but had been deployed sparingly before World War II. As the number of addicts grew dramatically, especially among young people, some Americans became alarmed. Harry Anslinger, whose Federal Bureau of Narcotics was being criticized for not being able to contain the spread of drugs, went on the offensive. He accused both organized crime and newly communist China of importing drugs into the United States. The People's Republic of China was not involved. The case for organized crime was overstated but partly true, and the sensational Kefauver Committee hearings about organized crime's involvement in many everyday activities in the United States raised the fear level still higher. In the aftermath of these hearings, Senator Hale Boggs worked with Anslinger to introduce new federal legislation to combat narcotics. The 1951 Boggs Act, also discussed in chapter 7, established the first federal mandatory minimums for drug convictions, at two, five, and ten years (for first, second, and third offenses, respectively) plus a $2,000 fine for violations of the law. This law pertained primarily to importing and selling, with little language in the statute about possession. The 1956 Narcotics Control Act applied the existing minimum sentences to people convicted merely of possession, increased the length of the minimums for importing or selling, and stipulated a minimum sentence of ten years for any offense of selling heroin to a minor, with a typical sentence of life and a possible sentence of death.[5]

Advocates promoted these laws as the solution to a growing drug problem. Anslinger exhorted state legislatures, saying, "There is no reason for any State to have a law which is any way weaker than the Boggs Act."[6] States quickly began passing similar laws, called Little Boggs Acts, some even with longer sentences, and mandating civil confinement for addicts. A few even criminalized addiction itself, with no proof of possession required for conviction. The Supreme Court struck down laws criminalizing addiction alone but allowed mandatory civil confinement for treatment. To addicts, it often looked like a distinction without a difference. From the mid-1950s to the mid-1960s, many people spent years in jail for minor possession, alongside those serving time for dealing and importing. The years of these mandatory minimum sentences coincided with decreased statistics characteristic of drug use, such as hospitalizations for addiction and overdose, voluntary and involuntary commitments to treatment programs, seizures, and arrests. Historian David Courtwright notes that the statistics were decreasing even before the laws took effect, suggesting the new law did not cause the improvements. Other observers at the time, such as scholars and some physicians, expressed skepticism about the statistics. They were concerned about the remaining addicts, both because those people were not getting treatment or support and because the increasing cost of their addiction meant they were more likely than ever to commit crimes to support it. There does not seem to have been as much concern about the social effects of mandatory minimums in the late 1950s and early 1960s as there would be in the 1980s, but there was a growing sense that these harsh laws were not solving the problem.

A number of voices were calling for a more well-rounded approach to the drug problem. Anslinger's retirement from the Federal Bureau of Narcotics in 1962 muted one determined and strident proponent of harsh sentences and supply control, although he served at the United Nations for two additional years. President John F. Kennedy listened to the voices calling for a new approach, though. Although the 1951 and 1956 laws remained in force until 1970, they were tempered somewhat in the 1960s by laws promoting rehabilitation and allowing for those who were receiving treatment to avoid some of the harshest penalties under the mandatory minimums. Federal monies supported state and local treatment programs, diverting some addicts from the criminal system altogether.

As we saw in chapter 9, most scholars identify Nixon's 1971 speech as the start of the War on Drugs. In many ways, though, the Nixon administration took a different approach to the issue of mandatory minimums than is usually associated with the War on Drugs. The Nixon administration took up legislation that President Lyndon B. Johnson's administration had been working on to try to replace the dozens of federal laws about drugs that had been passed since 1909 and were still on the books. These laws were often outdated, sometimes in conflict, and difficult to administer. They also did not seem responsive to the massive growth in drug consumption, particularly of marijuana, during the 1960s. The Nixon administration wanted a more rational approach, fitting with their sense that drugs were a problem partly because of their association with crime and partly because use was rising. Some in the Nixon administration, particularly staff in the Department of Health, Education and Welfare, wanted US drug policy to better reflect treatment options and scientific research. Many in Congress agreed, with some advocating in particular for lighter sentences, or none, for marijuana use. Other members of Congress and the administration wanted laws to reflect the harm done by drugs. The groups compromised and passed the 1970 Comprehensive Drug Abuse Prevention and Control Act. For the purposes of this chapter, the important outcomes were making possession of small amounts of marijuana subject to only modest punishment, changing all the sentencing guidelines back to maximum sentences for various levels of violations rather than mandatory minimums, and restoring eligibility for parole. The law reserved harsher punishments for those who sold narcotics to minors. In those cases, the usual sentences were doubled. But otherwise, the 1970 Comprehensive Drug Act looked like a resounding repudiation of mandatory minimum sentencing. This reversal does not indicate that Nixon wanted to ease up on the War on Drugs, though. His administration aggressively pursued both law enforcement and treatment programs, with the ultimate goal of reducing drug use by any means possible. Nixon believed that helping addicts get off drugs would pair well with arresting and convicting drug dealers and importers. One part of the 1970 act that was highly controversial at the time and has caused significant problems since was the adoption of the "no-knock" warrant, allowing police to forcefully enter someone's home without knocking under certain conditions. This kind of provision helps convey that the Nixon administration may have had a more humane approach to drug users but planned to use all the powers of government against dealers.

While the federal government was turning away from mandatory minimum sentencing, though, some state governments were imposing them ever more harshly, including states that had not adopted them in the aftermath of the Boggs Act. The most famous example is New York. New York State, and especially New York City, has always been perceived as having a heavy concentration of drug users, particularly the harder drugs such as heroin up to the 1970s, and cocaine in the 1970s and 1980s. New York's Republican governor Nelson Rockefeller was known as a liberal Republican, pragmatic in his approaches to policy and always willing to work across the aisle with Democrats. Passage of the harsh 1973 drug laws, which came to be called the Rockefeller laws, is not as much of a departure from that image as people often think. In the early 1970s in the areas in and near New York City, street crime seemed to be on the rise. People who lived there were fed up, and Black residents of Harlem were among the most frustrated. Reverend Oberia Dempsey, the Black pastor of Harlem's Park

Avenue Baptist Church, exclaimed in 1973: "In Harlem the non-addict has become the prisoner of the addict, afraid even to walk the streets."[7] Rev. Dempsey was not alone in his sentiment. Surveys of New Yorkers demonstrated that concern about crime and drugs was among their top worries. Governor Rockefeller responded to what he perceived as a crisis. He had to work a bit to convince upstate legislators, where the problem was less severe, to go along, but they did. The Rockefeller laws look eerily like the laws that would be passed at the federal level in the 1980s. Dealers could receive life in prison with nearly no chance of parole. People convicted of possession, for second and subsequent offenses, also faced increasingly stringent and inescapable long sentences. The coalition supporting these laws was broad, including not only Republicans, as might be predicted, but also Democrats, including Black Democrats, who were concerned about the effects of crime on their neighborhoods. Many people seemed to think a punitive approach was needed. Recent scholarship has demonstrated that even though these harsh laws were passed in the early 1970s, convictions under these laws did not rise much until the 1980s, after passage of the new federal drug laws in the early years of Ronald Reagan's presidency. The New York Police Department simply chose to not enforce the new laws as they had been envisioned, against street-level dealers or users. Low-level dealers, for instance, were allowed to "plead pre-indictment" to a misdemeanor to avoid being charged with a felony for selling narcotics, a crime carrying a mandatory life sentence. For police, collecting sufficient evidence for a conviction was time consuming, and they did not think it was a good use of scarce resources, especially given the federal funds flowing in to support other ways of addressing the drug problem.[8] Although in retrospect it is easy to see that policies adopted at the state and local levels in the 1970s had direct impact on the use of mandatory minimums in the 1980s, during the 1970s the policy and legal landscape of drug control were confusing and contradictory.

Some states even began to decriminalize marijuana in the 1970s, meaning that people received no jail sentence at all for possession, usually facing only a small fine if convicted, as discussed in chapter 12. Other states had retained their harsh mandatory minimums for possession and dealing adopted after the passage of the Boggs Act. Others embraced the treatment options receiving additional federal support. With all these different approaches, though, a key issue was that drug use seemed to continue to grow. In addition to the high levels of marijuana and heroin that had been in place from the late 1950s, cocaine also became much more popular in the 1970s. By the time Ronald Reagan was elected president in 1980, sentiment was turning back to a more punitive approach to drug users as well as drug dealers.

Parent groups became key advocates for a more aggressive response by the federal government. As youth acceptance of marijuana grew in the 1970s, accompanied by both experimentation and regular use, parents became increasingly concerned. Many times parents were unaware of their children's drug use until confronted with it at a party, after a concert, or when cleaning their rooms. Some parents took their outrage to elected officials or to other parents, forming education and lobbying groups. The most powerful of these was the National Federation of Parents for Drug-Free Youth, formed in 1980 to bring together a number of already existing groups founded in the late 1970s. Members were mostly white, mostly middle-class, mostly suburban. They were exactly the voters Reagan was trying to attract for his 1980 campaign, and he was happy to support their desires. After Reagan's election, his wife, Nancy Reagan, adopted as her primary cause the effort to stop drug use among young people. She appropriated her famous Just Say No slogan from an existing antidrug program developed in Oakland, California, by Joan Brann, a Black woman long active in Democratic and Progressive causes. Nancy Reagan also appropriated the structure of the Just Say No clubs, turning them into public relations opportunities as they proliferated in middle-class white communities.[9] Her broader attitude about drugs can be summed up in this statement she made: "Each of us has a responsibility to be intolerant of drug use anywhere, any time, by anybody."[10] Any drug use, by anybody, deserved punishment.

The Reagan administration moved in stages during its two terms to reinstitute mandatory minimums, with the additional twist of creating highly differentiated sentences for different types of drugs, particularly for cocaine and crack cocaine. The 1984 Federal Sentencing Reform Act established the framework for the "mandatory minimum" sentences at the federal level, which the states had been implementing since the early 1970s. Following the New York State example, by the time the 1984 federal legislation passed, forty-nine states already had state mandatory minimum laws for drug offenses.[11] These laws set immutable sentences for specific violations, with enhancements for committing the offense near a school or having a firearm. Judges could not reduce the sentences. This 1984 law set

Fig. 10.1. FBI agents raiding a so-called shooting gallery, where heroin was sold and used. In the 1980s in Washington, DC, drug use—especially of heroin—was a major social problem along Fourteenth Street NW, just north of the White House. Although crack cocaine and marijuana are usually considered the most common problem drugs of the 1980s, heroin was also popular. Photograph © Steve Raymer.

in motion a process for a commission to establish what were called "determinate sentences," meaning specified sentences more binding than mere guidelines, for a variety of serious federal offenses, including drugs.

These principles were applied more specifically to drugs in 1986. Members of Congress perceived a cocaine crisis in the United States in the mid-1980s. Testimony before Congress for the 1986 Anti-Drug Abuse Act dramatized the effects of crack cocaine. Senator Lawton Chiles (D-FL) spoke in favor of the bill. He especially advocated for provisions to strengthen sentences for crack cocaine. He claimed, "The whole Nation now knows about crack cocaine. They know it can be bought for the price of a cassette tape . . . and turn promising young people into robbers and thieves, stealing anything they can to get the money to feed their habit."[12] Members of Congress felt pressure to pass significant legislation. They agreed that they needed to bring back mandatory minimums, with differences for what they called "major" and "serious" drug dealers, and harsher penalties for drugs perceived as more dangerous. As a result, the 1986 law established sentences for crack that were one hundred times more severe than for cocaine: Possessing five grams of crack or five hundred grams of powdered cocaine resulted in a minimum of five years in prison for a first offense. For ten grams of crack or a kilogram of powdered cocaine, the sentence was ten years. Subsequent offenses earned much longer sentences.

In the late 1980s, media portrayed crack as dramatically more dangerous and addictive, in addition to giving the impression that crack was primarily used by Black Americans, despite the fact that white Americans used it in large numbers as well. The death of University of Maryland basketball star Len Bias of a cocaine overdose, in June 1986, dramatically shaped Congressional debate once it began that September. A House Judiciary staff member remembered how "The fearful image of crack in the public consciousness . . . drove the legislative package." Historian David Farber called the Congressional competition to show how tough they were being a "bidding war."[13] Given that initial proposals set the sentences for crack and powder cocaine as equal, then at 20:1, then at 50:1, before settling on 100:1, his assessment seems appropriate. Both the House and Senate bills had settled quickly on the five- and ten-year minimums for serious and major dealers, but the specific amount of drug required to earn each status decreased and the ratio increased without much discussion.[14] With everyone feeling that drugs were an emergency, it was easier to adopt stricter measures, despite the fact that there was no evidence of differential harm and the results were going to fall more heavily on urban minorities.

The final federal drug legislation of the 1980s, the 1988 Anti-Drug Abuse Act, was most notable for its emphasis on establishing drug-free schools and workplaces. This act required schools to inform students and employees at least once per year of the consequences of illegal use and to inform them about treatment options.[15] And, significantly, language in the 1988 act changed from using the phrase "alcohol and drugs" to "alcohol and other drugs," to reinforce the growing concern about the effects of alcohol consumption. This was the law mandating the health warning on alcoholic beverages, similar to that on tobacco products. The 1988 law also reinstated the possibility of the death penalty for "drug kingpins." The major drug dealers who have been executed to date have also been convicted of additional crimes, usually murder.

Studies since the 1990s have suggested that most of those convicted in federal courts and receiving mandatory minimums for crack were dealers, even if small ones. Many low-level dealers may well be selling only in support of their own habit, complicating the picture further. But these mandatory minimums received significant criticism for the racial disparity of their application. Black people received the vast majority of the long prison sentences, even though more white people used both crack and powdered cocaine. Although almost immediately controversial, these mandatory minimum sentences accurately reflected the fear driving US drug policy during the 1980s. Their racial disparity was troubling from the start, and a commission created in 1997 to study the effects of these disparities found that nearly 90 percent of those convicted in federal court for crack cocaine were Black, while the majority of crack users were white. Interestingly, the statistics for other drugs showed a high percentage of white people convicted. The 1997 *Sentencing Commission Report* found that 97 percent of those charged with LSD infractions and 68 percent of those charged for methamphetamine use also were white. Powdered cocaine in the same report saw its offenders as 48 percent Hispanic (the term of the time), 30 percent Black, and 21 percent white.[16] Despite these obvious disparities, it proved difficult to change the differences in sentencing mandates for powdered versus crack cocaine. An effort in the 1990s to eliminate the disparity was voted down in Congress. Some changes were made in 2010, during President Barack Obama's administration, reducing the ratios from 100:1 down to 18:1. As part of sentencing reform efforts during President Donald J. Trump's administration, those changed ratios were made retroactive so that people sentenced under the older law could leave prison more quickly. In his long career as a senator, President Joseph R. Biden had been a supporter, even an advocate, of mandatory minimums. He changed his mind after seeing the problems with them and made campaign promises in 2020 to propose legislation to eliminate them for drug offenses, along with other criminal justice reforms. His slim legislative majority in the Senate meant that by mid-2022, his administration had not yet addressed that issue with legislation.

Federal mandatory minimum sentences, especially for drug offenses, were most popular with the American public during the 1980s and 1990s. A host of other punitive laws passed at that time as well, particularly laws popularly called "three-strikes" laws after the California state legislation passed in 1994. More accurately termed habitual offender laws, versions of this approach have existed in the United States since the early 1950s and have been adopted by twenty-eight states. These laws call for lengthier sentences for people convicted of successive felonies (sometimes triggered only by violent felonies). The three-strikes version stipulates life in prison for the third felony conviction. On its face, this approach appeals: repeat offenders are causing more problems in society and should be removed; people who make a mistake and learn from it receive less punishment. Implementation proved problematic. One problem stemmed from the fact that poorer people and racial minorities often received less effective legal representation, meaning they more often received felony convictions than wealthy and white people charged with the same offense. Another problem stemmed from various ways the inflexibility of the laws made implementation unfair in some circumstances. For instance, someone might have two felony convictions from their teenage years, serve their time, turn their life around, and live well for decades, but if they then made some kind of mistake like getting in a physical fight, that third felony conviction meant a life sentence. Sentences being served for marijuana convictions, whether under mandatory minimums or three-strikes laws, have come to seem unfair to many people. People sit in state and federal prisons for marijuana violations even in places where marijuana is legal. Significant scholarship has also established the racial disparities in how sentencing occurs, further undercutting perceptions of their fairness. Incarceration remains a popular response to drug crime in the United States, but in recent decades there has been a robust debate about both its efficacy and its equity. The War on Drugs emphasis on punishment rather than prevention and treatment retains its appeal to many Americans, though, even in the midst of this debate.

11. ENVIRONMENTAL EFFECTS OF THE WAR ON DRUGS

The cost of a War on Drugs approach is usually tallied in dollars spent, numbers of people incarcerated for no crime other than possession, and the rise of narco-states. The environmental costs too often go uncounted, although they are also high. The War on Drugs prompts deforestation, clandestine dumping of chemicals used in illicit processing, and aerial spraying with dangerous herbicides. This approach to drug control has harmed the environment in the United States and other parts of the world.

Supply-control strategies for drug restriction or prohibition rely on interdiction, eradication, and crop substitution, more broadly known as alternative development. Interdiction intercepts drugs in transit, usually at a border or at a point of sale. Eradication means the destruction of drugs, whether growing in a field, at a processing or manufacturing plant, or after having been seized from a smuggler or dealer. Crop substitution transitions farmers who previously grew marijuana, opium poppies, or coca to a licit crop instead, so that they will still be able to make a living. Any focus on supply control has to rely on some combination of these three strategies, each of which has serious negative effects on the environment.

One of the earliest recorded efforts at interdiction and eradication likely had an unexamined environmental effect. Chinese commissioner Lin Zexu, who tried unsuccessfully to get British, American, and other European merchants to stop their illegal sale of opium in China in the 1840s, seized their stored opium and destroyed it by mixing it with water and flushing it out to sea. Since Chinese officials seized several tons of opium, the waters must have been full of the drug, but scholars have not paid attention to any effects. The British campaign to promote opium sales in China in the nineteenth century involved another environmental effect. Small farmers in India were forced to stop growing food stuffs to plant opium poppies instead, in a reversal of the crop substitution that takes place today. India rarely suffered famine before the British forced opium production but regularly did so after.

Early twentieth-century sources sometimes mention the three supply-control strategies, usually in passing. The Council of the League of Nations, in 1925, assured the Persian representative that it knew that if Persia was going to participate in efforts to "suppress this drug scourge," it had to identify "the best and most practical means of replacing the poppy by some other crop."[1] Illicit opium that had been seized would sometimes be destroyed, often by burning. Other times, if in a form making it useable, it would be added to the licit drug supply in the country where it had been seized. As discussed in chapter 6, even FBN commissioner Anslinger, as opposed to drugs as he was, kept the narcotics seized in the 1930s to add to the US stockpile, which proved useful during World War II. A careful search of existing records might reveal how much opium was destroyed before 1945 and the methods used, but it would be a challenging task. Since nonmedicinal narcotics remained legal or lightly controlled in most parts of the world before 1945, the quantity of drugs to be destroyed in order to maintain the supply-control regime was still low compared to later years. From what we can tell, the effects on the environment were minimal as well.

From 1945 to the late 1960s, as the United States and United Nations increased efforts to restrict drug production and enforce prohibition of nonmedicinal narcotics, governments increased their attention on all three methods of supply control. Government entities reported how much they had seized or how many acres had been planted in food crops instead of marijuana or opium, but international reports did not focus much on the specific methods by which drugs were destroyed. Sometimes the records give a few hints. A report by Anslinger commented on the "aerial survey" of poppy fields made by US and Mexican officials in spring 1947. Anslinger registered his disappointment that the "1947 opium poppy destruction campaign" had "achieved poor results."[2] At that time, Mexican soldiers and police carried out destruction manually, but in the early 1960s they started receiving equipment and financial assistance from the United States, including helicopters and flame throwers to facilitate poppy destruction. Flame throwers also increased the chances that destruction efforts would have the unintended consequence of fire escaping the targeted field.[3] As early as 1946, US officials also discussed using Agent Orange, the herbicide that became famous in the US war in Vietnam, to spray poppies and marijuana, although no programs developed at that time.[4] During these years, both US and UN efforts to control drugs focused most heavily on preventing people from newly cultivating drugs or from restarting cultivation after a hiatus in World War II. They encouraged economic development efforts to promote licit crops in areas where people were already engaged in agriculture. They also devoted resources to interdiction, in hopes of making drug trafficking less profitable. These efforts had modest environmental effects but set the stage for more interventions as drug production increased.

The environmental effects of drug eradication first drew attention in the mid-1970s, when the "paraquat scare" erupted in the United States. Americans had become increasingly aware of the harmful effects of pesticides and herbicides in the 1960s. By the early 1970s, an environmental movement channeled these fears into political action. In the mid-1970s, some Americans sounded the alarm about traces of the herbicide paraquat found in marijuana imported from Mexico. Since the early 1960s, the United States had been supplying Mexico with helicopters to facilitate aerial surveillance of illicit crops. Nixon administration officials, soon after taking office, began urging both Mexico and Jamaica to adopt aerial spraying. Initially US officials suggested using Agent Orange. They had used Agent Orange for the general eradication of vegetation during the US war in Vietnam as well as in a more targeted campaign during 1969–71 against the marijuana that grew locally.[5] As protests mounted against the harmful effects of Agent Orange, US officials switched to advocating use of either paraquat or glyphosate in Mexico. Mexican officials were reluctant, urging their US counterparts to conduct aerial spraying of these herbicides in the United States to test efficacy and safety. Negotiations during 1973–75, coupled with increased drug use by Mexican youth, convinced the Mexican officials to authorize use of the herbicides. At this time, US officials prioritized destruction of opium poppies, since Mexico had become the leading supplier of heroin to the United States. Mexican officials prioritized marijuana eradication, due to the growing use of that drug in Mexico. The forty helicopters and airplanes supplied by the United States to Mexico were used to accomplish both priorities. Tests conducted in early 1976 demonstrated that paraquat was significantly more effective at destroying marijuana, while glyphosate did well against poppies. Paraquat was so effective in part because it is highly toxic. Directly ingesting or inhaling paraquat, even in small amounts, can cause serious harm. Glyphosate is also toxic, although its harm was less easy to immediately detect. The long-term environmental effects to soil, water, and animal life were not yet well understood in the 1970s.

Farmers did not simply acquiesce in the destruction of their crops by herbicide spraying, whether aerial or by people using backpack sprayers. After spraying occurred, farmers rushed to harvest as quickly as possible, to save as much of their investment as they could. As a result, marijuana with paraquat residue was available for sale in both the United States and Mexico. Ordinary users could not tell if their marijuana was tainted with paraquat, sending a wave of panic across the United States. The public-interest advocacy group NORML (the National Organization for the Reform of Marijuana Laws, discussed further in chapter 12) argued that paraquat-laced marijuana could be dangerous to the health of consumers. After an investigation initiated by NORML, a sense of concern about the health effects grew. As historian Daniel Weimer notes, "anti-paraquat, pro-decriminalization rallies" took place in New York City and Washington, DC. Members of the California state legislature as well as Congress expressed concerns. Major media outlets from big city newspapers to *Time* magazine to, more predictably, *Rolling Stone* ran stories sympathetic to Americans who might unwittingly be smoking marijuana that could cause serious medical harm.[6] Defenders of the Mexican herbicide program noted that paraquat was easily available as an herbicide in the United States, used by farmers and home gardeners alike.

For a brief period in 1978–79, a variety of US federal government measures looked poised to limit US support of herbicide-spraying campaigns for drug eradication. One impetus for these actions was the lawsuit brought by NORML against the US Department of State to force the US government to conduct a full environmental review before supporting such campaigns outside US borders. The Percy Amendment, proposed by Senator Charles Percy (R-IL), stipulated that US funding could support herbicide programs only if chemical markers could be included in the spray so that the effects could be traced in any subsequent crops. This amendment, which passed, effectively ended support for paraquat, since the terms were too stringent to meet. President Jimmy Carter issued an executive order stipulating the terms for any US support, also effectively restricting some possibilities for spraying, at least against marijuana. These restrictions did not have much impact, though. Mexican officials noted that they could continue spraying if they wanted, since paraquat was legally available in their country. They wanted to continue to spray.[7] More importantly, atti-

Fig. 11.1. Using a powerful herbicide that kills everything in its path, Mexican police use a Bell Jet Ranger helicopter supplied by the United States government to spray opium poppies and latex-filled seedpods in a remote part of the Sierra Madre Occidental, 1985. Photograph © Steve Raymer.

tudes about illicit drugs in the United States hardened again as Ronald Reagan campaigned for president in 1980, as discussed further in chapter 12. Future spraying campaigns in Central and South America also targeted poppies and coca more than marijuana; in these regions, the lingering effects of herbicides were more difficult to detect.

Spraying of herbicides continued, but only in a few places with direct US support. Colombia had the longest, most intense spraying campaign, lasting from the 1980s to 2015. US-funded herbicide-spraying programs, both aerial and the more targeted backpack approach, also existed at various times in the United States, Panama, Belize, Venezuela, Guatemala, and Afghanistan (after 2001), among others.[8] In the 1980s, Colombia transitioned from a minor supplier of marijuana to the United States into the most important provider of cocaine along with significant amounts of marijuana and heroin. The Colombian government, facing a number of challenges to its authority, from antigovernment rebels to increasingly powerful drug-producing organizations, accepted US financial and equipment support for both aerial and backpack spray programs. The main target was coca rather than marijuana, so glyphosate was more appropriate than the more-controversial paraquat.[9] Americans did not protest this spraying program as they had the one in Mexico. The additional processing coca goes through to become cocaine made it impossible to detect the continued presence of herbicides, which may have been one reason for the diminished concern. Many Americans were familiar with glyphosate, under the name Roundup, since they used it in their own gardening and saw it used on food crops they ate regularly. It was said to be safe for the environment, animals, and people when used properly. The fact that glyphosate was mixed in stronger concentrations for spraying on coca and often used more intensely in Colombia was not widely known.

Farmers in Colombia protested this spraying. They had a formal mechanism for registering complaints with the Colombian government, to document and get compensation for spray drift that destroyed licit crops or harmed animals. This complaint process was slow, difficult to access, and rarely resulted in compensation for farmers. Advocacy groups sometimes tried to bring these problems to the attention of Americans, but in the 1980s and 1990s, most Americans thought the harm from illicit drugs outweighed the potential harm to the environment or to Colombian farmers, who most Americans thought were complicit in cocaine production.[10] Even spray campaigns in the United States did not prompt public outcry in the 1980s, although NORML and environmental groups protested and took legal action. Marijuana production in the United States had grown significantly during the 1970s in response to the paraquat scare as well as threats to supply from eradication and interdiction efforts in Central and South America. The DEA initiated the Campaign Against Marijuana Planting (CAMP) in 1982. The DEA plan relied on eradication and interdiction, as had campaigns in Mexico and Colombia and elsewhere. The DEA sprayed paraquat in Chattahoochee National Park in Georgia in 1982, prompting a lawsuit by NORML to require environmental review before future spraying of that herbicide. Glyphosate was not subject to the same controls, so the DEA scheduled additional spraying, such as two instances in 1985 at the Mark Twain National Forest in Missouri and federal-owned land in New Mexico. In some states, ordinary citizens joined state and local officials in protesting these DEA actions. Amid the legal battles, the DEA reduced its efforts, although spray programs did not end completely. Federal agencies worked with state governments in much the same way the US government worked with foreign governments, providing logistics and sometimes funding but allowing states from Oklahoma to Hawaii, to name only two, to purchase the herbicides and conduct the spray operations themselves. Eradication programs remain common. They often use manual eradication (cutting, hoeing, or burning) rather than spraying, but spray campaigns continue as well.[11] As public concern about the effects of herbicides and pesticides grew around the world, governments that still funded or permitted spray programs tried to keep them quiet. It is difficult to discover the full range of ongoing spray efforts.

Articles about antidrug efforts in Colombia often claim that the spray campaign there lasted from 1994 to 2015, sprayed nearly two million hectares over that time, and was the location of the only aerial-spraying program. Although as we have seen, there was aerial spraying before 1994, and in other locations then and since, these claims begin to convey the widespread environmental destruction imposed by the spray campaigns. Farmers and others living in rural areas had to learn to live with these spray campaigns. Spray drift, pilot error, or the interspersed nature of planting meant that many licit crops, such as plantains, yucca, corn, and pasture grass, were also sprayed and destroyed. In addition to suffering crop loss, people living in the areas that have been sprayed complain of health consequences: "respiratory distress, impaired consciousness, pulmonary edema, shock, arrhythmias and renal failure."[12] Anthropologist Kristina Lyons asked, "How do people keep on cultivating a garden, caring for forest or growing food when at any moment a crop-duster plane may pass overhead, dousing entire landscapes with herbicides?"[13] She studied the people's resilience, but their livelihood required resilience in the face of the harm done by this spraying. Colombia, faced with increasingly clear evidence that glyphosate is a carcinogen and harmful to insects and animals, suspended use of the chemical in 2015. Coca production increased in the aftermath of this decision. US president Donald Trump exerted significant pressure on Colombia to resume spraying, threatening to cut off US aid if the country did not do so. Colombian president Ivan Duque made an effort to resume spraying glyphosate, but a February 2022 decision by Colombia's highest court prevented the program from restarting.

Eradication, whether spraying or by manual methods, only works if the people living in that area have other crops they can grow or jobs they can do that will provide for them and their families. Alternative development programs, previously called crop substitution, sometimes accompany eradication efforts. They rarely work, however, to provide a sufficient standard of living. The Thai government initiated one of the few reasonably successful programs, despite the challenge of preventing people with a long tradition of opium growing from producing the crop. During the 1980s and 1990s, opium growing in Thailand decreased significantly. The Thai government provided consistent financial assistance and, importantly, did not punish those who still grew some opium during the transition to licit crops. Even this relative success story provides some cautions about alternative development. The hill areas where people traditionally grew opium were not naturally suited to licit cash crops. The new crops required more water, chemicals, and fertilizers to produce sufficiently to support local farmers.[14] Most alternative development programs suffer from this same dilemma: illicit drugs are often the easiest, most lucrative crop for farmers. Even worse, licit crops often do not generate sufficient income for even a subsistence life, or they require expensive and sometimes environmentally destructive inputs such as chemical fertilizers or pesticides. When farmers make what seems to them a sensible choice to grow just a little bit of drugs alongside subsistence food crops, they sometimes lose everything when governments spray or destroy all the crops. Supply control of drugs can never work until these ordinary farmers have crops they can grow sustainably, market easily, and use to generate sufficient income for their families.

Eradication, whether by manual methods such as cutting down or spraying, also prompts farmers to move to more remote areas where they can grow crops without detection. These efforts to hide both the plants and the initial stages of processing have caused extensive environmental destruction. Deforestation in countries producing illicit drugs was one of the first environmental effects to be noticed. Colombia expanded marijuana production in the 1970s to meet demands in the US market for marijuana from places other than Mexico. Environmental groups estimated that 100,000 hectares of "primary forests" were removed to make way for the marijuana.[15] Colombia increased production of coca and poppies from the 1980s on, with half of all deforestation in the country serving illicit drug production.[16] Often farmers moved into the most remote areas, never previously farmed, or into land with protected status for biodiversity, in order to escape detection. Deforestation was not just for the fields themselves. Illicit crops prompted other kinds of development in the area, particularly roads and airfields, but also building the initial processing plants to reduce the raw materials to a smaller, more manageable size for smuggling effectively. Indeed, one study found that Guatemala, Nicaragua, and Honduras experienced significant deforestation related to drug trafficking in the early 2000s, even though few drugs were grown in these countries. They were all transit countries, where roads, airfields, and storage facilities had to be built in remote, previously forested areas. Drug traffickers often cause deforestation through their need to launder the money they earn illegally. They buy real estate in remote areas and add various improvements so that they can demonstrate legal income and expenses. All these activities result in deforestation.[17]

Any kind of agriculture can result in deforestation, but the deforestation in support of drug production is particularly harmful in part because it is done in the context of the War on Drugs. The illicit nature of these crops means that there is no government oversight to try to choose appropriate places or put guidelines in effect to protect the environment. Growers and processors prioritize secrecy and production over safety, in order to avoid crop destruction or arrest. They use chemicals and fertilizers, both in growing the crops and in the initial processing done on site, in ways that may harm farmers, other crops, the soil, and/or water sources. They divert water from licit agriculture or the surrounding environment. They often lack reliable means to dispose of trash, so it piles up and harms the local environment as well. These harms accompany illicit drug production wherever it occurs. The harms are also difficult to study or to remedy. Those involved in illicit drug production, whether farmers, processors, or traffickers, are reluctant to allow anyone to assess their operations and have no incentive to comply with regulations. Scientists have resorted to indirect methods to investigate the situation. Biologists have studied the bird population in Colombia, Peru, and Bolivia, for instance, drawing a correlation between declining numbers and diversity of birds and the environmental damage in the region, much of it caused by illicit drug production.[18] Other times, anthropologists and geographers have been able to observe these effects in communities they have long studied. Joseph Hobbs, for example, provides fascinating insight into the Bedouin opium poppy growers in Egypt, who have turned to the practice out of economic distress. He observes that "the fields pose serious dangers to the natural environment, and they preclude other types of land use. Barbed wire, chemical fertilizers, and PVC hoses [for irrigation] are unsightly and disruptive elements on the natural landscape." He also notes that the farmers, living apart from their families for everyone's safety, grew bored and shot at local wildlife, for "food and sport." Government eradication efforts, both manual and herbicides, also had effects on the environment, including "damage to palms and ancient fruit trees in the vicinity of the drugs."[19] Even in this limited area, inhabited by relatively few people growing a small amount, comparatively, of drugs, signs of environmental damage are apparent.

Americans tend to think that drugs are grown and processed in other countries, then imported to the United States. To the extent that these Americans think about the environmental consequences of drug production, until recently they have imagined other countries experienced them. As marijuana production expanded in the United States from the late 1960s, however, the same patterns as elsewhere have emerged. Countercultural hippies initiated the surge in production in the late 1960s and especially during the 1970s from overlapping motives. Some people wanted to save money and reduce risk by growing their own. Others sought a simpler lifestyle, closer to nature. Growing and selling some pot helped finance their subsistence farming. The paraquat scare prompted another boom, as consumers wanted to know more about the product they were smoking. As marijuana consumption became more mainstream, as discussed in chapter 12, some growers also worked to improve the quality of American-grown marijuana by bringing in strains from Central and South Asia to hybridize with American plants. All these factors combined to lead to increased production in the United States.

Marijuana grown purely for personal consumption had little environmental impact, especially in areas where people could easily grow outdoors. Marijuana is easy to grow, and if people have sufficient land so that neighbors or law enforcement do not notice the marijuana, it can grow like any other plant. But when people needed to hide plants, they often chose to grow inside. Even amounts used for personal consumption, grown inside, require more water, warmth, and light than a person would usually consume. Still, the amounts needed to produce enough marijuana for personal consumption are negligible. The ease of growing the plant meant that many people who began growing for personal consumption transitioned into growing for the market. Author Ryan Stoa tells the story of Elaine, who grew marijuana in northern California from the early 1970s to the early 1980s, and then returned to it in the 2010s. She remembers that her housemate started growing a few plants on their small farm. "It was great; he was growing it, we didn't have to buy it anymore!" She started to help care for the plants and quickly learned how to produce a good crop. When a relationship change meant she needed to move, she took a job in a more remote area in northern California, growing marijuana clandestinely in national forests. Her boss, a former logger, knew how to clear a small area for growing marijuana while avoiding detection. They all learned how to move to and from their plots without creating paths that federal authorities could see. This pattern of production, replicated in national forests across the United States in the decades since the 1970s, echoes the deforestation of protected lands in other parts of the world. Elaine found the location a bit too remote, so she moved to Humboldt County, California. For a few years she grew marijuana in shifting locations: national forests, remote parcels of land owned by friends, and even sometimes on rented property. By all reports, Elaine took care of the land, even though it was not hers.[20] The system did not encourage that choice, though.

After Ronald Reagan was elected president in 1980, enforcement against marijuana increased. The CAMP program, mentioned previously in relationship to herbicide spraying, also supported manual eradication with helicopters. The helicopters engaged in aerial surveillance, then called in law enforcement to cut down marijuana plants and arrest any growers who remained. One effect of this intensified enforcement effort was, as in other parts of the world, to push growers into ever more remote areas, although in the United States the marijuana plots tended to be small, with the goal of blending into surrounding forest. Deforestation was not as extreme as in other parts of the world. Another effect, less common in traditional drug-producing areas but increasingly common in urban areas, was an increase in indoor growing for sale, not merely for personal consumption. Already by 1985, estimates showed that approximately a quarter of marijuana grown in the United States was grown indoors. The trend continued, with a further nearly 50 percent increase in indoor growing during 1986–87. Indoor operations were easier to hide, at least in the United States, since police needed a warrant to come into the property. Growers also liked being able to control all aspects of production: speeding up the cycle, producing specific strains, harvesting year-round, and precisely developing the strains consumers want. But at this scale, indoor growing has an environmental effect. The water and electricity consumption of indoor growing sites is enormous. In the 1980s and 1990s, before there was significant concern about climate change, this consumption was more likely to be how law enforcement discovered illicit indoor crops than to be criticized by those concerned about the climate. With growing demand in more recent years in the wake of decriminalization and legalization, though, electricity and water consumption are beginning to be serious problems. Not surprisingly, Colorado, California, and Oregon have seen significant increases in demands for electricity since 2010. In California, about 3 percent of total energy usage is for producing marijuana. In Denver, indoor growing is estimated to account for approximately half of the 1.2 percent annual increase in energy use each year since 2012.[21] Probably some marijuana would always be grown indoors, but its illicit status makes the percentage higher than it would otherwise be, increasing the drain marijuana production makes on water and energy resources.

Outside cultivation has also increased since the mid-1990s, with a variety of environmental effects. Some farmers in states where marijuana is legal want to grow responsibly, even organically, to meet market demand for safe, high-quality product. In theory their production should have no greater effect than any other kind of agricultural production, but the illegal status of marijuana at the federal level means that there is no legal way to distribute water rights to marijuana farmers. Since western states, where water is more scarce, were the first to legalize marijuana and also have significant land available for growing it, this is a serious environmental problem. Farmers often divert water from streams, nonagricultural water-supply lines, or irrigation systems. Water availability is already one of the most serious problems facing the western United States, which has experienced unprecedented drought and longer, more destructive wildfire seasons. The additional strain of increases in marijuana production makes an already precarious situation even more difficult.[22] In remote areas, both permanent and temporary marijuana plots show signs of unregulated pesticide and herbicide use. Abandoned sites have significant amounts of trash and discarded agricultural implements. Deforestation to grow marijuana is less common in the United States than in other parts of the world, but all the other environmental problems are similar.

The other significant recent development in drug consumption since the 1990s is the increase in the use of methamphetamines and synthetic opioids. Opioids still generally come from diverted pharmaceutical supplies or are imported into the United States from elsewhere, but meth is made locally at the point of consumption as well as imported. Meth production has serious environmental effects that have so far attracted only incidental attention. When produced licitly for the pharmaceutical market, care is taken to contain harmful chemicals. Illicit producers have neither means nor motive to do so, and so-called cook sites are often contaminated such that law enforcement and child protective services officials frequently require people found at a site to leave all their belongings behind. There has been some study of these effects, but not much. There's not much way to influence the actions of those producing illicitly, so the incentive to investigate the specific harms is low.

As has become all too obvious in recent decades, humans often negatively impact the environment just by traveling, producing food and other consumables, and heating or cooling our homes. Drug production would still have environmental effects, whether done licitly or illicitly. The War on Drugs approach substantially increases the negative effects, in both the methods of eradication and the changes producers make to avoid being caught. Any counting of the costs of the War on Drugs needs to include the harm to the environment alongside other harms.

12. MARIJUANA'S DIFFERENT PATH

In the United States, marijuana has sometimes been viewed as similar to "hard" drugs like heroin and cocaine and at other times more like "soft" drugs, such as alcohol and tobacco. Like opium, it has a long history as an ingredient in the patent medicines of the nineteenth and early twentieth centuries, prized for its pain-relieving qualities. It was never as popular a medicine as opium, and pharmaceutical companies did not adopt it as prescription medicine the way they did with opioids in the twentieth century. Recreational marijuana consumption in the nineteenth and early twentieth centuries was more prevalent in the southwestern part of the United States and was often associated with Mexican Americans, although marijuana was used throughout the country by a wide variety of people.[1] The Harrison Narcotics Act of 1914 did not outlaw marijuana, and its use grew during the 1920s and 1930s. Jazz musicians and other artists often smoked marijuana. During these decades, antidrug propaganda touted the dangers of "reefer madness," claiming that young people high on marijuana committed all kinds of wild and dangerous acts and seduced young women into sexual behavior they would never otherwise have engaged in. As had happened with opium, state and local governments passed laws outlawing marijuana consumption during the early twentieth century. Federal restriction came in the Marijuana Tax Stamp Act of 1937. This act didn't directly outlaw marijuana but stipulated that only certain people could get a license for it, and they had to pay a hefty fee for the appropriate "stamp." The states that had not already prohibited marijuana quickly did so, effectively making consumption illegal throughout the United States.[2]

During World War II, the US government encouraged farmers to grow more hemp, the generic name for the plant that can produce marijuana. Hemp, however, in this context meant hemp for rope, needed to fight the war. The countries from which the United States usually sourced hemp were in areas controlled by Japan. The hemp plants best suited to producing rope don't make the best marijuana for smoking, but the vast increase in domestic hemp production did divert some of this lesser-quality marijuana into the illicit market. During the war years, as it was more difficult than ever to get cocaine and especially heroin, many drug users switched to marijuana. When the war ended, they often went back to their previous drugs but didn't necessarily give up marijuana. During the 1950s, marijuana became a mainstay of counterculture. The Beat poets, among others, extolled the virtues of marijuana for helping them connect to a more authentic life, unencumbered by the materialism of consumer culture and more in touch with the arts, philosophy, and other people. Jazz musicians, painters, and others in the avant-garde smoked marijuana, and with this association it became "cool." In the 1950s, too, marijuana got its reputation as a gateway drug, something easy to try as a first or nearly first drug experience. Smoking cigarettes was common in the 1950s, so the method of ingestion was familiar. A marijuana high was believed to be less strong, less powerful than one from heroin. Those concerned about drug use worried that using marijuana made someone more susceptible to using other, harder drugs. Studies show a correlation between those who use hard drugs and smoking marijuana, but causation is more difficult to prove. Rates of marijuana use remained modest during the 1950s.[3] Those who opposed marijuana revived the "reefer madness" claims that marijuana users engaged in wild sexual or violent behaviors. Those who supported marijuana extolled its psychedelic qualities.

During the 1960s, marijuana use seemed to grow exponentially. The countercultural Beat poets and musicians often participated in the various antiestablishment movements during the 1960s, especially those protesting against the war in Vietnam. The peace movement, and youth culture more generally, embraced a variety of activities challenging traditional societal norms. Some young people, disgusted by a government they thought valued money and power more than the lives of ordinary people, rejected traditional paths to success, lived in communes, protested regularly against the war and other government policies they found oppressive, and celebrated the free spirit associated with rock and roll. Historian Emily Dufton argues that a small group of marijuana smokers introduced marijuana at some of the early peace rallies and rock concerts, distributing joints freely throughout the crowd. Many attendees found that smoking the drug elevated their sense of connection and calm, meaning that these protests were likely to end peacefully rather than in chaos and physical confrontation. Police often completely ignored the presence of marijuana at these protests. Dufton believes some were ignorant about the drug, quoting one who asserted, "I don't know if you know how to smoke pot, but you can't smoke it in the open air. It's probably banana anyway." The apparently bizarre banana reference reflects the practice some protestors had of opening protests by smoking banana peels, then believed (erroneously) to have hallucinogenic qualities. It may also be that police preferred to deal with large crowds of protestors who had been smoking pot and were often calm and compliant rather than crowds who had consumed other drugs, including legal ones like alcohol, that can promote belligerent behavior. Although rates of marijuana consumption in society as a whole remained relatively low, the rates for people in their late teens and twenties shot up during these years, with about one-third smoking at least occasionally.[4]

Although young people associated with the countercultural movements of the 1960s were the most prominent consumers of marijuana in that decade, pot use had begun to cross into other segments of society as well. It's not entirely clear how that happened, but a few trends are likely. Perhaps some of the 1950s participants in countercultural practices began during the 1960s to settle into careers and families, taking some habits with them. Additionally, although many of the people participating in peace protests were young, the peace movement was multigenerational and drew on people from all walks of life, all socioeconomic backgrounds, and all professions. It's highly likely that some older people tried marijuana at a protest and liked it. Research still needs to be done about how and why it happened, but we know that in the 1960s, marijuana consumption began to be more socially acceptable across society, although it of course was still far from common. Marijuana's relative acceptability was demonstrated by the fact that *Life* magazine, definitely a middle-class, socially acceptable publication, ran an even-handed story about it in 1969. The article noted that at least twelve million Americans had tried marijuana (about 6 percent of the population) and asked if the penalties for marijuana possession were too severe and if it should be legalized. Even more striking were the photos accompanying the story: middle-aged professionals at cocktail parties and formal dinners, passing around a joint.[5] It was both shocking and a sign of the growing use of marijuana by a wide variety of consumers. The fact that these people did not fear having their photos in a major, nationally circulating publication also demonstrates they did not much fear the legal consequences of being seen smoking pot. Police often ignored the drug, but if they arrested someone, the penalties could be harsh. Some states imposed long jail sentences for possession of even a small amount of the drug. The laws, societal attitudes, and people's behavior seemed to be in some conflict. Marijuana, more than opioids or cocaine, has often prompted this conflicted response. Laws governing its use have frequently been as harsh as for these other drugs, with potential for long jail sentences, but law enforcement sometimes has been more selective in choosing when to pursue it as a crime and when to ignore its use.

Groups at the state level, and after 1970 at the national level, began to advocate for the reform of marijuana laws to reflect growing acceptance of the drug. There were a number of groups, but the most significant group then and for some years was the National Organization for the Reform of Marijuana Laws (NORML), founded in 1970. Founder Keith Stroup, a lawyer, had previously worked for consumer protection, trying to promote safety standards and the publication of information about the safety record of many consumer products. Stroup smoked marijuana, but he advocated for legal changes more because he believed evidence showed marijuana was not as dangerous as other legally available products, and it should be an individual's decision to smoke or not in that case. Fundamentally, he took a libertarian approach: the government should restrict people's freedom only as necessary to promote safety. Stroup guided NORML's efforts to lobby elected officials at the state and national levels to reform marijuana laws, to decriminalize it, to reduce penalties, and perhaps to legalize it at some point.

This strategy attracted the support of some elected officials and many marijuana consumers, although many advocates wanted a more direct and radical approach. Despite growing support for marijuana, NORML did not immediately succeed in getting legislative change. Even as marijuana use became more widespread and more common among some mainstream groups, opposition to marijuana also increased. Middle-class, older Americans in particular worried about massive changes in society and associated marijuana with those other changes that they did not like. They worried about young people rebelling against societal norms as well as the consumption of both marijuana and heroin by soldiers in Vietnam, as discussed in chapter 8. Marijuana grew wild in Vietnam and so was readily available, consumed by soldiers on all sides of the conflict. President Richard M.

Nixon channeled this discontent from those he called the Silent Majority. Nixon disliked everything about the young countercultural movement. Partly he disliked it because they opposed most of his policies, and the rallies were often directed explicitly at Nixon and his efforts. But he disliked them on a more visceral level too. He did not like hippies, with their casual dress, long hair, and rejection of societal norms. Nixon associated marijuana use with all the changes in society that he found personally frightening and even threatening. He used his authority to advocate strongly for stricter controls on marijuana. As discussed in chapter 9, this atmosphere facilitated passage of the Comprehensive Drug Abuse Prevention and Control Act of 1970, which tightened control over all drugs and most importantly established the schedule for classifying drugs that is in use, with some modifications, to the present. All the drugs associated with the countercultural movement, including marijuana, were placed in Schedule I, the most restrictive level, generating the most significant penalties for possession and use and deemed not to have any medicinal purpose. It is in some ways ironic that as marijuana use became more widespread and common among a variety of groups in the United States, it was also put under the most restrictive status it had ever held in the nation's history.

Possibly this approach backfired, because these harsh laws at the national level were enacted at almost the same time that some states began to move toward decriminalization. Decriminalization is distinct from legalization. It usually means that possession of a small amount of marijuana (defined in ounces in most laws but intended to be the amount a person might have for his or her personal use) would be treated as a civil violation, punishable only by paying a fine, similar to a traffic ticket. Advocates of decriminalization are not necessarily in favor of marijuana consumption. Some are simply libertarians, believing the government should not have the right to tell people what to consume or not consume unless it can be proved to be seriously harmful. Others simply believe the law enforcement approach to controlling drug use has been ineffective and believe decriminalization allows the government to focus on other paths. Some do, of course, believe marijuana is relatively harmless, when compared to drugs already legal (such as alcohol and tobacco), and see decriminalization as a first step, with legalization the ultimate goal. In the early 1970s, all these people made common cause to begin working to get states to loosen their marijuana laws in the direction of decriminalization.

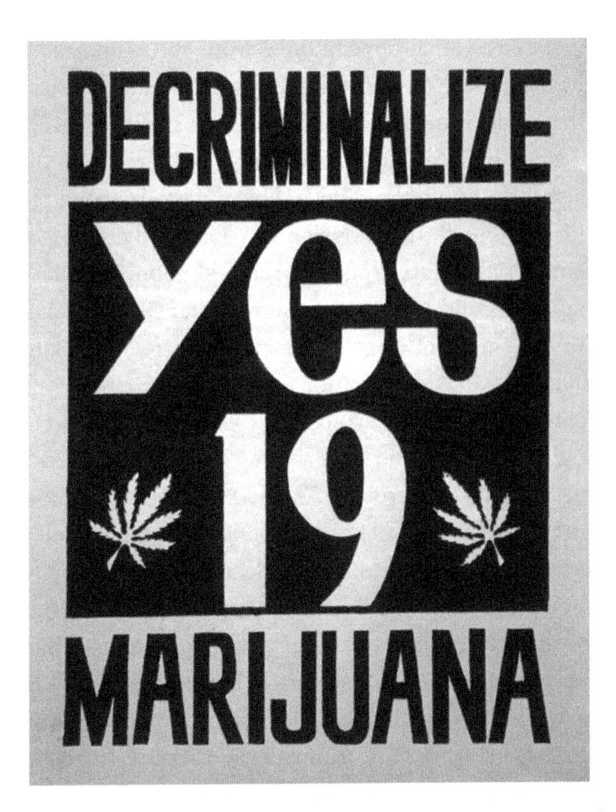

Fig. 12.1. Poster urging California voters to approve Proposition 19, the California Marijuana Initiative, in 1972. Library of Congress, Washington, DC.

The first state to actually decriminalize marijuana in the 1970s was Oregon, in 1973. The sponsor of the bill was a new, young legislator, Stephen Kafoury. When Kafoury campaigned door-to-door, he realized from the number of worried people who were slow to answer his knock, and smelled of pot when they did, that marijuana consumption was relatively common. And it was clear that people were afraid of getting caught. He introduced a bill to decriminalize marijuana, but as a new, young member of the legislature, he probably would not have gotten far with this proposal if he had not been joined in his effort by Stafford Hansell, a successful pig farmer in his sixties from rural (and more conservative) Oregon who had served in the legislature since 1965. Hansell gave a memorable speech before the legislature in which he brought samples of a variety of drugs: beer, whiskey, tobacco. He argued that they all, marijuana included, had similar levels of danger and benefit and that none of them would be eradicated by prohibition. He advocated decriminalization and was roundly applauded by the chamber. Oregon decriminalized marijuana that session, the first (and for a while only) state to do so using legislation.[6]

Some legislators at both the state and federal levels wanted to continue the decriminalization effort, but Nixon was adamantly opposed. He made it clear that he would cause trouble for any Republicans who supported these bills, and they did not move forward. After Nixon resigned in August 1974, under threat of impeachment, efforts revived. Senator Birch Bayh of Indiana introduced legislation to decriminalize possession of up to one ounce of marijuana. Many sympathetic witnesses testified to the harm caused to family members who were serving long jail sentences for possession of small amounts of marijuana. A good number of members of Congress supported Bayh's proposal but not enough to bring the bill to a formal vote. For similar reasons, state efforts to decriminalize also moved slowly. While Nixon was in office, governors feared he would punish their states in terms of contracts, grants, and other federal programs if they decriminalized. After Nixon left office, some states began to pass laws decriminalizing marijuana. Still, only a handful did: Maine, Colorado, California, and Ohio were in the first wave to decriminalize possession up to an ounce. By 1978, they were joined by another group: Minnesota, South Dakota, Mississippi, New York, North Carolina, and Nebraska. The decriminalization movement peaked in 1978, though. President Jimmy Carter was initially sympathetic, and there was talk in 1977 and 1978 that it was wiser to put drug prohibition and prevention efforts into harder drugs, like heroin, and not worry about marijuana. Even by the end of Carter's presidency in 1979 and 1980, however, the tide was turning back to worries about the effects of marijuana.[7]

Support for decriminalization coexisted with concern about the increasing use of marijuana, especially by young people. By the late 1970s, it appeared that teen marijuana use had increased. Marijuana was simply more prevalent in society, so more accessible to teens. And head shops, where marijuana-smoking paraphernalia was sold, appealed to the youth culture. The available statistics, which are always subject to some scrutiny since they are about illegal behaviors, suggest that the primary consumers of marijuana in the 1950s through early 1970s were young adults, but by the late 1970s and early 1980s, teens were trying marijuana in large numbers (60 percent or more reported having tried it) and regularly smoking it in numbers not previously recorded (up to 25 percent in some polls smoked once per month, and 5–7 percent reported smoking daily).[8] The numbers come primarily from surveys of young people. It is unclear how reliable the data are in absolute terms, but the self-reported rates of use were rising fast. Many parents began to be concerned about this drug use by their kids and thought that even if marijuana use by adults was not very harmful, there was no research into the effects on children and teens. Their own observations suggested it was problematic.

During the Reagan years, these parents founded groups to encourage more interventionist parenting, help parents set rules for whole sets of friends, and create educational efforts to discourage drug use. They also banded together to advocate for stricter laws regarding first marijuana and later all drugs. These efforts found success at the state level. States rolled back decriminalization laws and began to put in place other laws specifically making it more difficult to sell drugs or paraphernalia to kids. The Reagan administration favored these efforts. Both Ronald and Nancy Reagan believed antidrug efforts fit with their larger goal of promoting traditional values. They especially appreciated the parent-led groups, which emphasized the role of the family in teaching kids the best ways to live, rather than the government. Nancy Reagan took on the antidrug movement as her special cause. She attended the national conferences of some of these antidrug movements and donated a bit of her own money to the cause. She also helped funnel donations from other wealthy people. The Reagan administration took advantage of this focus on parent-led movements against drugs to shift the funding in the federal budget from education and prevention to a more militarized, law enforcement approach. So even though Nancy Reagan is associated with the famous Just Say No movement, a quintessential education and prevention program, the Reagan administration actually dramatically cut the funding going to education and prevention, spending that money instead on law enforcement and interdiction at the border. Many of the conservatives in the Reagan administration saw marijuana not as a libertarian issue, in which the small government philosophy should extend to not having the government intervene in people's choices about what kinds of substances to consume, but rather as a potential threat to traditional values.

In the midst of this harsh crackdown on marijuana, though, the beginnings of what would become a powerful medical marijuana movement emerged. The growing HIV/AIDS epidemic of the 1980s and 1990s provided an important impetus. Even before that, though, Robert Randall set a key legal precedent. Randall drove a taxi in the 1970s. His eyesight began to fail, and he learned he had glaucoma. His glaucoma did not respond to the existing medical treatments of the time, meaning his eyesight grew inevitably worse. By chance, he smoked a joint recreationally at a friend's invitation. The marijuana relieved the pressure in his eyes, making his vision clearer. He began to grow his own pot to smoke regularly and regained some eyesight. One day, while he was out of town, police were called to his neighbor's house and noticed his pot plants. He was arrested. His lawyer argued that Randall was within his rights to use marijuana because the harm from not using it (going blind) was worse than the benefit to society of prohibiting him from using. The judge ruled in his favor. As a result, in 1976, Randall became the first person to legally use marijuana for medicinal purposes. He even received a monthly supply from the one marijuana "farm" (in Mississippi) that produces the very small amount of marijuana the federal government grows for use in approved medical research. Randall became an advocate for medical marijuana during the 1980s, helping other people gain access to the drug for the same problem he had.[9]

During the 1980s and 1990s, San Francisco became a key center for experimentation with medical marijuana, in part because of the congruence of liberal politics, a large number of gay men who were affected by the growing HIV/AIDS epidemic, and proximity to one of the most prominent marijuana agricultural areas. Mary Rathburn's arrest for distributing marijuana brownies to people with HIV/AIDS to stimulate their appetites and reduce pain prompted enough protest that charges were dropped. She often worked with Vietnam veteran and gay rights activist Dennis Peron, who also distributed marijuana to people with HIV/AIDS. Physician Donald Abrams conducted private studies, since he was unable to get outside funding, with his patients and established beneficial effects on appetite and pain for HIV/AIDS patients.[10] San Francisco passed a resolution in support of medical marijuana in 1991. As a city, it didn't have the authority to change marijuana laws, but this legal change started a serious movement in California to get statewide approval. The California legislature approved a resolution in 1993, asking President Bill Clinton and Congress to take steps on legislation at the federal level to allow physicians to prescribe marijuana. This initiative went nowhere in Washington, but in California the movement continued.

In 1995, medical marijuana activists, working with a revitalized NORML, drafted a ballot initiative. California has a tradition of ballot initiatives, and the law there makes it relatively easy to get proposed laws on the ballot for all citizens to vote on. This measure stipulated that physicians could prescribe marijuana in treatment without fear of losing their license, and it exempted patients and caregivers from laws prohibiting the possession or cultivation of marijuana. It did not attempt to define or limit the medical uses of marijuana. Not surprisingly, the state attorney general and many others in law enforcement (especially prosecutors) opposed the initiative, especially warning that this proposed law directly clashed with federal law. Supporters understood the legal situation but argued vehemently that many people were suffering from medical conditions for which marijuana was the most effective treatment. They got people suffering from cancer, and their loved ones, to give moving testimony about the positive effects of this drug. The initiative was on the ballot in November 1996 and passed with 55.6 percent of the vote statewide. California started a trend, with Alaska, Oregon, and Washington also passing ballot initiatives for medical marijuana in 1998 and Maine in 1999.[11] As of 2022, thirty-seven states plus the District of Columbia, Guam, Puerto Rico, the US Virgin Islands, and the Northern Marianas allow medical marijuana in some form. An additional ten states allow medicines with very low tetrahydrocannabinol (THC) content. Only three states and American Samoa still prohibit all marijuana products, even those with limited THC. Additionally, many medicines have been developed that use cannabidiol (CBD).[12] The FDA has approved two medicines: one to treat a particular kind of seizure and another for nausea and loss of appetite in cancer and HIV/AIDS patients. There are a large number of over-the-counter medicines containing CBD. Overall, the usefulness of marijuana is being demonstrated by anecdotal investigations, but rigorous scientific research lags because marijuana remains a Schedule I drug. It is difficult to get permission to conduct research under these conditions, and drug companies face an uncertain future marketing medicines containing marijuana.

The movement for recreational use of marijuana followed in the footsteps of the medical marijuana movement. The first steps occurred, as with medical marijuana, in the western United States. The initial efforts came largely through voter ballot initiatives, which have a more robust history in the west than other parts of the country. The first states to legalize recreational marijuana, Colorado and Washington, did so in 2012. Two years later, Alaska, Oregon, and the District of Colombia joined them, and two years after that, California, Maine, Massachusetts, and Nevada also approved ballot initiatives to legalize recreational marijuana use. The first state to pass a law in the legislature to legalize marijuana was Vermont, in 2018. As of 2022, seventeen states plus the District of Colombia and Guam have laws allowing for the legal sale of recreational marijuana. At the federal level, no legal change has occurred, although the US House of Representatives passed a decriminalization bill in spring 2022. The Senate did not take up the legislation. All states with legal recreational marijuana have instituted strict controls over where marijuana can be sold and consumed and have age limits. In general, states have found few problems associated with legalizing marijuana and, not surprisingly, dramatically lower arrest and incarceration rates for drug possession.

It seems to be the case, which is perhaps not surprising, that youth consumption of marijuana has increased slightly, given that the drug is much more available. In many of the states with legal recreational marijuana, it is now not much more difficult to get a joint or, more likely, edible from an older sibling than it is to get a beer. Concerns about youth consumption will likely be an issue in coming years. In addition, marijuana remains a Schedule I drug in federal law. The contradictory legal status has proved most vexing for people in the marijuana industry due to complications with banking, variations in regulations in different states, and the inability to move produce across state lines. Making a mistake with regulations in an ordinary business might mean a fine; in the marijuana business, it could well mean being convicted of a Schedule I drug felony and going to prison for years. President Barack Obama's administration took a hands-off approach to the issue, allowing states in general to develop their own marijuana laws and seeing how things developed. Many members of his administration were sympathetic to the legalization movement and thought it would be easier to make a rational federal drug law after the states had some practice in dealing with the situation. President Donald Trump himself did not seem to have a strong opinion about marijuana, although his personal history as a sibling of an alcoholic makes him wary of all intoxicants. His first attorney general, Jeff Sessions, had promised to crack down on marijuana users in states with various levels of legal consumption. In practice, however, Trump administration officials also maintained a relatively hands-off approach. President Joseph Biden has acknowledged that the current system is not working and seems open to decriminalization and to getting people out of jail who are there only for marijuana convictions, but his administration has not prioritized this issue.

These legal changes in general have tracked with a more accepting view of marijuana from Americans. Gallup polls of the American people show a sharp increase in public support for marijuana, both recreational and medical, starting in the mid-1990s. In 1995, about 25 percent of Americans surveyed reported favoring the legalization of marijuana. In subsequent Gallup polls, the percentage climbed steadily through 2012, when it hit 50 percent. The line has continued upward since there, although sometimes dipping, but never below 50 percent. In late 2021, 68 percent of Americans favored legalizing marijuana, the same percentage as in 2020. People identifying as Democrats (83 percent) and independents (71 percent) overwhelmingly favored legalization, while Republicans were evenly split (with 50 percent in favor and 49 percent opposed). More than 95 percent of Americans polled favored medical marijuana in 2018. The numbers of people reporting that they had used marijuana also, not surprisingly, went up during the 2010s, but not nearly as quickly as those who supported a legal status for the drug.

Marijuana's status as an illegal drug seems destined to change in the United States, but the War on Drugs approach to drug control still shapes many of the legal issues around marijuana. Most dramatically, as of this writing, thousands of Americans sit in state and federal prisons, convicted of possessing or selling a substance now legal in the places where they are. The burgeoning businesses of growing, processing, and selling marijuana are hampered by the patchwork of state regulations and the potential for breaking federal law for doing something that would be legal if done in the service of any other business. Research into the full range of medicinal benefits is not taking place, given that pharmaceutical companies have no guarantee they can conduct clinical trials, let alone sell their product if they find something useful. The past century of history discussed in this chapter shows, too, that attitudes can quickly change. Prohibition may seem too irrational to impose after so many people have consumed marijuana for medical or recreational purposes, but the history of the War on Drugs shows that reason is not always the guiding force.

13. NEW CHALLENGES TO THE WAR ON DRUGS

The War on Drugs approach to drug control received significant criticism in the 1990s through 2020s but in large measure continues unabated. Efforts at sentencing reform and for the legalization of marijuana undercut some key aspects of the War on Drugs, as discussed in chapters 10 and 12. The crises that erupted in the 1990s and then again in the 2000s, of methamphetamines and opioids, respectively, have prompted a doubling down on the War on Drugs approaches of eradicating supply rather than addressing demand, and using law enforcement rather than treatment. But they have also focused some attention on harm-reduction measures and the underlying causes of problematic drug use. The War on Drugs approach has become more complicated to pursue with the drugs that have dominated the illicit market since the 1990s. Methamphetamine is a fully synthetic drug. Opioids (most fully, but some partly, synthetic) dominate the market over opiates, which come from the opium poppy. Both types of drugs are made from chemicals, whether in a crude meth cook site or a pharmaceutical factory. The agricultural eradication methods long pursued in the War on Drugs are irrelevant for these synthetic drugs. The illicit market has been flooded. This synthetic production did not replace previous agricultural production. Rather, synthetic production has supplemented the continued agricultural production, making for a world awash in drugs.

In the past thirty years, previous War on Drugs patterns related to both race and the fuzzy line between medical and recreational drug use have also both reemerged and shifted. Historically, the more closely drug use could be linked to an ethnic or racial minority or to urban life, the more that use would be portrayed as dangerous by government officials and mainstream media. But both the meth and opioid crises of the 1990s through 2020s have erupted first and most dramatically in rural areas and among white people. These drug users sometimes seemed to receive more sympathy than the kinds of condemnation that were common in the past. The surge in illicit use of methamphetamines and opioids also happened at the same time that prescriptions for amphetamines, chemically similar to methamphetamine, and opioids increased dramatically as well. For opioids especially, leakage from the licit, prescription market to the illicit market accounted for a large percentage of the problematic use, especially for people who began their use with a prescription. This chapter explores trends in the use of and attempts to control methamphetamines and opioids during the 1990s through 2020s, demonstrating the persistence of a War on Drugs approach to this problem.

Amphetamines are a stimulant, developed in 1929 and initially marketed as Benzedrine in 1934 by the pharmaceutical company Smith, Kline, and French. As discussed in chapter 6, soldiers from a variety of nations took amphetamines during World War II. After the war, as discussed in chapter 8, new versions were developed for a wide variety of ailments, from obesity and "pre-obesity" to anxiety and stress. They were widely prescribed, but some versions were also available without prescription. Not surprisingly, people took these versions for fun, to stay awake for activities such as studying and driving long-haul trucks, and for many other reasons. Federal policy changed to restrict amphetamines to prescription-only in 1959. The scale of prescribing was immense, however, also allowing for leakage of these white-market drugs (a term for legally prescribed medicines) into what is called the gray market (where pharmaceutical drugs are sold illicitly) and stimulating black-market sales. In this case, the black market is composed primarily of chemically similar drugs not produced by pharmaceutical companies. Amphetamines and methamphetamines were placed on Schedule II in 1970, leading the FDA to tighten up prescriptions. Their number dropped steeply.[1] Methamphetamine is related to amphetamine, as the name suggests, but its chemical composition allows the brain to access more dopamine, meaning it feels like a stronger high. A steady demand for amphetamines and methamphetamines continued during these years. Already by the 1980s, users and dealers had found ways to make methamphetamine from commonly available chemicals.[2]

Usage increased rapidly from a relatively small number of people, primarily in the western part of the United States, in the 1980s to almost 2 percent of the population by 1994 and almost 5 percent (approximately 1.5 million) using methamphetamine in 2004.[3] Usage rates stabilized for a decade after 2004 but began to increase again in 2015, to approximately 2 million in 2019. The public reaction to the growing use of meth followed a familiar pattern. Public relations campaigns claimed that meth is uniquely addictive and harmful. Ad campaigns featured before and after photos of people arrested for meth possession or dealing. The before photos usually featured a smiling, clear-skinned person with a full mouth of white teeth. The after photos showed sorrow or anger, blackened teeth, pock-marked skin, and usually extreme weight loss. These effects were not made up, even if they were exaggerated for purposes of the campaign. Meth could and did have devastating effects on those who became hooked, and it seemed frighteningly easy to become hooked. As with all drugs, though, many people use them without becoming addicted. Meth differed from previous drug scares, though. Users did not fit the scare-tactic mold of being urban and racially or culturally different from so-called mainstream America. Meth took hold most strongly, at least initially, in rural and small-town America, with white people, often working class and often women.

Most methamphetamine, from the 1990s to the present, seems to have been imported into the United States from labs in Mexico but also India and Myanmar, among other places. It also, however, came from local meth labs, sometimes called cook sites. Making meth is easy and can be done in spaces as small as the trunk of a car. It used to be simple to get the needed chemicals. It could be a small step from using to cooking and dealing. Making meth is a dirty process, with chemical by-products harmful to people and the environment. Local law enforcement came in close contact with these meth labs in ever-increasing numbers. In Indiana, for instance, state and local police uncovered more than 530 meth labs in 2000. In 2014, the number was more than 1,480.[4] These are the years of relatively flat usage rates in the United States. Each of these lab sites had to be decontaminated by people with special training. If at a house, all the belongings had to be discarded. This environmental hazard, which could be next door or in a neighbor's barn, meant that many people in these small towns and rural areas felt the meth crisis even when they did not use or know anyone who did.

Even though methamphetamine is chemically rather than agriculturally produced, the US policy against meth still used War on Drugs methods, primarily an attempt to control access to the key raw materials. Originally, the most important chemical in illicit amphetamines and methamphetamines was ephedrine, but its use was banned for over-the-counter medicines in the United States during the 1980s. Meth manufacturers then turned to pseudoephedrine as a substitute. Pseudoephedrine is found in many cold medicines, so addicts became "smurfs," or people whose job it was to buy cold medicine and deliver it to those making the meth. The name *smurf*, taken from the blue cartoon Smurfs popular in the 1980s, referenced the often blue blister packs from which the cold medicines came. As some states tightened control over pseudoephedrine in the early 2000s, dealers paid people (in money or more often in meth) to go store to store, buying packages one by one, often using fake names and IDs. When police raided a meth lab in a rural barn or abandoned house, they often found thousands of empty packages of cold medicines. For the addicts, this activity often bound them even more tightly to the source of their addiction and made this drug not only physically but also logistically difficult to escape. Most states adopted even stricter controls, but pseudoephedrine is still available over the counter most places in the United States. It's even more easily available in other parts of the world, and local meth producers can have it shipped to them with relative ease.

US efforts to stop methamphetamine usage followed the familiar policy of arresting users and dealers, attempting to control supply by stopping it at the border, and, since it was also made in the United States, controlling the supply of the key ingredient in meth. The specific ways this policy did not work with meth differed some from other drugs, but the overall effect was similar. In recent years, meth use has spread from its original base in rural or small-town, white America and has become more common among different ethnic and racial groups and in some urban areas. The massive surge in opioid abuse that began in the 1990s overshadowed media attention to methamphetamines, but usage rates remain high and are growing. Methamphetamine is more likely to be imported, especially from Mexico, than ever before. As a result, meth lab seizures in the United States have decreased dramatically while the purity of the drug on the illicit market has increased.

As with other drugs, US consumption rates outpace nearly every other country, but use of the full range of amphetamines, called amphetamine-type stimulants (ATS), which includes both amphetamines and methamphetamines as well as drugs like ecstasy, has increased everywhere. The 2000 United Nations *World Drug Report* called ATS in the 1990s "what cocaine had been in the previous decade: the key growth sector in the global drug market." This report noted that "youth in general" began to use, especially in the "music, dance and rave subculture."[5] Although use of so-called party drugs such as ecstasy increased during the 1990s, the much more

Fig. 13.1. A United States Customs and Border Protection dog and his handler checking luggage for narcotics at John F. Kennedy International Airport on Long Island near New York City, 1985. Despite the increase in the US production of illicit drugs, there are still substantial interdiction efforts at US borders. Photograph © Steve Raymer.

significant increase was in both amphetamines and methamphetamines. Seizures of these drugs increased from approximately 16 metric ton equivalents in 1998 to 43.7 metric ton equivalents in 2007, and more than 400 metric tons in 2019.[6] Both production and use rates grew fastest in East and Southeast Asia as well as what the United Nations calls the Near and Middle East / Southwest Asia. Production was concentrated in countries like Myanmar and Afghanistan and states bordering them. Many of these areas are also associated with heroin production. One consequence of a drug-control policy focusing on supply control is to encourage production to move into areas where effective government control is weak. These developments for ATS seem to reflect that assessment.

The upswing in ATS use in the United States did not replace more traditional opioid use fully. In the 1990s, heroin use rebounded, led by popular figures such as fashion models and musicians. A "heroin chic" developed.

Fashion models, whether or not they used heroin, sported the ultrathin bodies of an addict, the pale skin with dark circles under the eyes contrasted with bright-red lipstick, and baggy or ripped clothes. Overdoses and deaths only heightened the mystique for some, especially disaffected young people. Kurt Cobain, one of the founders of the iconic band Nirvana, struggled publicly with heroin, and his suicide in 1994 brought even more attention to the popularity of heroin in the 1990s.

Since the early 2000s, growing opioid use has attracted more public attention than the use of methamphetamine in the United States. Interestingly, the surge in prescription opioid use tracks alongside a surge in prescribed amphetamines, the former for pain and the latter for attention disorders. There is significant gray-market use of both opioids and amphetamines. People who want to take these medications at higher doses or for longer periods than their prescriptions access that gray market. Additionally, others who cannot or do not want to get a prescription from a doctor self-medicate with either amphetamines or opioids, depending on their ailment. These white- and gray-market users sometimes migrate to the black market of, for example, methamphetamine or heroin, although specific numbers are understandably difficult to establish. Since 2015, another worrying trend is the use of opioids and methamphetamines together, which increases the potential for fatal overdose.

The surge in opioid use, both licit and illicit, since the 1990s seems to have originated in a changed attitude about pain in the medical profession. This changed attitude dovetailed neatly with renewed efforts by pharmaceutical companies to get wider approval for their opioid products in the more relaxed regulatory environment following Ronald Reagan's presidency. Medical professionals had long debated the role of opioids in short- and long-term pain relief, trying to balance potential for addiction with pain reduction. Prescribing patterns also showed that young and old people, women, and Black people consistently received fewer and weaker prescriptions for pain medications. Some pain specialists began to publish work to demonstrate that more aggressive use of pain medication, particularly for end-of-life and cancer patients, was beneficial. Other pain specialists, by the 1980s, argued that pain sufferers deserved more medications and that for anyone truly suffering from pain, addiction was unlikely. The studies they touted were not as rigorous as they appeared at the time. But the US population was aging, and improvements in medicine overall meant that many people lived longer with chronic, pain-inducing illnesses than in the past. Granting pain relief allowed many people to improve their quality of life.

At the same time, though, pharmaceutical companies, particularly Purdue Pharma, were trying to figure out ways to more effectively promote opioid formulations they already had and were developing. Purdue Pharma infamously got FDA approval for OxyContin in 1995 despite doing no studies on its potential addictiveness and with a claim that it was less addictive than other opioids because its coating allowed for a time-release mechanism of the drug. The idea was that a steady release of the drug into one's system meant that people would never get the "craving" that prompted them to seek more of the drug. The problematic logic is evident: to avoid craving, one had to continue to take the drug, presumably forever. But even more problematic was the fact that for most people, the twice-a-day dose did not last a full twelve hours. At the end of each dose period, many people who took the drug exactly as prescribed experienced a decline in pain relief but often a resulting craving as well. In addition, of course, patients developed tolerance. And once the drugs entered the gray market, users quickly learned how to remove the coating so they could snort or inject or smoke the high dose of pure opioid. Purdue Pharma has received substantial criticism for its marketing of OxyContin, but other pharmaceutical companies also brought new opioids to market in the late 1990s and early 2000s, including a fentanyl lollipop and a fentanyl patch. These innovations in drug delivery were designed to seem safer by delivering the drug more slowly or in ways that did not mimic typical drug-consumption patterns. The companies spent substantial funds convincing doctors to prescribe these medicines, offering not only educational opportunities but also small perks such as carry-in lunches for the office from their pharmaceutical representative to much larger perks such as all-expenses-paid seminars in desirable vacation spots. In addition to direct efforts to convince individual doctors to prescribe, the pharmaceutical companies also paid millions of dollars to influential nonprofits in the medical field, such as the American Pain Society and American Pain Foundation. The nonprofits promoted the message pharmaceutical companies had devised, including one pain-care guide stating explicitly that addiction concerns were irrelevant due to "the fact that there is no evidence that addiction is a significant issue when persons are given opioids for pain control."[7]

The combination of a new approach to pain management in at least some parts of the medical profession and new, supposedly safer pain medications proved dangerous. In precisely the same parts of the country where methamphetamines had proved so popular, people started taking these new drugs in huge numbers. First-year sales for OxyContin were $44 million, with that number doubling in each of the next two years and reaching approximately $20 million a week by 1999. In the early 2000s, states began more closely tracking opioid prescriptions. In 2006, total opioid prescriptions in the United States numbered nearly 216 million. The number increased each year until 2012, when prescriptions numbered 255 million. The total US population in 2010 was just under 309 million. From this peak, prescriptions decreased steadily, and in 2020, just under 143 million prescriptions were written. The rates of prescriptions were consistently highest in West Virginia, Kentucky, Tennessee, Alabama, Mississippi, Louisiana, Arkansas, and Oklahoma, with Indiana and Ohio also having high rates. More urban states had somewhat lower rates, typically.[8]

Although the supply-control approach to drug control does not effectively eliminate illicit drug use, one part of the analysis underpinning it is useful in understanding drug consumption. If a location is awash in drugs, more people will consume them. In the 2000s, the United States was awash in drugs. Since the drugs were widely available, they became relatively inexpensive. If more people are consuming them, then more will become addicted. That is part of the explanation for what has come to be called the opioid crisis that began in the late 1990s. In the parts of the United States where drug use skyrocketed, there were other factors. Local economies were shrinking rather than growing. People lacked access to high-quality medical care, especially to alternatives to opioids for pain management. Untangling the legitimacy of the extremely high level of prescriptions will take years, but as historian David Herzberg noted, during these years, opioid addiction rates quickly surpassed the high rate of the 1960s, then the higher rate of the 1890s, to achieve "levels that had never been seen before."[9] As people lost access to prescriptions for a variety of reasons, they turned to the gray market. Opioids were so heavily prescribed that this market was also flush with drugs. For some, illicit pharmaceuticals eventually became too expensive, and they turned to heroin. More recently, the cheaper, more powerful fentanyl has increased in prevalence. Sometimes people know they are consuming fentanyl; other times other drugs are cut with fentanyl, making for an unpredictable and sometimes dangerous experience. Not all opioid users in the 2000s began with a prescription and ended with heroin or fentanyl, but the massive supply made that path a more likely one than in the past.

It took nearly two decades of quickly growing opioid prescriptions before prescription levels began to turn around. In this situation, the usual supply-control method applied to illicit drugs was not fully embraced. It was not that there was some fundamental chemical difference between heroin and pharmaceutical opioids. Rather, the claims and profits of the pharmaceutical companies, coupled with the fact that some level of opioid prescriptions is medicinally beneficial in society, prevailed. People who used drugs improperly, not the drugs themselves, initially took the blame. Pharmaceutical companies promoted that narrative. Societal sympathy for people who seemed to have become addicts for no fault of their own also grew, however. There were mixed messages: some media stories touted the sympathetic addict or overdose victim, such as young high school football players who received opioids for injuries on the field. Other media stories decried the drug-seeking behavior of addicts who went to pill mills, where doctors write thousands of prescriptions in a year for people they see only for a few minutes if at all, or who doctor shopped to collect as many prescriptions as they could. This contradictory attitude helped prompt a contradictory, insufficient response. Prescribing guidance was revised, with doctors encouraged to prescribe fewer opioids. This change may have reduced the number of people who would be newly introduced to potential opioid addiction but left some people without adequate pain management and left others, already addicted, without effective treatment.

Americans are somewhat more sympathetic to opioid addicts than they have been in the past. They are also skeptical about key aspects of the War on Drugs approach. Racial disparities in prison sentences for drug crimes are glaring. In addition, the high arrest rate for mere possession seems out of balance to many. In 2020, there were nearly 1.2 million Americans arrested for a drug crime, with nearly 87 percent of those for possession. And in early 2022, about 45 percent of people in federal prisons were serving time for a drug crime. Harsh drug sentences, especially at the state and local levels, have eased off from their peak, but it is still the case that much of the US response to drug use involves jail or prison.[10] Addicts rarely get treatment in jail, however, and some recent studies have shown that the few days after release are among the most dangerous for potential overdoses. Even with this knowledge, policies have been slow to change. US law and policy emphasize arrests for drug crimes and attempts to reduce supply as the most important ways to bring down use.

The effort to control supply has failed even more dramatically than in the past. The unsettled situation in both Myanmar and especially Afghanistan has created conditions for an increase in heroin production in many years since 2001. Before the US invasion of 2001, Afghanistan produced approximately 4,700 metric tons of opium. This dipped dramatically in 2001 to only 1,600 tons, but then it rose steadily each year until 2007 (8,890 metric tons), bounced around between about 5,000 and 7,000 metric tons until 2016, and has more recently been about 8,000 metric tons.[11] Most heroin in the United States comes from Central and South America, but when global production is high, then the cost of heroin is low and it is easier for people to access it. In 2018, not coincidentally the year after Afghanistan produced a bumper crop of more than 10,000 metric tons of opium, some reports put the price of a baggie of heroin (enough to get high once) at five US dollars or, as the report said, the price of a latte.[12] In addition to this massive supply of opium/heroin, illicit production of synthetic opioids is now a significant factor as well. Clandestine factories, often in Asia, produce highly pure opioids, particularly fentanyl and carfentanil. These drugs are so highly concentrated that they can ship small amounts in the regular mail to dealers in the United States, who mix them with other opioids or sometimes with methamphetamine. Under these circumstances, supply control becomes more difficult than it ever has been.

When the COVID-19 pandemic erupted in spring 2020, it was unclear what effect the virus, government lockdowns, and disruptions to global shipping might have on the illicit drug market. There was a moment, early on in the United States, when it appeared that the illicit drug trade would become substantially more difficult. People could not move freely, at least not without attracting attention. Border checks were tighter as a public health measure. It seemed more difficult to hide illicit activities because there was so much less activity of any kind. The illicit drug markets rebounded quickly, though, perhaps because they were accustomed to operating without attracting attention. Rather than a decrease in drug availability some hoped for at the pandemic's start, probably predictably, drug consumption increased. Risky consumption increased as well, with the number of fatal overdoses also increasing. The reasons for the increase in fatalities varied, from the unpredictable strength of opioids to the increased likelihood that people were alone when they consumed drugs to the mixing of drugs in ways that made a more severe overdose more likely.

If overdose was recorded separately as a cause of death in the United States, it would have been the sixth leading cause in 2020.

The advent of synthetic opioids and methamphetamines put further strain on the supply-side approach that the War on Drugs has followed since its inception. Not only did these drugs dramatically increase the overall supply of drugs, since they supplemented rather than replaced the existing agriculturally produced drugs, but they are also made from chemicals that are harder to control, since those chemicals also have other uses. The other primary strategy of the War on Drugs, in which users were demonized and jailed, also lost some appeal during the meth and opioid crises. To be sure, many addicts still evoked more judgment than sympathy. But other addicts seemed victim more of missteps or error than perpetrators of crime. The failures of the War on Drugs seem increasingly clear, but what will replace it is hard to discern.

Conclusion. Never-Ending War on Drugs?

In May 2016, Filipinos elected Rodrigo Duterte as their president. His pugnacious, brash attitude, willingness to flout convention, and harsh words for elites mean some have called him emblematic of the supposedly populist, opportunistic type of leader emerging in many places throughout the world. Duterte's most consistent campaign promise was to "kill all the drug lords." He meant it. As mayor of Davao for more than twenty years, he had already been overseeing harsh treatment for drug users and dealers. Many people identified as drug users or dealers had been killed by vigilantes. During Duterte's presidency, vigilante groups and both local and national police fulfilled his wishes. People suspected of any involvement in the drug trade, whether with justification or not, found themselves on a list, and often soon after were shot. From 2016 to 2022, the end of Duterte's term, at least eight thousand and perhaps as many as thirty thousand Filipinos lost their lives to Duterte's war on drugs.[1]

Duterte and his war on drugs are extremely popular too. Many Filipinos felt overwhelmed by the increasing use of methamphetamine, called "shabu" in the Philippines, and the crime accompanying it. Duterte's approval ratings often topped 91 percent. This is the logic of the US-initiated War on Drugs taken to its limit. The irony is thick. As we saw in chapter 2, it was the US acquisition of the Philippines that brought all the strands of US prohibitionist activism together to prompt the United States to embrace the War on Drugs approach first for the Philippines, and quickly after not only for the United States itself but for the rest of the world as well. Duterte also pointed to decreased crime rates during his term, as Reagan did in the 1980s, to justify his harsh tactics. And in this, the logic both replicates and travels, promoting War on Drugs approaches endlessly and everywhere.

The purpose of this book is to provide readers with ways to assess these types of claims. The book has traced the history of the varieties of War on Drugs approaches to controlling drugs, showing that many of the approaches have been tried again and again. Sometimes apparent successes led to claims of victory. A closer or longer look at the consequences, however, demonstrated that the strategies have only partial or temporary success. Sometimes apparent failures led to intensified efforts rather than changed tactics, often to the harm of many. And for people living in the United States, often the war is fought out of sight, with costs difficult to see let alone calculate.

Discerning an appropriate, effective policy for drug use is challenging. People, not all but perhaps most, seek mind-altering experiences that drugs provide. In the United States, we have decided that some drugs are so beneficial or harmless as to require no regulation, like caffeine, and others have a benefit sufficiently outweighing the harms that they are only very lightly regulated, such as alcohol, tobacco, and in some states marijuana. Nearly all other drugs are regulated by use, with medicinal use as determined by a doctor acceptable and other uses illegal. Drug laws and policies rarely depend on sound analysis of these harms and benefits, though. Alcohol can be addictive and cause physical and social harms. Many people consume illicit drugs without discernible harm. Many would claim a benefit from their consumption. There are no simple solutions for those problems drugs cause, and there are no definitive solutions, able to be adopted and simply implemented without further thought and modification. But this book has tried to use the history of the long War on Drugs to suggest some different ways of looking at the problems and solutions. The most obviously problematic part of the War on Drugs is the emphasis on supply control to the near exclusion of addressing issues of demand. So long as there is a demand for illicit drugs, they will be supplied. But the inverse is true as well: if there is an enormous supply of illicit drugs, people are more likely to take them than if the supply is limited. The lesson is not that there should be no supply control. Rather, supply control needs to take more account of why producers are willing to engage in making illicit drugs and attempt to address those causes. The more that supply-control efforts arise from the supply countries and locations rather than being imposed from outside, the more successful they will be. Supply control will continue to be elusive, however, since much illicit drug production occurs in places where political authority is weak. Supply control seems the most difficult way to address the drug problem of all those available. Reducing resources dedicated to supply control to allow more to be spent on demand reduction would be sensible.

Continued emphasis on supply control seems particularly problematic in the midst of the environmental crisis of the twenty-first century. Eradication methods harm the environment, whether by spraying or removing healthy plants from areas suffering drought or soil erosion. The illicit nature of production also harms the environment, as farmers pollute, steal water, and clear forests for their crops. Many agricultural producers of illicit drug crops live in places that might otherwise not support their livelihood due to the changing climate. Illicit producers of synthetic drugs also harm the environment with illicit dumping of chemicals. These risks are too great to tolerate anymore.

Addressing the demand side of the drug problem also seems daunting. As we have seen, humans seek mind-altering experiences and pleasure. The time period covered by this book, from the 1870s to the present, offered more and more of these mind-altering and/or pleasurable experiences. Historian David Courtwright explores the implications in his book *The Age of Addiction*, noting that "global industries . . . encourage excessive consumption and addiction."[2] Drugs are only one of many substances or practices to which one can become addicted. One observation might be that the ubiquity of the problem means that it is all the more important to study how to help people avoid and end addiction. It might be possible to tightly control opioid supplies; it will not be possible to so tightly regulate sugar or online games. A War on Drugs approach considers only the threats posed by drugs rather than assessing the range of harms and benefits, which may differ from person to person, to develop policies most likely to be both successful and effective.

Reducing the likelihood that one sample or a few uses of a drug turns into a habit and then an addiction offers promise as a way of reducing the drug problem. The War on Drugs approach criminalizes any use, typically. Most people who use a drug do so only a few times or for a short period. If they do not encounter the legal system during that minimal usage, they experience no harm. Many find great benefit in casual recreational use of drugs. There are a variety of ways, including decriminalization, to make it more likely that this typical user does not experience a lasting negative effect. Ryan Mears, the lead prosecutor in Marion County, Indiana, encompassing Indianapolis, announced, for instance, that he would not prosecute anyone whose only offense is having one ounce of marijuana or less. He said this kind of marijuana charge is "disruptive" to people's lives. Because marijuana use is still illegal in Indiana, he merely implied that the use of marijuana itself was not a problem.[3] Along with these steps to reduce the likelihood that a casual user encounters the criminal justice system, providing more support for harm reduction and addiction treatment would also reduce demand. The research exists to support the effectiveness of these measures. Their implementation requires only changing funding priorities.

Another theme of this book has been that people historically have taken drugs for legitimate reasons. Nearly all types of drugs discussed in this book have legitimate medical uses. We have also seen, however, that public health measures reduced the need for opiates in the nineteenth and twentieth centuries. A renewed commitment to research into and support for alternatives to the addictive drugs that people take, whether by self-medicating or through prescription, could also reduce demand. Physical therapy and nutrition counseling, for instance, can help with many of the ailments causing pain, but these treatments are often difficult to access. The vast increase in the number of Americans using opioids in the early twenty-first century should also prompt alarm about what broader societal reforms might be needed. It is more difficult to initiate a research program to solve that more existential problem, but the need is clear.

The more than one hundred years of the War on Drugs has changed the United States. Its failures are well known, but politicians have difficulty imagining the alternatives, or at least imagining how to achieve the alternatives. But as we have seen, it is not merely that the War on Drugs does not work to reduce the harm of illicit drugs. In many ways, the War on Drugs spreads that harm. The harm is greatest in the poorest countries of the world where governance is already weak, since they have become the drug producers. They suffer precarity when crops are destroyed, destruction and sometime danger from their environment, and continued poverty. In the United States, the harm is greatest for racial minorities, particularly Black people, who have been targeted unjustly by drug laws, and for people in poor, rural areas. The harm is not limited to these groups, however. The War on Drugs has distorted US politics, development aid, international relations, policing practices, and medical care. Changing from war tactics to ones more suited to reducing the number of people experiencing the harms of drugs will be difficult. But it is necessary.

GLOSSARY

Amphetamine: Central nervous system stimulant with many medical uses, from preventing narcolepsy to helping people with ADHD. It is commonly used by prescription. People use it illicitly to stay awake or, when self-medicating, for the same conditions that it is commonly prescribed for. A synthetic drug.

Barbiturates: This class of drugs suppresses the central nervous system. It was used for sedative and hypnotic effects. Now mostly superseded by benzodiazepines, it was commonly used in the mid-twentieth century. A synthetic drug.

Coca/cocaine: Coca leaves traditionally grew in Peru and Bolivia, where people chewed the leaves for a mild stimulant. The processed form, cocaine, provides a powerful stimulant high. Coca leaves were not a global product because they lose potency with time, but cocaine became popular. Cocaine can be consumed by sniffing/snorting, injecting, or dissolving in liquid. It can also be prepared as crack cocaine and consumed by smoking or injecting. Cocaine also has medicinal uses and originally was used as a topical anesthesia for eye surgeries and dental work. This usage persists in such drugs as Novocain.

Hallucinogens: A group of drugs that produce alterations in perception, mood, or thought. Examples include cannabis, LSD, and mescaline. Interestingly, the group of drugs do not have a common means by which they cause these effects.

Licit/illicit: These terms are quite similar to the terms *legal* and *illegal*. Licit and illicit are more often used a little more loosely than legal and illegal but also to indicate that there are substances that may be permitted to be taken under some circumstances but not under others.

Marijuana/cannabis: This is a psychotropic drug that grows as a plant. The leaves, buds, and sometimes young stems are harvested. Traditionally they were then smoked in water pipes or rolled into joints, and that method is still common. The psychoactive substance in marijuana, delta-9, is now also processed and available in other forms, called edibles.

Methamphetamine: A form of amphetamine that also has some medical uses. The chemical composition facilitates a stronger dopamine reaction, so users experience a stronger high when taken recreationally. It is commonly manufactured and used illicitly.

Narcotics: The word *narcotics* has two meanings, which can be confusing. The 1914 Harrison Narcotics Act contributed to this confusion by stating that it (a narcotics act) covered "opium and coca leaves" and their derivatives, salts, etc. We continue to use the term in this general sense to refer to what we might informally classify as the illegal "hard" drugs, such as opioids but also cocaine. This usage is confusing because the word *narcotic* refers in an even more general sense to something that is soothing or lulls you into relaxation, which is the opposite of the effect of cocaine. More properly, the word *narcotics* refers to those drugs that have a soothing effect and can induce sleep. The overlap with opioids is strong. The broader usage was common in the early twentieth century and appears frequently in this book.

Opium/opiates/opioids: Opium is a product of the poppy plant. Once the petals fall off, the seed head is exposed and if scored, a sap oozes out. This sap is collected and boiled down to make opium. Various preparations of opium have been used throughout history, including opium prepared for smoking on its own or mixed with tobacco or sometimes with hash; opium dissolved in liquids, especially alcohol (often called laudanum); and in pill form. It used to be that natural opium processed into the drugs morphine or heroin were collectively called opiates, and synthetic versions of opiates were called opioids. Nearly all drugs based on the chemical structure of opium are now either fully synthetic or partly synthetic, so most people today just use the word *opioids* to refer to this class of drugs. The most common, always illegal version is heroin. Prescription versions include morphine, oxycodone, codeine, fentanyl, etc.

NOTES

INTRODUCTION. The Meaning of Drugs

1. The CDC counts overdoses in the "accidents" category when enumerating deaths. See CDC, National Center for Health Statistics, "Drug Overdose Deaths in the U.S. Top 100,000 Annually," press release, November 17, 2021, https://www.cdc.gov/nchs/pressroom/nchs_press_releases/2021/20211117.htm.

2. US Department of Health and Human Services, Substance Abuse and Mental Health Services Administration, "Highlights for 2020 National Survey on Drug Use and Health," accessed May 23, 2022, https://www.samhsa.gov/data/release/2020-national-survey-drug-use-and-health-nsduh-releases.

CHAPTER 1. The Many Uses of Drugs

1. Neil C. M. Carrier, *Kenyan Khat: The Social Life of a Stimulant* (Boston: Brill, 2007), esp. chapter 1. This work is an anthropological, not historical, approach. One of the few historical studies of khat is Ezekiel Gebissa, *Leaf of Allah: Khat and Agricultural Transformation in Harerge, Ethiopia, 1875–1991* (Athens: Ohio University Press, 2004). For peyote, see Mike Jay, *Mescaline: A Global History of the First Psychedelic* (New Haven, CT: Yale University Press, 2019), especially chapters 1 and 2.

2. For a useful overview, see Roderick Phillips, *Alcohol: A History* (Chapel Hill: University of North Carolina Press, 2014).

3. Benjamin Breen, *The Age of Intoxication: Origins of the Global Drug Trade* (Philadelphia: University of Pennsylvania Press, 2019), 157–58. Breen also provides an excellent introduction to the history of drugs in the early modern era.

4. For a useful introduction to the history of tobacco, see Marcy Norton, *Sacred Gifts, Profane Pleasures: A History of Tobacco and Chocolate in the Atlantic World* (Ithaca, NY: Cornell University Press, 2008).

5. Sidney W. Mintz's classic *Sweetness and Power: The Place of Sugar in Modern History* (New York: Penguin, 1986) remains the best starting point for this topic.

6. Martin Booth's *Opium: A History* (New York: St. Martin's, 1996) is useful for the modern period.

CHAPTER 2. **Identifying the Problem**

1. Steffen Rimner, *Opium's Long Shadow: From Asian Revolt to Global Drug Control* (Cambridge, MA: Harvard University Press, 2018), 56–64.

2. The colony Burma is the country now known as Myanmar. The country retained the name Burma upon independence in 1948. In 1989, following a coup to suppress the government democratically elected in 1988, the military leaders of Burma changed the name to Myanmar. Official US policy still recognizes the name Burma for the country.

3. Chan Laisun, speech to Society for the Suppression of the Opium Trade, in *Friend of China* 1 (March 1875): 15. Chan Laisun's name is rendered as reported in the journal.

4. Statistics from John F. Richards, "The Opium Industry in British India," *Indian Economic and Social History Review* 39, nos. 2–3 (2002): 156–63.

5. James Rush has the best discussion of TeMechelen's efforts in James R. Rush, *Opium to Java: Revenue Farming and Chinese Enterprise in Colonial Indonesia, 1860–1910* (Ithaca, NY: Cornell University Press, 1990): 159–78.

6. W. P. Groeneveldt, *Rapport over Opium-Monopolie in Fransch Indo-China* (Batavia: Landsdrukkerij, 1890).

7. Great Britain, Royal Commission on Opium, *First Report of the Royal Commission on Opium*, vol. 6, *Final Report* (London: H. M. Stationary Office, 1895), 93 for the quote and 93–96 for the general points.

8. Rimner, *Opium's Long Shadow*, 87–97.

9. As reported in Rimner, *Opium's Long Shadow*, 107–9.

10. M. T. H. Perelaer, *Baboe Dalima* (Amsterdam: Elsevier, 1886); English translation by E. J. Venning published in 1888 by Vizetelly and Co., London.

11. William Rosser Cobbe, *Doctor Judas: A Portrayal of the Opium Habit* (Chicago: S. C. Griggs, 1895), 17.

12. Joyce A. Madancy, *The Troublesome Legacy of Commissioner Lin: The Opium Trade and Opium Suppression in Fujian Province, 1820s–1920s*, Harvard East Asian Monographs (Cambridge, MA: Harvard University Press, 2004), esp. 110–33.

13. Virginia Berridge, *Opium and the People: Opiate Use and Drug Control Policy in Nineteenth and Early Twentieth Century England* (London: Free Association Books, 1999), 97–122.

14. Howard Padwa, *Social Poison: The Culture and Politics of Opiate Control in Britain and France, 1821–1926* (Baltimore: Johns Hopkins University Press, 2012), 67–78.

15. David T. Courtwright, *Dark Paradise: A History of Opiate Addiction in America* (Cambridge, MA: Harvard University Press, 2001), esp. chapter 1.

16. Diana Ahmad, *The Opium Debate and Chinese Exclusion Laws in the Nineteenth-Century American West* (Reno: University of Nevada Press, 2007), 58–62.

CHAPTER 3. **Deciding on Prohibition**

1. Diana S. Kim, *Empires of Vice: The Rise of Opium Prohibition across Southeast Asia* (Princeton, NJ: Princeton University Press, 2020).

2. Anne L. Foster, "Opium, the United States, and the Civilizing Mission in Colonial Southeast Asia," *Social History of Alcohol and Drugs* 24, no. 1 (January 2010): 6–19.

3. Carl A. Trocki, *Opium, Empire and the Global Political Economy: A Study of the Asian Opium Trade, 1750–1950* (London: Routledge, 1999), 118–28.

4. W. P. Groeneveldt, *Rapport over Opium-Monopolie in Fransch Indo-China* (Batavia: Landsdrukkerij, 1890), 127–238.

5. John M. Jennings, *The Opium Empire: Japanese Imperialism and Drug Trafficking in Asia, 1895–1945* (Westport, CT: Praeger, 1997), 17–38.

6. Lori Loeb, "Doctors and Patent Medicines in Modern Britain: Professionalism and Consumerism," *Albion: A Quarterly Concerned with British Studies* 33, no. 3 (Autumn 2001): 409–10.

7. Paul Gootenberg, *Andean Cocaine: The Making of a Global Drug* (Chapel Hill: University of North Carolina Press, 2008), especially chapters 2–5. For the Dutch effort, see Arjo Roersch van der Hoogte and Toine Pieters, "From Javanese Coca to Java Coca: An Exemplary Product of Dutch Colonial Agro-Industrialism, 1860–1920," *Technology and Culture* 54, no. 1 (January 2013): 90–116.

8. Anne L. Foster, "The Philippines, the United States and the Origins of Global Narcotics Prohibition," *Social History of Alcohol and Drugs* 33, no. 1 (March 2019): 16–21. Much of the discussion in this chapter draws on this article.

9. Letter from William H. Taft to Elihu Root, July 13, 1903, Theodore Roosevelt Papers, Library of Congress Manuscript Division, Theodore Roosevelt Digital Library, Dickinson State University, accessed October 10, 2022, https://www.theodorerooseveltcenter.org/Research/Digital-Library/Record?libID=o41275.

10. See Philippine Opium Commission, *Use of Opium and Traffic Therein*, S. Doc. 59-265 (Washington, DC: Government Printing Office, 1906), 55, for the recommendation in the Philippines.

11. Philippine Opium Commission, *Use of Opium*, 20.

12. Philippine Opium Commission, *Use of Opium*, 51.

13. Philippine Opium Commission, *Use of Opium*, 54.

CHAPTER 4. **International Conferences**

1. These international efforts are covered well in Mark Harrison, *Contagion: How Commerce Has Spread Disease* (New Haven, CT: Yale University Press, 2012), especially chapter 7.

2. Maartje Abbenhuis has written about the peace conferences. For an introduction to the issue, see Abbenhuis, "'This Is an Account of Failure': The Contested Historiography of the Hague Peace Conferences of 1899, 1907 and 1915," *Diplomacy and Statecraft* 32, no. 1 (January 2021): 1–30. For efforts against "white slavery," see Jessica R. Pliley, *Policing Sexuality: The Mann Act and the Making of the FBI* (Cambridge, MA: Harvard University Press, 2014), chapter 1.

3. The discussion of the Shanghai Commission draws on Anne L. Foster, "Prohibition as Superiority: Policing Opium in South-East Asia, 1898–1925," *International*

History Review 22, no. 2 (June 2000): 253–73; Helena Barop, "Building the 'Opium Evil' Consensus: The International Opium Commission of Shanghai," *Journal of Modern History* 13, no. 1 (2015): 115–37.

4. *Report of the International Opium Commission, Shanghai, China, February 1–26, 1909*, vol. 1, *Report of the Proceedings* (Shanghai: North-China Daily News and Herald, 1909), 84.

5. William B. McAllister, *Drug Diplomacy in the Twentieth Century: An International History* (New York: Routledge, 2000), 30–35. McAllister remains the most important source for the history of international developments in drug control. Much of this chapter draws on his work in addition to my own research in primary sources.

6. League of Nations, *Treaty Series: Publication of Treaties and International Engagements Registered with the Secretariat of the League of Nations*, vol. 8 (1922). The International Opium Convention (January 1912) is found in pages 187–240. For the quotes, see p. 195.

7. Secretary's Notes of a Conversation held in M. Pichon's Room at the Quai d'Orsay, Paris, April 17, 1919 (Paris Peace Conf.180.03201/5), in *Papers Relating to the Foreign Relations of the United States* (hereafter FRUS) (1919), vol. 4, *Paris Peace Conference*, document 35, 567.

8. McAllister, *Drug Diplomacy*, 65.

9. McAllister, *Drug Diplomacy*, 108.

10. Douglas Clark Kinder and William O. Walker III, "Stable Force in a Storm: Harry J. Anslinger and United States Narcotic Foreign Policy, 1930–1962," *Journal of American History* 72, no. 4 (March 1986): 908–27.

CHAPTER 5. **Changing Practice and Policy in Medicine and Public Health**

1. Samuel O. L. Potter, *Handbook of Materia Medica, Pharmacy, and Therapeutics, Including the Physiological Action of Drugs* (Philadelphia: P. Blakiston's Son, 1897), 366–68.

2. Samuel O. L. Potter, *Therapeutics, Materia Medica and Pharmacy: The Special Therapeutics of Diseases and Symptoms* (Philadelphia: P. Blakiston's Son, 1917), 349–52.

3. E. P. Hennock, "Vaccination Policy against Smallpox, 1835–1914: A Comparison of England with Prussia and Imperial Germany," *Social History of Medicine* 11, no. 1 (1998): 49–71; Michael Willrich, "'The Least Vaccinated of Any Civilized Country': Personal Liberty and Public Health in the Progressive Era," *Journal of Policy History* 20, no. 1 (2008): 76–93, quote on 77.

4. Mary Augusta Brazelton, *Mass Vaccination: Citizens' Bodies and State Power in Modern China* (Ithaca, NY: Cornell University Press, 2019), 5.

5. For one example, see Francis Dube, "Public Health at the Zimbabwean Border: Medicalizing Migrants and Contesting Colonial Institutions, 1890–1960," *Histoire Sociale / Social History* 52, no. 105 (May 2019): 93–108.

6. Tom Koch and Kenneth Denike, "Crediting His Critics' Concerns: Remaking John Snow's Map of Broad Street Cholera, 1854," *Social Science and Medicine* 69, no. 8 (2009): 1246–48.

7. Warwick Anderson, *Colonial Pathologies: American Tropical Medicine, Race and Hygiene in the Philippines* (Durham, NC: Duke University Press, 2006).

8. Vidya Mahambare, "The Hidden Truth behind India's Low Refrigerator Ownership," *Economic Times*, March 24, 2017, https://economictimes.indiatimes.com/blogs/et-commentary/the-hidden-truth-behind-indias-low-refrigerator-ownership/.

9. W. J. Keith (secretary to the Financial Commissioner, Burma), "Report on the Working of the Revised Arrangements for the Vend of Opium in Lower Burma during the Year Ended 31st March 1904" (Rangoon, Office of the Superintendent, Government Printing, Burma, November 1904), IOR/V/24/3127, British Library, London.

10. Walter A. Bastedo, *Materia Medica: Pharmacology, Therapeutics and Prescription Writing for Students and Practitioners* (Philadelphia: W. B. Saunders, 1913), 357.

11. Roy Porter, *The Greatest Benefit to Mankind: A Medical History of Humanity* (New York: W. W. Norton, 1999), 364–69.

12. Paul Gootenberg, *Andean Cocaine: The Making of a Global Drug* (Chapel Hill: University of North Carolina Press, 2008), 23–25.

13. Of course, not all people managed their pain this way. Some did nothing and just endured the pain. Others drank alcohol, which was less effective but may have seemed more culturally appropriate.

14. Some examples from the *British Medical Journal*: "Section of Surgery: Intractable Pain," August 12, 1939, p. 350; "The Surgeon and Pain," January 12, 1935, pp. 47–50; G. F. Rowbotham, "Treatment of Pain in the Face by Intramedullary Tractomomy," November 26, 1938, pp. 1073–76.

15. Miriam Kingsberg, "Abstinent Nation, Addicted Empire: Opium and Japan in the Meiji Period," *Social History of Alcohol and Drugs: An Interdisciplinary Journal* 25, no. 1/2 (Fall 2011): 99–100.

16. Attempted treatment in these early years has received too little scholarly attention. Daniel J. P. Wertz briefly discusses it in "Idealism, Imperialism and Internationalism: Opium Politics in the Colonial Philippines, 1898–1925," *Modern Asian Studies* 47, no. 2 (March 2013): 488.

CHAPTER 6. **Opportunities of World War II and Its Aftermath**

1. Dennis B. Worthen, *Pharmacy in World War II: Serving at Home or in the Military* (New York: Pharmaceutical Products Press, 2004).

2. Bernard L. Rice, "Recollections of a World War II Combat Medic," *Indiana Magazine of History* 93, no. 4 (December 1997): 323.

3. Mark Harrison, *Medicine and Victory: British Military Medicine in the Second World War* (Oxford: Oxford University Press, 2004), 203.

4. Nicolas Rasmussen, *On Speed: The Many Lives of Amphetamine* (New York: New York University Press, 2008), 78–79; Stephen Snelders and Toine Pieters, "Speed in the Third Reich: Methamphetamine (Pervitin) and Drug Use from Below," *Social History of Medicine* 24, no. 3 (December 2011): 686–99.

5. As quoted in Suzanna Reiss, *We Sell Drugs: The Alchemy of US Empire* (Berkeley: University of California Press, 2014), 18.

6. Bureau of Narcotics, *Annual Reports* (Washington, DC: Government Printing Office, 1937–41).

7. Library of Congress, Legislative Reference Service, "Raw Materials," in *Bibliographies of a World at War*, vol. 3–4 (Washington, DC: Government Printing Office, 1942). See especially the Chemicals and Drugs section, in Supplement 1, pp. 85–87. For the correspondence about opium purchases from Turkey, see FRUS (1942), vol. 4, *The Near East and Africa*, 699–714 and FRUS (1943), vol. 4, *The Near East and Africa*, 1112–19.

8. William B. McAllister, *Drug Diplomacy in the Twentieth Century: An International History* (New York: Routledge, 2000), 136–41.

9. Douglas Clark Kinder and William O. Walker III, "Stable Force in a Storm: Harry J. Anslinger and United States Narcotic Foreign Policy, 1930–1962," *Journal of American History* 72, no. 4 (March 1986): 920–21.

10. Reiss, *We Sell Drugs*, 12–38. Reiss provides an excellent analysis of the ways US economic and political power influenced the intersection of pharmaceuticals, illicit drugs, and foreign relations, primarily focusing on the Americas.

11. W. van Boetzelaer (Minister Plenipoteniary of the Netherlands) to US Secretary of State, September 29, 1943 (890.114 Narcotics/30), in FRUS (1944), vol. 2, *General, Social and Economic Matters*, document 898, p. 1076. The discussion of this issue draws on documents in this volume of FRUS.

12. British Embassy to the Department of State, "Aide-Memoire," November 6, 1943 (890.114 Narcotics/44), in FRUS (1944), vol. 2, *General, Social and Economic Matters*, document 900, p. 1080.

13. See the discussion in Matthew R. Pembleton, *Containing Addiction: The Federal Bureau of Narcotics and the Origins of America's Global Drug War* (Amherst: University of Massachusetts Press, 2017), 115–27.

14. See Alfred W. McCoy, *Politics of Heroin: CIA Complicity in the Global Drug Trade* (Chicago: Lawrence Hill Books, 2003), chapter 1.

15. Chief of the Division of International Labor, Social and Health Affairs (Otis E. Mulliken) to Under Secretary of State (Joseph Grew), Memorandum, February 3, 1945 (511.4A5/1-1345), in FRUS (1945), vol. 2, *General Political and Economic Matters*, document 795, 1534–35.

CHAPTER 7. **US Laws and International Conventions**

1. William B. McAllister, *Drug Diplomacy in the Twentieth Century: An International History* (New York: Routledge, 2000), remains the classic treatment for international agreements related to narcotics control.

2. "United Nations Opium Control," *New York Herald Tribune*, November 18, 1946, A23.

3. Peter Kihss, "U.N. for War by China, Mexico to Uproot Opium Plantations," *New York Herald Tribune*, June 6, 1948, A2.

4. United Nations Conference for the Adoption of a Single Convention on Narcotic Drugs, *Official Records*, vol. 1, *Summary Records of Plenary Meetings* (New York: United Nations, 1964), 5 (quote by Green), 15 (quote by Barona), 7 (quote by Banerji).

5. United Nations Conference for Adoption of a Protocol on Psychotropic Substances, *Official Records*, vol. 2, *Summary of Plenary Meetings* (New York: United Nations, 1973), 9.

6. Anslinger retired as head of the FBN in 1962 but remained US representative to the Commission on Narcotics for an additional two years.

7. Harry J. Anslinger, "Organized Protection against Organized Predatory Crime: VI. Peddling of Narcotic Drugs," *Journal of Criminal Law and Criminology* 24, no. 3 (September–October 1933): 650, 652.

8. The Boggs Act, excerpted in David F. Musto, ed., *Drugs in America: A Documentary History* (New York: New York University Press, 2002), 276–77.

9. See Michael Lassiter, "Pushers, Victims and the Lost Innocence of White Suburbia: California's War on Narcotics in the 1950s," *Journal of Urban History* 41, no. 5 (2015): 787–88.

10. David T. Courtwright, *Dark Paradise: A History of Opiate Addiction in America* (Cambridge, MA: Harvard University Press, 2001), 156.

11. Joint Committee of the American Bar Association and the American Medical Association on Narcotic Drugs, *Drug Addiction: Crime or Disease?* (Bloomington: Indiana University Press, 1961), quote on 163.

12. Quoted in David F. Musto, *The Quest for Drug Control: Politics and Federal Policy in an Age of Increasing Substance Abuse, 1963–1981* (New Haven, CT: Yale University Press, 2022), 16.

CHAPTER 8. **Who Is Using?**

1. Both had been invented in the nineteenth century but saw much greater use in the twentieth century after pharmaceutical companies began producing them in mass quantities.

2. Nicolas Rasmussen, *On Speed: From Benzedrine to Adderall* (New York: New York University Press, 2008), 113.

3. As quoted in David Herzberg, *White Market Drugs: Big Pharma and the Hidden History of Addiction in America* (Chicago: University of Chicago Press, 2020), 182.

4. Hugh J. Parry, "Use of Psychotropic Drugs by U.S. Adults," *Public Health Reports* 83, no. 10 (October 1968): 802.

5. As quoted in Rasmussen, *On Speed*, 132.

6. Stephen Kinzer, *Poisoner in Chief: Sidney Gottlieb and the CIA Search for Mind Control* (New York: Henry Holt, 2019), esp. 63–72 for the initial authorization.

7. Eric Schneider, *Smack: Heroin and the American City* (Philadelphia: University of Pennsylvania Press, 2013), esp. chapter 3.

8. Herzberg, *White Market Drugs*, discussion on 183–87, charts on 292–93.

9. Robert P. Goldman, "Dope Invades the Suburbs: Teen-Age Addiction Is Spreading Fast in our 'Best' Communities," *Saturday Evening Post* 237, no. 13 (April 4, 1964): 22.

10. Jeremy Kuzmarov, *Myth of the Addicted Army: Vietnam and the Modern War on Drugs* (Amherst: University of Massachusetts Press, 2009), especially chapter 3.

11. Alfred W. McCoy, *The Politics of Heroin: CIA Complicity in the Global Drug Trade* (Chicago: Lawrence Hill Books, 2003), especially chapter 5.

12. Paul Gootenberg, *Andean Cocaine: The Making of a Global Drug* (Chapel Hill: University of North Carolina Press, 2008), 275–86.

13. Lloyd D. Johnston et al., *Trends in Drug Use and Associated Factors among American High School Students, College Students and Young Adults: 1975–1989* (Ann Arbor: University of Michigan Institute for Social Research, 1991), 52–54.

14. Martha Smilgis et al., "The Big Chill: Fear of Aids, How Heterosexuals Are Coping with a Disease That Can Make Sex Deadly," *Time Magazine* 129, no. 7 (February 16, 1987): 51.

CHAPTER 9. **War on Drugs Declared**

1. Richard Nixon, "Remarks about an Intensified Program for Drug Abuse Prevention and Control," June 17, 1971, The American Presidency Project, UC–Santa Barbara, https://www.presidency.ucsb.edu/documents/remarks-about-intensified-program-for-drug-abuse-prevention-and-control.

2. David Musto, *The American Disease: Origins of Narcotics Control*, 3rd ed. (Oxford: Oxford University Press, 1999), 248.

3. Table 9.1 was created by summarizing the definitions and examples in the 1970 Controlled Substances Act: An Act to Amend the Public Health Service Act (Comprehensive Drug Abuse Control and Prevention Act of 1970), Public Law 91-513, US Statutes at Large 84 (1970), 1247–52.

4. David Herzberg argues that for a few years after 1970, consumer advocates succeeded in using the schedules to effectively regulate the pharmaceutical market. But the antiregulation movement associated with the Reagan presidency gave more power to the pharmaceutical companies. They began to effectively lobby for scheduling favorable to themselves. See Herzberg, *White Market Drugs: Big Pharma and the Hidden History of Addiction in America* (Chicago: University of Chicago Press, 2020), 200–210 and chapter 7.

5. Eric C. Schneider, *Smack: Heroin and the American City* (Philadelphia: University of Pennsylvania Press, 2008), 166–70.

6. Amitai Etzioni, "Methadone: Best Hope for Now," *Smithsonian Magazine* 4, no. 1 (April 1973): 50.

7. Interview with John R. Bartels Jr., DEA administrator, in *Drug Enforcement Administration* (Washington, DC: Department of Justice, 1974), 2.

8. Alfred W. McCoy, *The Politics of Heroin: CIA Complicity in the Global Drug Trade* (Chicago: Lawrence Hill Books, 2003), 387–96.

9. McCoy, *Politics of Heroin*, 432.

10. Brian Mann, "After 50 Years of the War on Drugs: 'What Good Is It Doing Us?,'" *Morning Edition*, National Public Radio, June 17, 2021, https://www.npr.org/2021/06/17/1006495476/after-50-years-of-the-war-on-drugs-what-good-is-it-doing-for-us.

11. John F. Kennedy, "Remarks to the White House Conference on Narcotic and Drug Abuse," September 27, 1962, The American Presidency Project, UC–Santa

Barbara, https://www.presidency.ucsb.edu/documents/remarks-the-white-house-conference-narcotic-and-drug-abuse.

12. Lina Britto, *Marijuana Boom: The Rise and Fall of Colombia's First Drug Paradise* (Berkeley: University of California Press, 2020), especially chapter 5, is illuminating. McCoy, *The Politics of Heroin*, chapter 9, provides a global overview.

CHAPTER 10. **Mandatory Minimums**

1. David Musto, *The American Disease: Origins of Narcotic Control* (Oxford: Oxford University Press, 1999), 101–7.

2. Bureau of Internal Revenue, Department of the Treasury, *Compilations of Treasury Decisions Relating to the Act of December 17, 1914 known as the Harrison Narcotic Act* (Washington, DC: Government Printing Office, 1917), section 11, p. 9.

3. Musto, *The American Disease*, 131–32.

4. Caroline Jean Acker, *Creating the American Junkie: Addiction Research in the Classic Era of Narcotic Control* (Baltimore: Johns Hopkins University Press, 2002), 156–73; Nancy D. Campbell et al., *The Narcotic Farm: The Rise and Fall of America's First Prison for Drug Addicts* (Lexington, KY: South Limestone Books, 2021), 12–14.

5. To Amend the Penalty Provisions Applicable to Persons Violating Certain Narcotics Laws (Boggs Act), November 2, 1951, Public Law 82-255, US Statutes at Large 65-767; Narcotics Control Act, July 18, 1956, Public Law 84-728, US Statutes at Large 70-567.

6. David Courtwright, *Dark Paradise: A History of Opiate Addiction in America* (Cambridge, MA: Harvard University Press, 2001), 156.

7. Quoted in Jessica Neptune, "Harshest in the Nation: The Rockefeller Drug Laws and the Widening Embrace of Punitive Politics," *Social History of Alcohol and Drugs* 26, no. 2 (June 2012): 170.

8. Mason B. Williams, "How the Rockefeller Laws Hit the Streets: Drug Policing and the Politics of State Competence in New York City, 1973–1989," *Modern American History* 4, no. 1 (2021): 75–76.

9. Emily Dufton, *Grass Roots: The Rise and Fall and Rise of Marijuana in America* (New York: Basic Books, 2017), 165–76.

10. Musto, *The American Disease*, 267.

11. Musto, *The American Disease*, 273–74.

12. Senator Lawton Chiles, *Congressional Record-Senate*, 99th Congress, 2nd session, vol. 132, part 18, September 26, 1986, p. 26447.

13. David Farber, *Crack: Rock Cocaine, Street Capitalism, and the Decade of Greed* (New York: Cambridge University Press, 2019), 139–40.

14. United Sentencing Commission, *Special Report to the Congress: Cocaine and Federal Sentencing Policy* (Washington, DC: Government Printing Office, 1995), 116–20. See also Michael Massing, *The Fix* (Berkeley: University of California Press, 2000), 184.

15. Musto, *The American Disease*, 278.

16. Quoted in Musto, *The American Disease*, 276.

CHAPTER 11. **Environmental Effects of the War on Drugs**

1. Advisory Committee on the Traffic in Opium and Other Dangerous Drugs, "Extract from the Minutes of the Thirty-Fifth Session of the Council, September 5, 1925," C.500.XI.1925, League of Nations, Geneva, September 10, 1925.

2. US Secretary of State to US Embassy in Mexico, enclosing Statement of the United States Representative on the Commission on Narcotic Drugs of the United Nations, Mr. Harry J. Anslinger, Regarding the Narcotics Situation in Mexico, August 9, 1947, 812.114 Narcotics/8-947, in FRUS (1947), vol. 8, *The American Republics*, document 713, 837.

3. William O. Walker III, ed., *Drugs in the Western Hemisphere: An Odyssey of Cultures in Conflict* (Wilmington, DE: Scholarly Resources, 1996), 173.

4. As discussed by Daniel Weimer in "The Politics of Contamination: Herbicides, Drug Control, and Environmental Law," *Diplomatic History* 41, no. 5 (November 2017): 851. Weimer is one of the few historians to study this issue in depth.

5. Jeremy Kuzmarov, *Myth of the Addicted Army: Vietnam and the Modern War on Drugs* (Amherst: University of Massachusetts Press, 2009), 127.

6. Weimer, "The Politics of Contamination," 858.

7. Weimer, "The Politics of Contamination," 865.

8. Martin Jelsma, *Vicious Circle: The Chemical and Biological "War on Drugs"* (Amsterdam: Transnational Institute, 2001), 14–20.

9. Daren G. Fisher and Alexander A. Meitus, "Uprooting or Sowing Violence? Coca Eradication and Guerrilla Violence in Colombia," *Studies in Conflict and Terrorism* 40, no. 9 (2017): 790–92.

10. Kristina Lyons, "Chemical Warfare in Colombia: Evidentiary Ecologies and *Senti-Actuando* Practices of Justice," *Social Studies of Science* 48, no. 3 (2018): 1–24.

11. For an overview of activities through the mid-1980s, see Rosa del Olmo, "Aerobiology and the War on Drugs: A Transnational Crime," *Crime and Social Justice*, no. 30 (1987): 28–44. Sometimes NORML press releases are the best way to track activities by US states. For example, see "DEA Herbicide under Fire from Hawaii Residents," October 17, 1996, and "Oklahoma Legislature Ready to Approve Aerial Spraying of Controversial Anti-Marijuana Herbicide," March 27, 1997, both available at https://norml.org/news/.

12. Fisher and Meitus, "Uprooting or Sowing Violence?," 791.

13. Kristina Lyons, "Decomposition as Life Politics: Soils, *Selva*, and Small Farmers under the Gun of the Colombia-U.S. War on Drugs," *Cultural Anthropology* 31, no. 1 (2016): 64.

14. Chupinit Kesmanee, "Dubious Development Concepts in the Thai Highlands: The Chao Khao in Transition," *Law and Society Review* 28, no. 3 (1994): 673–86.

15. Lina Britto, *Marijuana Boom: The Rise and Fall of Colombia's First Drug Paradise* (Berkeley: University of California Press, 2020), 101.

16. Maria D. Alvarez, "Illicit Crops and Bird Conservation Priorities in Colombia," *Conservation Biology* 16, no. 4 (2002): 1087.

17. Kendra McSweeney et al., "Drug Policy as Conservation Policy: Narco-Deforestation," *Science* 343, no. 6170 (January 31, 2014): 489–90.

18. Alvarez, "Illicit Crops," 1088–89; Jon Fjeldsa et al., "Illicit Crops and Armed Conflict as Constraints on Biodiversity Conservation in the Andes Region," *Ambio* 34, no. 3 (May 2005): 205–11.

19. Joseph J. Hobbs, "Troubling Fields: The Opium Poppy in Egypt," *Geographical Review* 88, no. 1 (January 1998): 77–79.

20. Ryan Stoa, *Craft Weed: Family Farming and the Future of the Marijuana Industry* (Cambridge: MIT Press, 2018), chapter 3.

21. Nick Johnson, *Grass Roots: A History of Cannabis in the American West* (Corvallis: Oregon State University Press, 2017), chapter 5.

22. Johnson, *Grass Roots*, especially chapter 5.

CHAPTER 12. **Marijuana's Different Path**

1. David T. Courtwright, *Forces of Habit: Drugs and the Making of the Modern World* (Cambridge, MA: Harvard University Press, 2001), 43–46.

2. See the discussion in William B. McAllister, "Harry Anslinger Saves the World: National Security Imperatives and the 1937 Marihuana Tax Act," *Social History of Alcohol and Drugs* 33, no. 1 (Spring 2019): 38–42.

3. Nick Johnson, *Grass Roots: A History of Cannabis in the American West* (Corvallis: Oregon State University Press, 2017), 59–68.

4. Emily Dufton's book provides the most comprehensive overview of the history of marijuana in the United States after 1950. Emily Dufton, *Grass Roots: The Rise and Fall and Rise of Marijuana in America* (New York: Basic Books, 2017), quote on 22.

5. "Marijuana," cover story, *Life* magazine, October 31, 1969.

6. Dufton, *Grass Roots*, 57–62.

7. Dufton, *Grass Roots*, 65–72; Johnson, *Grass Roots*, 85–86, 100–101.

8. Lloyd D. Johnston et al., *Trends in Drug Use and Associated Factors in American High School Students, College Students and Young Adults, 1975–1989* (Washington, DC: National Institute on Drug Abuse, 1991), 51–58.

9. Dufton, *Grass Roots*, 208–13; Johnson, *Grass Roots*, 104–6.

10. Martin A. Lee, *Smoke Signals: A Social History of Marijuana—Medical, Recreational, and Scientific* (New York: Scribner, 2012), 222–47.

11. Dufton, *Grass Roots*, 216–24.

12. In marijuana, THC is the compound that causes the feeling of being high; CBD binds more weakly with the receptors that make people feel high.

CHAPTER 13. **New Challenges to the War on Drugs**

1. David Herzberg, *White Market Drugs: Big Pharma and the Hidden History of Addiction in America* (Chicago: University of Chicago Press, 2020), 213–20.

2. Nicholas Rasmussen, *On Speed: The Many Lives of Amphetamine* (New York: New York University Press, 2008), provides the best overview. See especially chapter 8.

3. Rasmussen, *On Speed*, 222–25; Christopher M. Jones et al., "Patterns and Characteristics of Methamphetamine Use among Adults—United States, 2015–2018," *Morbidity and Mortality Weekly Report* 69, no. 12 (March 27, 2020): 317–23.

4. Taken from the Statistics area of the Indiana Methamphetamine Investigation System website, accessed May 4, 2022, https://www.in.gov/meth/statistics/.

5. United Nations Office for Drug Control and Crime Prevention (UNODCCP), *World Drug Report 2000* (Oxford: Oxford University Press, 2000), 51.

6. United Nations Office on Drugs and Crime (UNODC), *World Drug Report 2009* (Vienna: UNODC, 2009), 127; UNODC, *World Drug Report 2021*, vol. 2, *Global Overview: Drug Demand / Drug Supply* (Vienna: UNODC, 2021), 55.

7. Quoted in Chuck Grassley and Ron Wyden, "Findings from the Investigation of Opioid Manufacturers' Financial Relationships with Patient Advocacy Groups and Other Tax-Exempt Entities," Committee on Finance, United States Senate, December 16, 2020.

8. The OxyContin data comes from Patrick Raden Keefe, *Empire of Pain: The Secret History of the Sackler Dynasty* (London: Picador, 2022), 215–16; the total numbers for post-2006 come from Centers for Disease Control and Prevention, "U.S. Opioid Dispensing Rate Maps," accessed October 17, 2022, https://www.cdc.gov/drugoverdose/rxrate-maps/index.html.

9. Herzberg, *White Market Drugs*, 276.

10. For federal prison statistics, see "Offenses" Statistics from the Federal Bureau of Prisons, accessed May 10, 2022, https://www.bop.gov/about/statistics/statistics_inmate_offenses.jsp; Ben Grunwald, "Toward an Optimal Decarceration Strategy," *Stanford Law and Policy Review* 33, no. 1 (March 2022): 21–26.

11. UNODCCP, *Global Illicit Drug Trends 2002* (New York: United Nations, 2002), 45; UNODC, *World Drug Report 2009*, 33–34; UNODC, *World Drug Report 2021*, vol. 3, *Drug Market Trends: Cannabis, Opioids*, 87.

12. Michael Hufford and Donald S. Burke, "The Costs of Heroin and Naloxone: A Tragic Snapshot of the Opioid Crisis," *Stat*, November 8, 2018, https://www.statnews.com/2018/11/08/costs-heroin-naloxone-tragic-snapshot-opioid-crisis/.

CONCLUSION. **Never-Ending War on Drugs?**

1. Sheila Coronel provides the consistently best coverage. Read especially Sheila Coronel, "'I Will Kill All the Drug Lords': The Making of Rodrigo Duterte," *Atlantic*, September 20, 2016; Sheila Coronel, "Duterte Says Safety Comes at a Price: Filipinos Should Know What That Price Is," *Rappler*, August 20, 2019.

2. David T. Courtwright, *The Age of Addiction: How Bad Habits Became Big Business* (Cambridge, MA: Belknap Press of Harvard University Press, 2019), 6.

3. Crystal Hill and Ryan Martin, "Marion County Will No Longer Prosecute Simple Marijuana, Officials Say," *Indianapolis Star*, September 30, 2019.

SUGGESTIONS FOR FURTHER READING

CHAPTER 1

Benedict, Carol. *Golden-Silk Smoke: A History of Tobacco in China, 1550–2010*. Berkeley: University of California Press, 2011.

Breen, Benjamin. *The Age of Intoxication: Origins of the Global Drug Trade*. Philadelphia: University of Pennsylvania Press, 2019.

Courtwright, David T. *Forces of Habit: Drugs and the Making of the Modern World*. Cambridge, MA: Harvard University Press, 2001.

Goodman, Jordan, et al., eds. *Consuming Habits: Global and Historical Perspectives on How Cultures Define Drugs*. New York: Routledge, 2007.

Mintz, Sidney W. *Sweetness and Power: The Place of Sugar in Modern History*. New York: Viking, 1985.

Norton, Marcy. *Sacred Gifts, Profane Pleasures: A History of Tobacco and Chocolate in the Atlantic World*. Ithaca, NY: Cornell University Press, 2008.

Zheng, Yangwen. *Social Life of Opium in China*. Cambridge, UK: Cambridge University Press, 2005.

CHAPTER 2

Berridge, Virginia. *Opium and the People: Opiate Use and Drug Control Policy in Nineteenth and Early Twentieth Century England*. New York: Free Association Books, 1999.

Courtwright, David T. *Dark Paradise: A History of Opiate Addiction in America*. Cambridge, MA: Harvard University Press, 2001.

Kadia, Miriam Kingsberg. *Moral Nation: Modern Japan and Narcotics in Global History*. Berkeley: University of California Press, 2014.

Madancy, Joyce A. *The Troublesome Legacy of Commissioner Lin: The Opium Trade and Opium Suppression in Fujian Province, 1820s–1920s*. Harvard East Asian Monographs. Cambridge, MA: Harvard University Press, 2004.

Padwa, Howard. *Social Poison: The Politics and Culture of Opiate Control in Britain and France, 1821–1926*. Baltimore: Johns Hopkins University Press, 2012.

Rimner, Steffen. *Opium's Long Shadow: From Asian Revolt to Global Drug Control*. Cambridge, MA: Harvard University Press, 2018.

Rush, James R. *Opium to Java: Revenue Farming and Chinese Enterprise in Colonial Indonesia, 1860–1910*. Ithaca, NY: Cornell University Press, 1990.

CHAPTER 3

Foster, Anne L. "The Philippines, the United States, and the Origins of Global Narcotics Prohibition." *Social History of Alcohol and Drugs* 33, no. 1 (March 2019): 13–26.

Gootenberg, Paul. *Andean Cocaine: The Making of a Global Drug*. Chapel Hill: University of North Carolina Press, 2008.

Kim, Diana S. *Empires of Vice: The Rise of Opium Prohibition across Southeast Asia*. Princeton, NJ: Princeton University Press, 2020.

Pliley, Jessica R., et al., eds. *Global Anti-Vice Activism, 1890–1950: Fighting Drinks, Drugs, and "Immorality."* New York: Cambridge University Press, 2016.

Trocki, Carl A. *Opium, Empire and the Global Political Economy: A Study of the Asian Opium Trade, 1750–1950*. New York: Routledge, 1999.

Tyrrell, Ian R. *Reforming the World: The Creation of America's Moral Empire*. Princeton, NJ: Princeton University Press, 2010.

CHAPTER 4

Abbenhuis, Maartje. *The Hague Conferences and International Politics, 1898–1915*. New York: Bloomsbury Academic, 2019.

McAllister, William B. *Drug Diplomacy in the Twentieth Century: An International History*. New York: Routledge, 2000.

Pedersen, Susan. *The Guardians: The League of Nations and the Crisis of Empire*. New York: Oxford University Press, 2015.

Wright, Ashley. *Opium and Empire in Southeast Asia: Regulating Consumption in British Burma*. Houndmills, UK: Palgrave Macmillan, 2014.

CHAPTER 5

Amador, José. *Medicine and Nation Building in the Americas, 1890–1940*. Nashville, TN: Vanderbilt University Press, 2015.

Anderson, Warwick. *Colonial Pathologies: American Tropical Medicine, Race, and Hygiene in the Philippines*. Durham, NC: Duke University Press, 2006.

Chakrabarti, Patik. *Medicine and Empire, 1600–1960*. Basingstoke, UK: Palgrave Macmillan, 2014.

Dube, Francis. *Public Health at the Border of Zimbabwe and Mozambique, 1890–1940: African Experiences in a Contested Space*. Cham, Switzerland: Palgrave Macmillan, 2020.

Monnais, Laurence, and Harold J. Cook. *Global Movements, Local Concerns: Medicine and Health in Southeast Asia*. Singapore: National University of Singapore Press, 2012.

Spillane, Joseph F. *Cocaine: From Medical Marvel to Modern Menace in the United States, 1884–1920*. Baltimore: Johns Hopkins University Press, 2002.

CHAPTER 6

Andreas, Peter. *Killer High: A History of War in Six Drugs*. Oxford: Oxford University Press, 2020.

Harrison, Mark. *Medicine and Victory: British Military Medicine in the Second World War*. Oxford: Oxford University Press, 2004.

McAllister, William B. *Drug Diplomacy in the Twentieth Century: An International History*. New York: Routledge, 2000.

McCoy, Alfred W. *The Politics of Heroin: CIA Complicity in the Global Drug Trade*. Chicago: Lawrence Hill Books, 2003.

Pembleton, Matthew. *Containing Addiction: The Federal Bureau of Narcotics and the Origins of America's Global Drug War*. Amherst: University of Massachusetts Press, 2017.

Rasmussen, Nicolas. *On Speed: From Benzedrine to Adderall*. New York: New York University Press, 2008.

Reiss, Suzanna. *We Sell Drugs: The Alchemy of US Empire*. Berkeley: University of California Press, 2014.

CHAPTER 7

Bradford, James Tharin. *Poppies, Politics, and Power: Afghanistan and the Global History of Drugs and Diplomacy*. Ithaca, NY: Cornell University Press, 2019.

Carey, Elaine. *Women Drug Traffickers: Mules, Bosses, and Organized Crime*. Albuquerque: University of New Mexico Press, 2014.

McAllister, William B. *Drug Diplomacy in the Twentieth Century: An International History*. New York: Routledge, 2000.

McCoy, Alfred W. *The Politics of Heroin: CIA Complicity in the Global Drug Trade*. Chicago: Lawrence Hill Books, 2003.

CHAPTER 8

Campbell, Nancy D. *Discovering Addiction: The Science and Politics of Substance Abuse Research*. Ann Arbor: University of Michigan Press, 2007.

Dyck, Erika. *Psychedelic Psychiatry: LSD from Clinic to Campus*. Baltimore: Johns Hopkins University Press, 2008.

Herzberg, David. *White Market Drugs: Big Pharma and the Hidden History of Addiction in America*. Chicago: University of Chicago Press, 2020.

Kuzmarov, Jeremy. *Myth of the Addicted Army: Vietnam and the Modern War on Drugs.* Amherst: University of Massachusetts Press, 2009.
Schneider, Eric. *Smack: Heroin and the American City.* Philadelphia: University of Pennsylvania Press, 2013.
Tomes, Nancy. *Remaking the American Patient: How Madison Avenue and Modern Medicine Turned Patients into Consumers.* Chapel Hill: University of North Carolina Press, 2016.

CHAPTER 9

Britto, Lina. *Marijuana Boom: The Rise and Fall of Colombia's First Drug Paradise.* Berkeley: University of California Press, 2020.
Dufton, Emily. *Grass Roots: The Rise and Fall and Rise of Marijuana in America.* New York: Basic Books, 2017.
Farber, David R., ed. *The War on Drugs: A History.* New York: New York University Press, 2022.
Gootenberg, Paul. *Andean Cocaine: The Making of a Global Drug.* Chapel Hill: University of North Carolina Press, 2008.
Koram, Kojo, ed. *The War on Drugs and the Global Colour Line.* London: Pluto Press, 2019.
McCoy, Alfred W. *The Politics of Heroin: CIA Complicity in the Global Drug Trade.* Chicago: Lawrence Hill Books, 2003.
Musto, David. *The American Disease: Origins of Narcotics Control.* 3rd ed. Oxford: Oxford University Press, 1999.

CHAPTER 10

Alexander, Michelle. *The New Jim Crow: Mass Incarceration in the Age of Colorblindness.* 10th anniversary ed. New York: New Press, 2020.
Farber, David. *Crack: Rock Cocaine, Street Capitalism, and the Decade of Greed.* New York: Cambridge University Press, 2019.
Fortner, Michael Javen. *Black Silent Majority: The Rockefeller Drug Laws and the Politics of Punishment.* Cambridge, MA: Harvard University Press, 2015.
Kohler-Hausman, Julilly. "'The Attila the Hun Law': New York's Rockefeller Drug Laws and the Making of a Punitive State." *Journal of Social History* 44, no. 1 (September 2010): 71–96.
Lassiter, Matthew D. "Impossible Criminals: The Suburban Imperatives of America's War on Drugs." *Journal of American History* 102, no. 1 (June 2015): 126–40.
Massing, Michael. *The Fix.* Berkeley: University of California Press, 2000.
Sherry, Michael S. *The Punitive Turn: How the United States Learned to Fight Crime Like a War.* Chapel Hill: University of North Carolina Press, 2020.
Tallaksen, Amund R. "Junkies and Jim Crow: The Boggs Act of 1951 and the Racial Transformation of New Orleans' Heroin Market." *Journal of Urban History* 45, no. 2 (2019): 230–46.

CHAPTER 11

Johnson, Nick. *Grass Roots: A History of Cannabis in the American West.* Corvallis: Oregon State University Press, 2017.

Lyons, Kristina. "Decomposition as Life Politics: Soils, *Selva*, and Small Farmers under the Gun of the Colombia-U.S. War on Drugs." *Cultural Anthropology* 31, no. 1 (2016): 56–81.

Miller, Char, ed. *Where There's Smoke: The Environmental Science, Public Policy and Politics of Marijuana.* Lawrence: University of Kansas Press, 2018.

Stoa, Ryan. *Craft Weed: Family Farming and the Future of the Marijuana Industry.* Cambridge, MA: MIT Press, 2018.

Weimer, Daniel. "The Politics of Contamination: Herbicides, Drug Control, and Environmental Law." *Diplomatic History* 41, no. 5 (November 2017): 847–73.

CHAPTER 12

Campos, Isaac. *Home Grown: Marijuana and the Origins of Mexico's War on Drugs.* Chapel Hill: University of North Carolina Press, 2012.

Dufton, Emily. *Grass Roots: The Rise and Fall and Rise of Marijuana in America.* New York: Basic Books, 2017.

Johnson, Nick. *Grass Roots: A History of Cannabis in the American West.* Corvallis: Oregon State University Press, 2017.

Smith, Benjamin T. *The Dope: The Real History of the Mexican Drug Trade.* New York: W. W. Norton, 2021.

Stoa, Ryan. *Craft Weed: Family Farming and the Future of the Marijuana Industry.* Cambridge, MA: MIT Press, 2018.

CHAPTER 13

Campbell, Nancy D. *OD: Naloxone and the Politics of Overdose.* Cambridge, MA: MIT Press, 2020.

Courtwright, David T. *The Age of Addiction: How Bad Habits Became Big Business.* Cambridge, MA: Belknap Press of Harvard University Press, 2019.

Garriott, William. *Policing Methamphetamine: Narcopolitics in Rural America.* New York: New York University Press, 2011.

Herzberg, David. *White Market Drugs: Big Pharma and the Hidden History of Addiction in America.* Chicago: University of Chicago Press, 2020.

Keefe, Patrick Radden. *Empire of Pain: The Secret History of the Sackler Dynasty.* London: Picador, 2022.

Szalavitz, Maia. *Undoing Drugs: The Untold Story of Harm Reduction and the Future of Addiction.* New York: Hachette, 2021.

INDEX

Page references in italics indicate illustrations and t *indicates a table.*

Printed and bound by CPI Group (UK) Ltd, Croydon, CR0 4YY

01/07/2024

14522386-0001